MY LIFE AND TIMES
OCTAVE THREE:
1900-1907

A

BY COMPTON MACKENZIE

Novels and Romances

SINISTER STREET
SYLVIA SCARLET
GUY AND PAULINE
CARNIVAL
FIGURE OF EIGHT
CORAL
THE VANITY GIRL
ROGUES AND VAGABONDS
THE ALTAR STEPS
THE PARSON'S PROGRESS
THE HEAVENLY LADDER
HUNTING THE FAIRIES
WHISKY GALORE
KEEP THE HOME GUARD TURNING
THE MONARCH OF THE GLEN
THE RIVAL MONSTER
THE RED TAPEWORM
ROCKETS GALORE
THE LUNATIC REPUBLIC
POOR RELATIONS
APRIL FOOLS
RICH RELATIVES
BUTTERCUPS AND DAISIES
WATER ON THE BRAIN
VESTAL FIRE
EXTRAORDINARY WOMEN
THIN ICE
EXTREMES MEET
THE THREE COURIERS
OUR STREET
THE DARKENING GREEN
THE PASSIONATE ELOPEMENT
FAIRY GOLD
THE SEVEN AGES OF WOMAN
PARADISE FOR SALE
THE FOUR WINDS OF LOVE:
- THE EAST WIND
- THE SOUTH WIND
- THE WEST WIND
- THE NORTH WIND

MEZZOTINT

Play

THE LOST CAUSE

Verse

POEMS 1907
KENSINGTON RHYMES

History and Biograph

EASTERN EPIC. VOL. I
ALL OVER THE PLACE
GALLIPOLI MEMORIES
ATHENIAN MEMORIES
GREEK MEMORIES
AEGEAN MEMORIES
WIND OF FREEDOM
MR ROOSEVELT
DR BENES
PRINCE CHARLIE
PRINCE CHARLIE AND HIS LADIES
CATHOLICISM AND SCOTLAND
MARATHON AND SALAMIS
PERICLES
THE WINDSOR TAPESTRY
THE VITAL FLAME
I TOOK A JOURNEY
COALPORT
REALMS OF SILVER
THE QUEEN'S HOUSE
MY RECORD OF MUSIC
SUBLIME TOBACCO
GREECE IN MY LIFE
CATS' COMPANY
CATMINT

Essays and Criticism

ECHOES
A MUSICAL CHAIR
UNCONSIDERED TRIFLES
REAPED AND BOUND
LITERATURE IN MY TIME
ON MORAL COURAGE

Children's Stories

SANTA CLAUS IN SUMMER
TOLD
MABEL IN QUEER STREET
THE UNPLEASANT VISITORS
THE CONCEITED DOLL
THE ENCHANTED BLANKET
THE DINING-ROOM BATTLE
THE ADVENTURES OF TWO CHAIRS
THE ENCHANTED ISLAND
THE NAUGHTYMOBILE
THE FAIRY IN THE WINDOW BOX
THE STAIRS THAT KEPT ON GOING DOWN

Autobiography

MY LIFE AND TIMES: OCTAVE ONE
MY LIFE AND TIMES: OCTAVE TWO

"Gunner" from the painting by Seymour Lucas

MY LIFE AND TIMES

OCTAVE THREE

1900-1907

Compton Mackenzie

1964
CHATTO & WINDUS
LONDON

Published by
Chatto & Windus Ltd
42 William IV Street
London, W.C. 2
*
Clarke, Irwin & Co. Ltd
Toronto

Printed in Great Britain by
T. & A. Constable Ltd
Hopetoun Street, Edinburgh

To

JIM and ALICE THOMSON,

gratefully and affectionately

CONTENTS

★

Note

There will be an index in Octave Four, to be published next year, which will have all entries in Octaves Three and Four.

PLATES

★

SEVENTEEN YEARS OLD: 1900

THE Bournemouth Hydropathic Establishment had been under the direction of Dr Johnson Smyth for about a year when I arrived there in that first week of March 1900. Dr Smyth had been a Major in the R.A.M.C. attached to the Grenadier Guards; on festive occasions at the Hydro he used to gratify his guests by appearing in mess-kit. The establishment was situated in Durley Gardens and consisted of five or six adjoining houses put together. The corridors thus created had a low step as one passed through them from house to house because Durley Gardens sloped slightly down toward the promenade along the West Cliff. At the back of these converted houses the Doctor had built a Turkish bath and installed various forms of hydropathic equipment. The public rooms consisted of a drawing-room, a dining-room large enough to seat all guests at small tables, a gymnasium, a billiards-room, and immediately beyond the front door a small and cosy lounge which was the centre of the Hydro's life, presided over as it were by Mr Finnigan, a small man with a trim grey beard and florid laughter-crinkled countenance, who was in a continuous state of exuberant geniality shared by his family, of whom I recall two or three sons in their early twenties. He and they twinkled like the silver in their Liverpool shop window, and the sheen of their good nature rivalled the sheen upon the leather of their dressing-cases. The decision to extend the Finnigan trunk line from Liverpool to London had just been taken and Bond Street had been chosen for the new shop, which is still there as I write of it in 1963.

I owe a great debt to old Mr Finnigan who, though I think of him as old, was probably in his mid-fifties; he immediately made me welcome and by his bubbling Irish good nature dissolved in a moment the self-consciousness of a boy of just seventeen when he alighted from the fly and walked into that Bournemouth Hydro straight out of school. I owe a great debt to those jolly sons of his whose Christian names I have forgotten, though I have a notion that my particular favourite was called Herbert who if he be still alive must be about 85 to-day. I should confess at this point that I claimed to be eighteen years old with a suggestion that nineteen was not far away. I do not believe that any of the guests in the Hydro suspected me of being only just seventeen.

Before I left London I had been to say good-bye to Reggie Turner in Clement's Inn, and on that Saturday morning Ranger Gull came in. He had recently had a successful novel published by Greenings, who were Reggie Turner's publishers. This was called *The Hypocrite* and it had enjoyed the same kind of 'shocking' success at the end of the Victorian age as we are familiar with to-day from the Four Letter School. Later, under the pseudonym of Guy Thorne, he would write a novel called *When It Was Dark*, which thanks to widespread pulpit advertisement would be the first 'best seller' in a big way. On hearing that I was going to Bournemouth Gull gave me a card of introduction to his brother who, still up at Oxford, would be staying for the Easter vac in one of the big Bournemouth hotels.

Ranger Gull was a drinker in the grand style. When he went to live in Cornwall he made a habit of concealing bottles of whisky all over the moors so that on country walks he could boast he was never more than a quarter of a mile away from refreshment. On that February morning in 1900 he paced up and down Turner's room while he was talking, until suddenly he said: "Well, I have to see Leonard Smithers at twelve o'clock, when the real drinking of the day will begin."

With this Ranger Gull shot out of the room; I recall Reggie Turner's saying he hoped that Leonard Smithers would keep sober for poor Ernest Dowson's funeral.

When I look back to those three months I spent in the West Cliff Hydro I am puzzled to know why I was accepted as worthwhile company by so many elderly men, all of whom treated me as a contemporary. I have told already of my friendship with Lord Chalmers when I was fifteen, and I am inclined to call these friendships with older men when I was young the most valuable experience of my youth. Now in my old age I find its most valuable experience is my friendship with much younger men than myself.

Surgeon McMorris talked to me severely when he heard me declare that the vote to erect a statue to Oliver Cromwell in Parliament Square was a disgrace to the House of Commons. Surgeon McMorris, who had retired from service in different parts of the world in order to devote himself entirely to golf, was a thin tall Ulsterman, and I rejected all his claims for Cromwell's greatness except one. I admitted that he was a military commander of the highest class but insisted that the Protectorate had been as great a moral disaster for England, Scotland, Wales and Ireland as the way William of Orange had squeezed himself on to the throne. That led to a fiercer argument because the Surgeon was an Orangeman. He was also a teetotaller, and I regret that at this date I was unaware that Dutch William's Torbay invasion, with the treachery of Marlborough to reinforce it, had been financed by the gin-makers in Holland, and that to repay the loan William had granted them a monopoly, thus depriving the English for a century of Scotch or Irish whisky and almost rotting London with gin. Our arguments were always political, and in the end Surgeon McMorris decided we must agree to differ and that as a sign of such agreement he would teach me how to putt.

The Surgeon's lessons were given along the corridor on the first floor, the hole being one of the roses in the Brussels carpet. I have mentioned the little step down where one house led to another. "These bunkers are a confounded nuisance," he used to say. "And much as I'd like to show you how to play a good mashie stroke we might hit one of the old ladies coming out of her room."

One of the Surgeon's idiosyncrasies was to sprinkle a semi-circle of Keating's Powder outside his bedroom door before retiring to rest. This, he told me, was to keep the beetles out. I never saw a blackbeetle anywhere in the Hydro, but the Surgeon never failed to secure himself against them by sprinkling that semi-circle of Keating's Powder round the door of his bedroom. I can see him now standing in the entrance in grey frogged pyjamas, a triumphant expression on his thin distinguished countenance at the thought of the disappointment he was going to inflict on predatory blackbeetles.

Another veteran was Colonel George Sartorius, brother of a V.C., who had been a junior subaltern in the year of the Mutiny, fought through many Eastern campaigns and shot the biggest buffalo ever killed in India, the horns being forty-seven inches across.

The Colonel and I paced the West Cliff frequently, and often sat together in a shelter; but the real exercise was taken by my fancy as I fought through the Afghan campaigns of '70 and '80, in the Sudan in '84 and in Burma from '86 to '89, not to mention an exciting interlude when the Colonel was a Pasha in the Turkish army and fighting the Russians with Baker Pasha in '76. Baker Pasha had been cashiered from the Guards for kissing a young woman in a train, but he distinguished himself so much against the Russians that Queen Victoria, who had insisted on his being cashiered, relented and he was restored to his rank in the British Army as Colonel Valentine Baker.

On one of our walks together I had occasion to borrow sixpence from Colonel Sartorius to buy cigarettes; that afternoon at tea in the lounge he said to me gruffly, his little round brick-red face darkening, "You owe me sixpence." I hastily paid him, but after tea he took me aside and growled, "Always pay your debts at once." I tried to explain that I was only waiting for a suitable moment after tea. "Shouldn't wait at all," he went on growling, "borrowed money should always be paid back at once."

I can acquit myself of the slightest intention to evade the debt. Nevertheless, it was an impressive reminder, and being impressionable I benefited by it. Colonel Sartorius certainly forgave me, for he invited me to stay with him at Godalming, but I never went, so swift and crowded was life after I was released from the penal servitude of school.

The third veteran was Major Nugent, who had been in one of the Irish cavalry regiments—a Hussar not a Lancer. He was from the South, a complete contrast to Surgeon McMorris, and a great favourite with the elderly maiden ladies. "God help them, poor dears," he used to say to me, "when I see them drinking that Australian burgundy with their dinner, my heart bleeds for them."

Once a week there was an evening of entertainment in the Hydro gymnasium, on which occasions Major Nugent always sang '*O lucky Jim, how I envy him*,' followed by *When we are Married*, and winding up with *Where are the Boys of the Old Brigade?* to which the maiden ladies, knitting away among the rowing-machine and the riding-machine and the punch-ball and the parallel bars, used to tap their feet genteelly. Caruso himself would not have charmed those elderly maiden ladies as sweetly.

The Major taught me euchre; he and I and two of the young Finnigans had many a four. I never see euchre played to-day, but it is a good game for two, three or four players. The top card is the knave of trumps followed by the knave of the same colour. These are known as the Right Bower and the Left Bower, which may be derived from bow oar, the game having been popular with the lumbermen. Later the Joker was introduced to take precedence of all cards.

I still hear from that Spring of over sixty years ago one particular round when two of the young Finnigans were partners against the Major and myself in the billiards-room. Clubs were trumps, and one Finnigan led the ace. I beat it with the knave of spades.

"The Left Bower, b'George," muttered the Major.

The other Finnigan played the knave of clubs;

"The Right Bower, b'Jove," muttered the Major.

And then taking a card from his hand, and holding it high above his head for a moment before he brought it down with a triumphant crash upon the table, he shouted,

"The Joker, b'God!" and scooped up the trick.

I recall a Sunday afternoon when the Major and I decided to break the Hydro rules by playing a game of billiards. I can see the expression on the Doctor's face as he abruptly came into the room and flung the cover over the table without a word and left us standing in the billiards-room like a couple of schoolboys who had been found out.

"Begad," exclaimed the Major when the Doctor had swept out of the room without speaking to either of us, "you'd think the man had been commissioned by Moses himself."

Then there was J—, six feet six inches tall, who had been either in the Life Guards or the Blues. He was a melancholy man who used to pace up and down the corridors without speaking to anybody, both hands in his pockets in which he kept chinking bunches of keys. "Makes me think I'm still in uniform," he said to me once. "Accoutrements, you know, and all that."

His wife was with him, a charming and good-looking woman in her early thirties with light brown hair, but always with a worried look, evidently wondering what was going to become of her husband, and indeed she had good reason to worry; some months later he killed himself.

More remarkable than J— or his wife was their daughter just three years old. This lovely little creature was nearer to fairyland than any child I have known. She would sit beside me and in a rhythmic chant recite long phantasies composed by herself. I have often wondered whether she lived to grow up and I am tempted to give her name in the hope of hearing what became of her. Yet I cannot bring myself to profane the privilege I once enjoyed of wandering with that three-year-old child through the realms of poesy. It shall remain for me an unique intimacy.

At this date the smart attire for a young man was a blue serge suit with a red knitted tie and brown shoes. This is what I wore myself with a choker collar, but mercifully no photograph of myself in such a rig has survived. T— was attired like this. T— had just returned from South Africa, having been invalided out from the Imperial Yeomanry and was recuperating at the Hydro in the company of his handsome sister. T— inspired a good deal of whispering among the maiden ladies and not a few ribald comments from the men because he spent so much time in his sister's bedroom. He was my first experience of a great liar, and although his accomplishment would be surpassed later in my life by greater liars, like Axel Munthe and Ford Madox Ford, he still occupies a minor place in my memory. A more accurate word than 'liar' would be the Italian *improvisatore* or perhaps 'romancer', and I withdraw 'liar'.

On one occasion cannibalism was a topic in the billiards-room. "I expect I'm the only one here who knows what human flesh tastes like," said T—.

We exclaimed in astonishment.

"Yes, when I was on safari in Matabeleland soon after the war we had an unusually good soup one night. When I told my cook-boy how good it was he beamed and said it was because he had put in it a dead baby he had bought from its mother. Of course, I gave him a flogging and forbade him ever to do such a thing again."

"But didn't you feel horribly sick when you heard what your cook-boy had done?" we asked.

"Yes, I suppose I felt a bit squeamish but I have to admit that it was a really excellent soup."

I was still much preoccupied with ecclesiastical affairs in that spring of 1900 and I recall my pessimistic gloom about the future of the Anglican Church when the gathering of bishops at Lambeth condemned Reservation of the Blessed Sacrament. Yet the idea of becoming a Roman Catholic never entered my mind even after being presented to Cardinal Vaughan, who was on a visit to Bournemouth and came to tea with Mr Finnigan at the Hydro. What a magnificent figure of a Cardinal he was! There has been no Archbishop of Westminster of comparable appearance. I see that superb figure seemingly carved from ivory as he sat there in the Hydro lounge where all the old maiden ladies goggled at him over their knitting, their chaste Protestantism thrilled to the marrow. I was wondering how so impressive a man could have supposed that the condemnation of Anglican Orders would bring hesitant clergymen over to Rome. I wished I had the courage to ask him how it was possible to offer Archbishop Laud a Cardinal's hat if he would abjure Anglicanism without any suggestion of his having to be reordained or reconsecrated. I believe that if there had not been so many other people at tea that afternoon I might have asked him questions about

Anglican Orders, but there they were and I lacked the courage to commit what I considered would be a breach of good manners.

I was a regular communicant at St Clement's Church of which I have written in my second Octave, and I think it was here that I met a son of John Porter, the famous racehorse trainer whose Kingsclere stables were renowned. As I remember, the great jockey Mornington Cannon always rode for him. Young Porter was an unlikely colt to come out of Kingsclere; he told me that his father gave him a small allowance to keep away from home.

"But it's not my fault, is it, if I hate horses and want to lead an artistic life of my own?"

I, always a strong supporter of anybody who did what he felt compelled to do, sympathized with young Porter.

"My father is always on at me to find a nice girl and get married, but I don't like girls any more than I like horses," he complained.

I was less sympathetic with him over this prejudice because I was myself much in love with Kitty, an Irish girl who was staying at the Hydro with her elder sister.

There will seem something absurd in a boy of seventeen and a quarter seriously set on marrying a girl eight years older than himself; in justice to Kitty she did suppose that I was nearly nineteen and she did try to persuade me that an engagement was impossible. Yet, however much it may have been against her notion of what was suitable, she did fall in love with me, and as I look back to that last April of the nineteenth century the sun seems to be shining all the time as Kitty and I sit side by side on a secluded cliff looking down on wide sands and a tranquil sea. I remember wondering in the fever of our kisses how I should ever be able to tell her what would happen on our marriage night; the seventeen-year-old of to-day would be spared such an embarrassing reflection. When we could not escape together to that secluded cliff we proposed bicycling expeditions to which Kitty's elder sister always attached herself as chaperon. We usually managed to elude that dumpy elder sister on these expeditions, because we could ride faster and always took the turning which did not lead to where we were supposed to be going.

At last that sister, who must have been quite thirty, decided that Kitty was getting completely out of control and wrote to her mother. That mother was as near to what Ensign Beverley called a weather-beaten she-dragon as anybody I have met. She decided immediately that the only thing to do was to take Kitty away from Bournemouth at once. Somehow we contrived a last meeting at which I reiterated my determination to marry her and was given an address to which I could write without her mother's knowledge. Then came the miserable morning when Kitty and her sister with their weatherbeaten she-dragon of a mother got into the waiting fly and drove away from the Hydro.

I went up to Kitty's empty room. The forsaken bedroom of my beloved, littered with the waste of packing in the sunshine of a May morning, was desolation itself. I gazed miserably at the bits of tissue paper lying about. Then I saw in the soap dish on Kitty's washstand the pink oval of soap with which she had washed her hands. This was a more precious souvenir than tissue paper and I carried that pink cake of soap up to my own bedroom where its faint perfume would speak to me of my beloved Kitty.

How empty the Hydro drawing-room seemed that evening after dinner without the sight of Kitty. I have never been able to describe women's dress but as I look back at that spring of 1900 they seem excessively upholstered to the eyes of to-day. Yet no amount of upholstery could spoil the trimness of Kitty's figure or dull the sparkle of her hazel eyes when I came in to sit beside her after dinner.

"You will be missing Miss —" one after another of the maiden ladies would say sympathetically.

Surgeon McMorris prescribed golf as a cure for love's sickness, but Major Nugent took me to dinner at the Grand Hotel, and over a bottle of champagne begged me to believe that his heart had been broken at least half a dozen times without the slightest deleterious effect either upon his career in the Army or his zest in single blessedness.

It must have been shortly before the relief of Mafeking that I was parted from Kitty, and when a Lancashire visitor to the Hydro urged me to come out and revel with him I had no heart to do so. The door of the Hydro was closed and locked up sharp at eleven every night and the Lancashire commercial traveller asked me if I would let him in when he returned from celebrating the news from Mafeking any time after midnight. The Finnigans told the reveller to climb over the hydropathic annexe at the back and promised to let him in from the window in the lounge if he made it before one o'clock. At midnight the electric light was turned off but we agreed to play euchre by candlelight until the reveller returned and we could open the window for him.

About half-past twelve we heard the crash of glass. We wondered what had happened, but there was no way of finding out and when the reveller had not returned by two o'clock we went off to bed. Next morning Dr Smyth was on the warpath. The reveller had crashed through the glass roof of the Turkish bath and in trying to find his way out had somehow got into the hot room in which from a combination of liquor and heat he had fallen asleep. When discovered by the attendant he was brought before Dr Smyth, who expelled him from the Hydro and warned him that if there was the least delay in settling the bill for damages he would be sued.

"You'd think a chap who'd been in the Grenadiers would have a bit more patriotism," the reveller complained to us as his luggage was taken out to the waiting fly.

In the autumn of 1899 Dom Aeldred Carlyle acquired a tiny temporary monastery to house his little community of Benedictines at Milton Abbas in Dorset, where they remained until January 1901, moving from there to Caldey Island. Here later with most of the community he submitted to Rome. Those who remained Anglican went to Pershore. I have seen it stated that the original of Dom Cuthbert Manners of Clere Abbey in *Sinister Street* was Dom Aeldred Carlyle. This is not so. Dom Cuthbert Manners existed entirely in my imagination. I take this opportunity of repeating how little there is of my own past in the story of Michael Fane and I hope that by the time these first three octaves of *My Life and Times* have been published *Sinister Street* will be recognized as a genuine feat of imagination and not presumed to be autobiography concealed as fiction. The only personal fact preserved from those months in the West Cliff Hydro is that piece of pink soap left behind by Kitty who was an infinitely more attractive young woman than the Kathleen McDonnell of *Sinister Street* and shared nothing with her except Irish nationality.

I had first met Aeldred Carlyle when he was a medical student all day and became a monk at night in Ealing. Then he set to work and started his Community on the Isle of Dogs, whence it moved for a while to Great Titchfield Street, where they were joined by my friend George Chambers. In the autumn of 1899 they moved again to Milton Abbas in Dorset and George Chambers wrote to ask me to visit them. On a blazing day at the beginning of June I set out on my bicycle for a fairly long ride. I recall being defeated by the chalky road uphill out of Blandford and unwillingly dismounting to walk up it. I was still enough of a schoolboy to consider it a reflection upon one's prowess to be defeated by a hill. When I read *The Mayor of*

Casterbridge it always revives the memory of that hot white dusty road.

I have but the vaguest picture of the little monastery itself, but I recall vividly the tiny thatched choir built of mud and stone by the brethren themselves. I also remember losing half a sovereign, a very heavy loss indeed in those days, and being advised by Dom Aeldred to pray to St Anthony for its recovery. To my gratified amazement the prayer was successful and I found the half-sovereign in the grass of a meadow across which George Chambers and I had walked to look at the view of Milton Abbas Minster, which rather to my disappointment was not a gothic ruin. I also recall my disapproval of the way the Squire—a Hambro as I remember—had built a model village which seemed to bring a touch of suburbia into Dorset in spite of the green uniform of the local constable. How many people to-day remember those green Dorset policemen whose uniform became the conventional dark blue during the First World War? They were so appropriate to that lovely wooded shire once upon a time. I had not read a word of Thomas Hardy at this date; George Meredith would remain my idol until my second year at Oxford when I forsook him for Hardy, though I remained faithful to the poems and that exquisite short story *The Tale of Chloe*.

Among a few scraps of paper which have survived since 1900 I find the record of my having gone to have my 'bumps told' by a phrenologist, as the phrase went. Do phrenologists still exist? They always used to call themselves professors; the one I consulted in Bournemouth on April 19th was Professor W. Cross. Under the bald bearded head on the outside of the Phrenological Chart is a table of his fees. For a Verbal Statement with marked Chart he charged five shillings. A Written Analysis cost one or two guineas. But a 'Most exhaustive and detailed Analysis of Physical and Mental Capabilities' cost five guineas. I need hardly say that five shillings was all I could afford. For this I received the figures against the various bumps, 48 in all, to show whether they were very large, large, full or moderate. My biggest bumps were Constructiveness, Locality, Comparison and Agreeableness. At the end was 'the Trade or Profession best adapted for'. I was suited to be an art critic, an analytical chemist, a judge of stock, a civil engineer, or if I made literature my profession I might be an editor or writer of romance. Against 'Business' is one word, 'bad', and the Professor added 'nervous system far too active.' After looking through his analysis of my bumps I am wondering whether phrenology has not been unjustly ridiculed.

My time at Bournemouth came to an end in the first week of June. How infinitely more valuable to my future those three months in the Hydro had been than if I had passed wearily through them still at school!

My father had decided to spend the first fortnight of his holiday by joining a tour to Switzerland with a party of about a dozen people not a single member of which can I extract from memory's coffer. What I do remember was that I had a light grey flannel suit made by a tailor in Oxford Street called Kingston which cost £4, 10s, a grey Homburg hat bought at Heath's, and half a dozen Aertex shirts bought at the very shop in Oxford Street in which they are still being sold to-day.

Our first destination was Lucerne where we stayed at the Schweitzerhof Hotel. It was here I realised once and for all that the proper way for me to begin a new day was with coffee not with tea. The dependence of British men and women on that early morning cup of tea remains for me to this day incomprehensible.

In Lucerne the party did all the conventional things such parties do when visiting Lucerne, but wherever we drove in char-à-bancs I felt we were driving about round a salad bowl. After going up in the funicular to the top of the Rigi I was continually surrounded by tourists. If I could have escaped from the chatter and sat among the flowers, listening to the cow-bells, I might have surrendered to the beauty of Switzerland, but that was impossible.

One evening I set out alone to explore the night life of Lucerne. I wandered along by the lake, meeting hardly a soul and at last sat down outside a small café among the pollarded acacias. Presently a waiter came along to ask what I would take to drink. I must have known the names of other liqueurs but the first one that came to me was maraschino of which I ordered myself a glass. There I sat, the sole customer of that café, sipping my maraschino and wondering why people liked liqueurs.

We went to Grindelwald for the second week of our tour and this, in spite of the oppressive exclusion of the world by the bulk of the Eiger, the Mönch and the Wetterhorn, I liked much better than Lucerne. The meadows in front of it powdered with St Bruno's lilies were a delight. We went to Interlaken, where it rained all day and we ascended the Jungfrau in the funicular. The view of mountains all round was superb no doubt, but what remains to me of that view is a large patch of lavender-blue violas in bloom.

Luckily for me I made the acquaintance of the Duncans in the

Bear Hotel and life was transformed for me by Norah and Myra, two Scottish girls from Glasgow. Their mother was a formidable personality who owned tea-plantations in Ceylon. She was a small dark woman with a mocking tongue and ruled her daughters with matriarchal authority. The eldest of them was engaged to be married to one of the Welbys, the firm of diamond-merchants at the corner of Long Acre. Norah and Myra who would have been twenty and eighteen, talked of their elder sister's betrothal as if she had entered a nunnery by getting engaged to be married. They seemed to think that for her the gaiety of life was ended. I fancy Mrs Duncan thought I was too young to be a serious suitor for the hand of either of her two younger daughters, both of whom would be catches for any impecunious young man she would feel bound to discourage severely. So with Mrs Duncan's approval Norah, Myra and I set out with a guide to survey the great glacier from a narrow path along the mountainside. The ground on either side of that path was crimson with those little azaleas called Alpine roses, and we picnicked at the end of it in a silence that was suddenly broken by the dull roar of an avalanche on what I think was the Wetterhorn opposite. Soon afterwards we saw three mountaineers hurrying down the slope towards the glacier below. I never had any ambition to climb mountains; any ambition I might have had would have been cured by the roar of that avalanche and the sight of those hurrying mountaineers.

I parted with the Duncans very regretfully at the end of that delightful week in their company. They were going on to Pontresina and later in September would be staying by Lake Maggiore, but they promised to write to me and made me promise to come and stay with them in Glasgow after Christmas.

As for me I should be leaving the touring party at Geneva to spend the summer with my French uncle, Claude Greppo, at Charnay-Bayère in the Lyonnais. The party stayed a night at the Hôtel Bristol in Geneva before returning to London and I was left to travel on next day to France. My father gave me the money to pay my hotel bill and buy a second-class railway ticket to Lozanne, the nearest station to Charnay.

That evening after dinner I went to the Kursaal and captivated by *petits chevaux* I proceeded to back the horses with five-franc pieces. I do not know what the rules are to-day for *petits chevaux* but in 1900 horse number 5 of the 9 horses meant that the bank won and the odds against the players were heavy. I kept putting on five-franc pieces, losing every time, until I had lost the whole of my railway fare. In a vain attempt to recover it I lost the whole of my hotel bill. All that was now left was about thirty francs of pocket money, and presently I had only one five-franc piece left. I forget which of the nine horses I put it on, but it was the five which won and I walked out of the Kursaal, literally without a sou.

In the morning I asked the bulky head-porter of the Hôtel Bristol to send a telegram for me to Avonmore Road. '*Have lost money for ticket and hotel bill please telegraph amount Hotel Bristol Geneva.*'

I felt the head-porter was regarding me with growing suspicion next day when no reply came, and when by the afternoon of the following day there was still no reply I felt I could not return to the hotel and spent the night on a bench beside Lake Geneva. This may be considered fatuous behaviour, but at seventeen worldly wisdom is not remarkable. When I got back to the Hôtel Bristol the money had arrived and I let the porter suppose I had spent the night with a girl. Since that absurd behaviour of mine in Geneva I have never been able to gamble desperately. I have backed horses; indeed, I kept myself by betting while I was writing *Carnival*, but I have never been able really to enjoy even roulette. I have always been tickled by the thought that the lesson of this cautionary tale should have been administered by Geneva, the fount of Puritanism, where surely if anywhere one should have been safe from the temptation to gamble.

The journey to France gave me a variety of experience. There were four of us in the grey-upholstered second-class carriage as we rumbled along through the sunny June landscape. In one corner were an Italian honeymoon couple, the bridegroom in a white suit fast asleep on one side, and the bride fast asleep opposite. I was in the other corner on the same side as the bride; opposite me was a Frenchman. I hear now the buzz of a bluebottle-fly against the pane in the warmth of that summer day.

I do not know how long we had been travelling when, waking from a doze, I saw that the sleeping bridegroom's white tunic was splashed with blood. I drew the Frenchman's attention to it whereupon he rose from his seat with a finger to his lips and moved cautiously along to take down a bag in the rack above the bridegroom. He opened it and showed me a broken bottle of red ink which had been dripping from the bag.

"*Ne dites rien,*" he murmured. "*Ce n'est rien du tout.*" With this he threw the broken bottle out of the carriage window and settled himself back in his seat.

We rumbled on for a while until there came from the bride a loud scream.

"*Carlo!*" she cried, "*sveglia-ti. Guarda! Guarda!* [wake up, look, look.] *Tu hai un emorraggio, o sei già morto?*" [You have a haemorrhage, or are you already dead?] The bridegroom now woke up and saw what he supposed was blood upon his tunic.

"*Dio mio, che cosa è successo?*" [My god, what has happened?]

At this the Frenchman put his hand in his waistcoat pocket and produced a small phial which he offered to the bridegroom with a courtly gesture. The bridegroom, supposing that he was being offered a restorative, put the bottle to his lips and gulped down some of the contents; at once he let out a louder yell than ever. "*Sono stata avvelenato!*" [I've been poisoned!] he yelled.

What the Frenchman had offered him was a phial of ammonia to take out as much of the ink stain as possible, which he tried to explain. It was no use. The bride was determined to believe the Frenchman had tried to poison her husband and pulled the communication cord. The train came to a stop among green meadows, and a quarter of an hour of excitable argument went on during which various passengers alighted to take part. At last the guard decided that nothing could be done until the train reached Lyons. What happened there I do not know because I alighted at Lozanne, some twenty kilometres before we reached Lyons, where a trap was waiting to drive me the six miles or so to Charnay-Bayère.

Strange the freaks of memory! I cannot recall who met me on that sunny day at the end of June, nor a yard of the five or six miles from Lozanne to Charnay, nor the vehicle I drove in, and yet the picture of that small French railway station, and of the train going on its way to Lyons is perfectly clear at this moment.

The house of my uncle, Claude Greppo, a severe grey house with green jalousies, stood well above the dusty road, the garden in front buttressed by a massive wall on the mossy top of which one could sit at ease with one's feet on the ground and watch the great white cows, that did the work of oxen when they were not being milked, move slowly and softly by. Beyond the house was my uncle's vegetable garden, of which the melons were his pride, and beyond this garden was an orchard of peaches. The windows of the house looked over a wide prospect of lush green water meadows to the little town of Châtillon-d'Azergues, two or three miles away, which stood on rising ground among vineyards and had a ruined castle. At the height of noon the place was the colour of a Victoria plum but it used to deepen with the westerly sun until by dusk it looked like a deep-bloomed damson. The particular charm of that castle for youth was the oubliette; a small aperture at the top of the stone steps that wound round the inside of the tower wall was pointed out as the window through which the condemned man was allowed to take his last look at earth before he was precipitated through a trap upon the knives of the oubliette below. It was a fair prospect they gave him over the red roofs of the little town, over the blue river, to vine-covered slopes crowned by forest beyond.

Behind my uncle's house the land ran up to a ridge dotted with small oak-trees and thickets of broom. From here one could look across a hundred miles of fat cultivated plain to where along the horizon sailed, like a fleet of mighty frigates, the Alps. This ridge was frequented by large green lizards with black lozenges along their backs and by hundreds of Swallow-tail butterflies. Why Swallow-tail butterflies should haunt this kind of country in France, and in England never move outside the Fens is a mystery. Few butterflies have so majestic a flight, and I used to watch that multitudinous sarabande for hour after rapturous hour of utter beauty. The trunks of the oak trees were haunted by dark Hipparchias, sheened with bronze, but whether Circe or Hermione I do not know. Yet perhaps the most memorable sight of butterflies that year was of myriads of Clouded Yellows above a field of lucerne, dancing above it like the spirits of Wordsworth's daffodils.

My uncle Claude Greppo was now in his mid-sixties, asthmatic, irritable, speaking English with a strong accent but disinclined to speak French with his family. How my grandparents had ever consented to his marrying my aunt Ellen I cannot guess. He had come to New York as traveller for a firm of Lyons silk-merchants when Ellen Bateman, after a fantastic career as a child actress, was making up for her lost schooldays by working with governesses and tutors.

However, married she was at fifteen and had her first child, who died at a year old, when she was sixteen. She might have been a dramatic soprano and prima donna; she might have been an actress of outstanding quality, as good in comedy as she was in tragedy. At eight years old she was playing a poor little newsboy in a play written by her mother, and one night she suddenly asked the audience of a San Francisco theatre to buy her papers, and the stage was covered with money flung on it by the audience. I have told earlier about the goblet made of virgin gold given her by the miners of '49, engraved *To Ellen Bateman from the Sierra Nevada.*

Claude Greppo was doing well as a traveller when unfortunately his friends persuaded him to become a manufacturer on borrowed capital and he lost it all. It was a struggle for my aunt to bring up a family of five, and life continued to be a struggle until her eldest daughter Claudia married Charles Danforth. I have told of the impression made on us as children by the visit of those rich American cousins.

When I came to Charnay in 1900 Charles Danforth had died in Athens of pneumonia three years before, and two years later his wife had died. My aunt Ellen was entrusted with the guardianship and bringing up of the three Danforth children, Charlie, Claudia and Marian, who were all at Charnay this summer. So too was her youngest daughter Ellen, now 29, dark, languid and handsome, much more French than American.

I was glad to find a well-stocked library of Tauchnitz novels bought during the visits the Danforths had paid to Europe. Those English novels published during the last twenty years were invaluable to my future as a novelist.

After my devotion to French decadence during the last year, after the Satanism of *Là-Bas* and the necrophily of Rollinat, and the voluptuous horrors of Baudelaire's black Venus, it was high time I should be able to be moved by Rhoda Broughton's love-stories. I have not ventured to re-read them because I do not want to spoil a past experience by possible disillusionment. Then I read nine novels of Henry Seton Merriman right off the reel. He could provide youthful and unsophisticated readers with an illusion that they were moving behind the scenes of European politics, and he shared with Rudyard Kipling an ability to present commonplace people with an apparent omniscience that deceived the reader into supposing it was possible to generalize about a man's behaviour from his superficial characteristics. Somerset Maugham would do the same kind of thing for youth twenty years later and provide it with ready-made cynicism about life in general and women in particular. I have written about these novels of the 'eighties and 'nineties in *Literature in My Time* and need not say more about them now.

The great discovery in my reading was Balzac. What would I not give now to recapture the emotion with which I read *Eugénie Grandet* at seventeen! It was the habit of Eugénie's father to present her with money on her birthday, and this gift she was enjoined not to spend but to keep in a money-box. Every year on her birthday she was told to fetch her money-box for this year's present to be added to it and always her father counted what was in her box and praised her for not having spent a single sou. Then Eugénie fell in love with a young man who needed money and she lent him her savings. In due course her birthday came round and her father as usual told her to bring down her money-box. Eugénie was shattered with dread of what her father would say when he found the money-box empty. So was I. She was going upstairs at the bottom of the page to fetch that fatal money-box, and I could not bring myself to turn the page to learn what happened when old Grandet found it was empty. I hardly slept that night, knowing that in the morning I should have to turn that page and learn the worst. I have never dared to read *Eugénie Grandet* since because I cannot bring myself to read that incident with the blunted emotion of age; I must preserve inviolate the memory of that agonizing suspense.

My uncle Claude was under the delusion that he was a philosopher and he had published an unreadable work, the unsold copies of which were stacked in the garret of the Charnay house. He had a habit of testing me with his metaphysical theories, when I learnt the valuable accomplishment of appearing to be listening to somebody while I was pre-occupied with my own thoughts. Sometimes, however, he would question me so sharply that I had to listen. I hear him now:

"Est-ce que rien peut venir de rien?"

"Non, mon oncle."

"You have understood what I am saying? Can nothing come out of nothing?"

"No, Uncle Claude."

"Bon! Can something come out of nothing?"

"No, Uncle Claude."

"Bon."

"Can nothing come out of something?"

I hesitated. Nothing had come out of a lot of things in my experience.

"Oui, mon oncle."

At this he would raise his hands above his head in despair at such stupidity. "It is useless to teach you even the elements of philosophy if you cannot grasp that nothing cannot come out of something."

"Pardon, mon oncle."

"And do not speak French to me. Your accent is terrible. Do not speak French until you can pronounce '*fauteuil*'." And this I was never able to do to his satisfaction.

One day he asked me if I should like him to teach me piquet, and when I told him I knew the game already he snorted. "No doubt you can play piquet as well as you pronounce '*fauteuil*'."

We sat down to piquet and I was about 400 points up on him after three hands. "Beginner's luck," he growled.

After a fortnight, by the end of which I was over 6000 points up on him, he suddenly threw his hand into the air after a repique and declared that it was useless to play against somebody as lucky as I was. We never cut for a deal again.

Not long after I came to Charnay my mother wrote to say that my father had been deeply upset over my behaviour in Geneva, and said she thought it would make him feel relieved about my future if I asked him to get me articled to his solicitors, Colyer and Colyer. I told my aunt Ellen that the last thing on earth I wanted was to become a solicitor, and she agreed with me that it was an absurd idea.

"Your dear mother gets foolish notions sometimes. I shall write to her."

And write she did to say that the proper thing would be for my father and mother to agree I should go to Oxford in the autumn and that, as I had already settled which college I wanted to go to, she should write to Magdalen and find out if they were willing to accept me.

"I'll have to pass Smalls first."

"Smalls?"

"Responsions. You have to pass Responsions before you can go up to Oxford."

"Is it a difficult examination?"

"Oh no, it's very easy. It's held some time at the end of September or beginning of October."

My aunt's letter was effective. I heard no more about being articled to a firm of solicitors.

Some time at the end of July my aunt Isabel came out to Charnay, bringing with her my sister Viola. Isabel Bateman was now Sister Isabel Mary in the white habit of a novice of the Community of St Mary the Virgin at Wantage, which she had joined in her forty-fifth year and of which some twenty years hence she would become Mother-General. She was now in the St James's home for penitents in Fulham. Her last appearance on the stage had been in *Trelawney of the Wells* at the Court Theatre.

Since her daughter Claudia's death a year before, my aunt Ellen had lost her faith and at this date was a passionate atheist. So naturally she was depressed by Isabel's becoming a nun. After a while she recovered her faith and the happiness of her younger sister in the conventual life was her own greatest happiness. I myself was faintly irritated by my godmother's attitude as a novice. I had too much Bateman in myself to tolerate being told that Balzac was deplorable reading for somebody of my age.

"I really cannot be told what I should and should not read, because I think I am probably going to write myself one day."

She asked to see a short story I had written and found it ridiculous, as I have no doubt it was. However, she did agree with my aunt Ellen that the notion of becoming articled to a firm of solicitors was foolish. So I felt with some relief that she would not encourage my mother's plan to set my father's mind at rest. Nevertheless, I was glad when she went back to England after a fortnight. When my mind was made up in youth I could not argue about it; I used to enclose myself in a kind of crystal and become oblivious of everybody. When I decided not to be a parson I could not accept such a decision as a disappointment to anybody else; it concerned only myself.

That Summer in the Lyonnais floats like a golden cloud in my memory. I found plump little Claudia, who was then about ten years old, delightful company; I enjoyed talking to my languid cousin Ellen.

There was a feast in which the local band promenaded all over the village with the *brioche*, with a slice of which the household was presented after healths had been drunk. I had a Kodak camera and still have a snapshot I took of the band on its round.

Not even the arrival of the *Daily Mail* with the news that every member of the Foreign Legations had been massacred at Peking and that a memorial service was being arranged in St Paul's Cathedral could startle me out of that peace. Nor, indeed, was there any reason to be startled; a couple of days later it turned out that the *Daily Mail* announcement was without any foundation, and the memorial service was cancelled just in time.

It may be worth recalling that the appellation of Hun, which the Germans so much resent, was given to them that Summer by their own Kaiser when he harangued the troops embarking at Bremerhaven to give the Chinese a lesson: "No quarter will be given, no prisoners will be taken. Let all who fall into your hands be at your mercy. Just as the Huns gained a reputation in virtue of which they still live in historical tradition, so may the name of Germany become known in such a manner in China that no Chinaman will ever again even dare to look askance at a German."

And at the end of that July on board the *Hohenzollern* the Kaiser, preaching a sermon on a text from *Exodus* declared: "The heathen spirit of the Amalekites is again astir in far off Asia—with great might and cunning, with fire and with slaughter, is the attempt being made to bar the way of European commerce and of European intelligence."

In that autumn of 1900 the voters of England and Scotland would return at the Khaki Election that disastrous Unionist Government which made the Anglo-Japanese Alliance; only in Wales was there some prescience of disaster to inspire the electors to turn away in greater numbers from imperialists without the imagination, the courage, or the self-denial to act imperially.

Not that I myself was any more of an imperialist at that date than I am to-day, and the 63 years of varied experience I have enjoyed since 1900 have scarcely even modified my political outlook. However, politics whether foreign or domestic, are inappropriate to the mood of that Summer I am looking back at. It is marked more deeply in my memory by my own zest in its simple delights. I recall a visit to Lyons and sitting on a boulevard between the slow bottle-green Sâone and the swift ice-blue Rhône and eating five exquisite small melons green and golden-netted and costing 30 centimes apiece. I recall marvellous ices and *petits fours* and cream pastries eaten in a crowded square with a view of the cathedral on its hill, looking like an elephant with gilded legs upside down. I recall the rapid shallow stream in which I searched for crayfish or fished for small insipid dace and roach. I recall endless conversations with old peasants and being entertained with their milk and wine and peaches. I recall the threshing with flails when the grain overflowed into the narrow village street until one waded in it almost knee deep. That experience remained unique until seventeen years later in Naupaktos I waded through such gold above the waters of Lepanto. I recall the evening meal of lettuce and skimmed milk cheese that seemed the perfect end of miles of wandering in the sun. I recall days when it was too hot even for me to hunt butterflies and I would sit in an arbour covered by jasmine with a view of the winding white dusty road and deep-bloomed Châtillon flickering in the heat on the other side of the water meadows in a cream of meadow-sweet. Here I would read novels like *The Heavenly Twins* and *The Woman who Did* which had been the topics of the At Home Day, that genteel convenience of late Victorianism. When I was not reading I was writing long letters on crackling foreign notepaper to various girl friends, planning among so many other plans to visit the Duncans at Cadenabbia in October should my hopes of Oxford be frustrated.

But my outstanding memory of that summer is the dinner given in honour of my cousin Theodore Greppo, the eldest son, who had come over from America to visit the scenes of his youth. Theodore was a Wall Street stockbroker who had married a fashionable New York beauty and was the only conventional son of my aunt Ellen. He was very much the slave of his wife in the way that Americans so often are; she must have given him leave to make this trip without her.

There were at least a dozen of his old friends who sat round the circular table in the Charnay dining-room, among them Monsieur Boeuf the *maire*, who looked exactly like his name. There was also a Captain Desgouttes of the Zouaves who had been Theodore's greatest friend in boyhood. We ate course after delicious course, all cooked by my aunt, the culmination of which was a marvellous game-pie. We sat down at one o'clock, and it was nearly six o'clock before we rose from the table to walk about a bit and sit down again a couple of hours later to supper.

I found myself strolling in the orchard with the Captain of Zouaves. Having been irritated by the self-righteous attitude of the British Press over the Dreyfus case, I had felt compelled to become an anti-Dreyfusard when everybody else was pro-Dreyfusard at home, not from any real feeling for justice but because the French papers had been so rude to us over the Boer War.

"*Vous savez, mon capitaine,*" I said. "*Moi, je suis anti-Dreyfusard.*"

The Captain adjusted his pince-nez and looked at me with contempt.

"*Alors, vous êtes idiot,*" he snapped. "*Vous êtes imbécile.*"

He went on to say that every honest soldier knew what a disgrace it was that Dreyfus should have been condemned for a crime he had never committed. And he added bitterly that honest soldiers were suffering for their honesty. "I myself am ordered to Cochin-China next week and that means the end of my military career." As he said this Captain Desgouttes looked eastward to where the last rays of the setting sun were flushing with rose the snowy tops of the Alps.

But it was not the end of his military career. He would become General Jean Desgouttes who commanded the Army of the Rhine; my cousin Theodore, who enlisted in the American Army when the

United States came into the First World War, was one of his schoolday friend's *aides* and was with him on that triumphant march into Germany.

On the evening of Friday, September 21st I left Lyons for Paris. Why I know the date is because I travelled with a carriageful of provincial *maires*, all the provincial *maires* in France having been invited by President Loubet to spend the weekend being entertained at the Exhibition when 22,000 of them would sit down to lunch in the Tuileries gardens. The other nine travellers in the second-class compartment were *maires*. I was lucky to have a corner seat facing the engine. I was not allowed to open the window and the heat was suffocating as those nine paunchy *maires* tucked into their supper-baskets. It was a great relief when at last they all fell into sonorous sleep and as cautiously as if I were breaking into a house I managed to open the window for about a couple of inches and let a bit of air into the garlic-hung atmosphere. I suppose I must have dozed fitfully myself during that night but I was wide awake at six of a sparkling morning when the train was running through Fontainebleau. I can see as vividly as if it were a journey I had taken last night the limpid blue of the September sky and the forest a luminous, almost an ardent green, and the tallowy faces and black alpaca jackets of my travelling companions, all a-snore in the morning light, on the frowsty grey upholstery of that second-class carriage.

When the train reached the Gare de Lyon I drove to the Gare du Nord and put my bags in the left luggage office to be collected by me for the railway journey to Le Havre, where I was to catch the night boat to Southampton. Then I set off for the Louvre where, reciting to myself that page Walter Pater wrote about La Gioconda, I gazed at that immortal woman in a rapture. She was strangely like my aunt Ellen. Indeed, all the Leonardo da Vinci women resemble either my aunt Ellen, my aunt Isabel or my mother. I was also much impressed by the Venus of Milo, but most of all by the Winged Victory from Samothrace.

From the Louvre I drove in a fiacre to the Exhibition and was so fascinated by the moving platform that I spent the rest of the day on it. The first platform was stationary; one about a couple of inches above went round at two kilometres an hour, and another two more inches above went round at four kilometres an hour. If one walked against this at ordinary speed one remained where one was, a curious effect. On the other hand if one walked with it on the faster of the moving platforms one was going round the Exhibition at about eight miles an hour. It was great fun watching children escaping from governess or nurse by running along the faster platform, and one had a view of every pavilion as one glided round some thirty or forty feet above the grounds of the great Exhibition.

I have always wondered why the moving platform was not developed as a means of progress in large cities. Escalators are a commonplace, and an escalator seems a more complicated piece of mechanism. The problem of motor transport in the future should have been obvious to men of vision by 1900, but human beings with rare exceptions seem incapable of foresight and those who possess it are usually treated like Cassandra.

When I went on board the boat for Southampton I found there was not one vacant berth and I had to spend a queasy night on deck. Feeling chilled, I asked for a hot bath, but when I was comfortably immersed I found it impossible to get a lather from the soap. I discovered that the bath was half oil, which had somehow got into the water, and on emerging I found myself greasy all over. By this time there was no more hot water and I had to run an absolutely cold bath before I could rid myself of the oil; it was most disagreeable.

When I reached the railway station at Southampton on Sunday morning I found that the train for Alton had left five minutes ago and that there would not be another until late in the afternoon. I tried two Southampton churches; finding that glorified morning prayer would have to be endured before the bisected so called second service was reached, I decided that I should get more spiritual benefit from visiting the big Netley Hospital crowded with South African wounded in convalescence. One of these was due to leave hospital next day and he suggested we should go for a sail on Southampton Water. We had a great time under a sky of billowy cumulus and the perfect breeze, fortified internally by some ham sandwiches which a kind nurse had cut for us, after exacting from my companion a firm promise to be back in hospital by three o'clock. There I left him and set out to wander back to Southampton by country lanes.

On the way a ludicrous incident occurred. Turning a corner, I intruded upon a domestic scene. A girl of fifteen or sixteen wearing a great floppy hat was standing in the middle of the lane holding up her skirt and petticoats while her mother was sewing a button on to the flap of her long white lace-fringed drawers.

"Peeping Tom, eh?" demanded a small indignant man with mutton-chop whiskers, who with paternal modesty had turned the back on the operation. The girl dropped her skirt and petticoats and glowered at me indignantly; her mother with needle and thread in her hand glowered with equal indignation.

"Well, I'm afraid I can't walk back in the opposite direction because you choose to turn a country lane into a bedroom," I said. With this I walked on with the elaborate nonchalance of seventeen.

I devoted the week at Beech to reading the Greek and Latin books set for Responsions; and in due course went up to Oxford and passed the examination. Yet I cannot remember anything about it. What I do remember is my mother coming up to Oxford and looking at rooms at 7 Longwall, which were booked for the opening of the Michaelmas Term. I recall that the name of one of the other lodgers was Gathorne-Hardy; he must have been an uncle of Bob Gathorne-Hardy who would be associated with me on the staff of *The Gramophone* a quarter of a century later.

Those rooms in Longwall had to be cancelled a day or two afterwards because the college authorities decided that at seventeen I was too young to be out of college in my first year and there were no rooms vacant in college; I was to come up in April and take my matriculation. I was much disappointed at the time but it turned out all for the best.

Father Dolling, the much loved head of the Winchester College Mission at Landport, who had been put out of St Agatha's by Randall Davidson when he became Bishop of Winchester, was now at St Saviour's in Arcadia Street, Poplar, and when I went to visit Uncle Robert (as he was to us) he took me down with him to Trant's House for a night. He wanted me to meet Johnny Bramston, now entering his second year at Magdalen, because he would be able to tell me something about the College. However, Johnny Bramston was away. The Reverend Trant Bramston was the best known and best loved of the Winchester dons, a great eccentric figure of the period. All the Asquiths were in his house, and I recall from that evening Arthur (Oc) Asquith reciting one of Herrick's poems to Clarissa Bramston (Kissa) in which there was a line about a leg as white as any egg. Davidson, who five years later would be playing the Just Argument in the *Clouds* of Aristophanes when I should be playing Phidippides, was also there that evening, bound for Balliol next year. It was a magical evening and I regretted that Uncle Robert's plan for me to go to Trant's House had not materialized. Yet, again it was all for the best because, profoundly as I admire what was then Winchester's adamantine mould, it might have landed me in the Civil Service in spite of every effort I made to keep out of it.

The question now was where and how was I to spend the year before I went up to Oxford. I tried to persuade my mother that the most useful prologue to Oxford would be to let me travel alone all over Europe, but that unfortunate business at Geneva had spoilt any chance of my doing that. In the end it was decided that I should go to the Reverend Arnold Overton, the Vicar of High Cross, two or three miles out of Ware in Hertfordshire.

By now that bicycle with the wide handlebars and the thick Clincher tyres which had been the joy of my schooldays was too old-fashioned an affair for enterprising youth; it was too old-fashioned even for my young brother, and Frank scornfully rejected my suggestion that he should inherit it. My heart was set on a free-wheel bicycle and after wrestling with catalogues I decided upon a Rover model costing 18 guineas. The salesman shook his head when I told him I wanted a free-wheel.

"It's a bit soon for one of these new free-wheel bicycles," I was told. "If you take my advice, you'll wait a bit to see how they develop. We haven't had time yet to judge what they can do."

I was not to be shaken by such cautious advice and insisted on a free-wheel. I rode that Rover for eight years until I acquired a green Raleigh and gave my Rover to our gardener in Cornwall, who rode it for at least another eight years. How many bicycles made to-day could last as long as that?

The distance between High Cross and Earls Court was about 25 miles and I rode those miles many times during the next year—along the Commercial Road through the Whitechapel that once upon a time had been a name of dread and now seemed so jolly, from Whitechapel turning left northward through Cheshunt, Waltham, Hoddesdon, and Ware to High Cross.

The village began in a wooded hollow and rose up to the fairly modern church and red brick vicarage at the top of the hill, whence the country ran level on either side of the old North Road into Cambridgeshire. The Reverend Arnold Overton, who was always laconic but never taciturn, was an old Exeter College man and most of his pupils were bound for Exeter. He had the sense to recognize at once that I knew what was best for myself. He did suggest that German might be a useful addition to French, and when I suggested reading a translation into German of Ibsen's *Doll's House* he did not immediately propose Goethe or Schiller as a better approach to

German literature. His wife may have argued that it was wiser to let me concentrate upon writing poetry and for the sake of scholastic appearances to toy with *The Doll's House*.

Mrs Overton was an influence of inestimable value to that critical eighteenth year of boyhood's end. She was a daughter of Dr Edersheim, the distinguished authority on Palestine. I suppose she would have been in her late thirties at this date, tall and handsome, with a mind that cut like a razor through pretentiousness, snobbery, and complacency. She used to review books every week for the *Guardian* (not the *Manchester Guardian*) and I recall her endorsing my mother's opinion of Charles Marriott's novel *The Column* which had been the great success of that autumn. I had fallen for it completely and had been shocked by my mother's inability to appreciate it because for her there was not a real person in it. I had confided to Mrs Overton what I believed was my mother's inability to appreciate a great novel.

"Your mother is perfectly right."

And when some years later I tried to re-read *The Column* I wondered how I could have been taken in by such an ado about nothing. *The Column*, and *The Gadfly* by E. L. Voynich, are the two novels the re-reading of which has made me feel most apologetic for a youthful indiscretion.

Besides having infallible good taste Mrs Overton was a superlative housewife and ran the vicarage with a Swiss cook and house-parlourmaid. She herself managed the poultry, Golden Wyandottes with brown eggs in one run and Black Minorcas with white eggs in the other. She was a wonderful gardener, too, and I learned much about growing flowers in that walled garden of the vicarage; it was here, marvelling at the first *Iris reticulata* in bloom, that my passion for bulbous irises began.

I can see Mrs Overton looking at me sadly when I had taken her advice to read *Emma* and confessed that it had bored me. It has required courage to confess in public that I was once upon a time bored by *Emma*; that it could ever have happened shows how much immaturity of taste was still mine. To be bored by *Emma* and to be captivated by *The Column*!

The Overtons had two small boys—Ted and Tom. The former was on the edge of seven when I came to High Cross that October, and Tom would have been about a year younger. We became close friends and I spent many hours in their company while I was at the Vicarage. Ted was a very solemn little boy full of earnest questions, sensitive and if offended liable to fall into a gloom. Tom was touched with genius and the most enchanting small boy I have known. To-day Ted is Sir Arnold Overton, K.C.B., K.C.M.G., M.C., who after a fine war record had a brilliant career in the Civil Service. Tom was killed at Gallipoli.

Dr Boyd, a delightful Irish doctor who commanded the Ware Company of the 1st V.B. Battalion (Herts) of the Bedfordshire Regiment, came on a visit to the Vicarage one day early in that October and asked me why I did not join the Volunteers. I was much taken by the idea and asked Mr Overton if he would write and suggest such a step to my father. He at once agreed, and to my great satisfaction my father consented without a murmur in spite of the fact that my uniform and equipment was going to cost him over £100. So I was commissioned before the end of that October and notified of as much by Mr Brodrick, the Secretary of State for War. The formal commission signed by Queen Victoria did not arrive so quickly. In order to spare the Queen the fatigue of signing commissions a stamp had been made; this outraged Her Majesty's sense of military decorum and she forbade them to be issued, declaring she would be able to sign them personally very shortly. During that autumn Queen Victoria was moving towards her end, and she never did sign those commissions. In the last week of January I received mine stamped Victoria R.I. in purple ink, but countersigned across the top by Edward VII in his own hand. Nevertheless, the commission is dated in that October of 1900 and so I think I can claim to be the youngest man alive with Queen Victoria's commission.

The 1st Herts considered itself one of the crack volunteer battalions in Great Britain. There were two companies in Hertford, and a company each for Ware, Welwyn, Stevenage, Hitchin, Hoddesdon, Royston and Bishop's Stortford. Every company was over a hundred strong. The uniform was scarlet with white facings. The 2nd Herts, which drew its recruits from St Albans, and other places in the west of the county, wore a grey uniform and was looked down upon by the 1st Herts. The right half-company of the Ware Company was commanded by Henry Croft, who would one day be Lord Croft and Under-Secretary of War during the Second World War. I commanded the left half-company. Henry Croft would command the battalion when it became Territorial and it would be brigaded with the Guards in September 1914. It was in recognition of the part played by that Hertfordshire Territorial battalion that the old 14th Foot became the Bedfordshire and Hertfordshire Regiment.

Buying my uniform at Hawke's was a thrill for seventeen—scarlet tunic with silver lace for ceremonial occasions, scarlet service tunic, blue service tunic for undress occasions, mess jacket and tight overalls, greatcoat, cape, haversack, waterbottle, half-wellingtons and marching boots from Wildsmith in Jermyn Street. My father was spared the expense of a sword because Colonel Stephenson, who had retired from the command of the Queen's Westminster Rifles, lent me his for as long as I should need it; it was one of his typical kindnesses.

Throughout that autumn I was drilled three times a week with the other recruits in the hall of the Ware Company and then I had to drill them. Henry Croft, the senior subaltern, was at Cambridge, and when he came down for the Christmas vac. I was back in London. So I saw little of him until the summer manoeuvres at Aldershot. My colour-sergeant was everything a young subaltern could hope for; he was always close at hand to give me good advice. I remember vividly the moment of crisis. Captain Boyd had been called away to a case and so it fell to me to take a squad of some 40 men to the shooting-range on the other side of Hertford. When we were marching through Hertford the Ware chaps started chai-aiking the girls and blowing kisses. There was a good deal of local rivalry between Hertford and Ware and my colour-sergeant said: "You must hold them in, sir, or there may be trouble. And it's up to you now to show 'em once and for all that you'll stand no nonsense."

"Shall I march them at attention, colour-sergeant?"

"That's a very good idea, sir."

And march them at attention I did for the whole two miles to the shooting-range. I never had any trouble with them again.

Route marches at night were a feature of that autumn. Most of the company commanders were local squires and could afford to entertain the rank and file lavishly. I look back to delicious cold suppers after tramps of ten miles, with plenty of champagne to sustain one for the ten miles march home. I recall a particular evening when one of the Gilbeys, who commanded the Bishop Stortford company, entertained us like a Roman emperor.

Back in London for the last Christmas I should spend in Avonmore Road, from which my mother was set on moving as soon as a bigger house could be found, I spent a lot of time with the Stephensons in Addison Court Gardens. I think Violet was still at my aunt Katie's dramatic school in Philbeach Gardens, from which as Miss Violet Sterne she would join the Compton Comedy Company in the following summer. I spent more time with her elder sister Ivy that winter. She and I went to midnight Mass at the Carmelite church in Kensington Church Street. The music was Mozart's and there was an exquisite *Incarnatus* sung by a soprano which I have never heard since. As Ivy and I walked back afterwards along Kensington High Street there comes back to me a fragment of our conversation.

"I wonder whether we shall ever go again together to midnight Mass," Ivy said, half to herself.

"Why on earth shouldn't we?"

"You'll be forgetting us soon."

I protested against this.

"Don't you realize that you'll be famous one day?"

"What difference will that make?"

"You'll be living in another world."

I protested again but she shook her head.

"I know I am right."

"Well, whatever happens, I shall never forget how much you and Violet and your father have done for me."

Ivy Stephenson is no longer alive to read this small tribute of a grateful heart for what the Stephensons did for me sixty-five years ago, but that I should still remember a fragment of conversation from a walk home along the Kensington High Street of the last week of the nineteenth century is surely proof of what I owe to Ivy and Violet Stephenson.

It was earlier in that December that I went to the prize-giving at my sister Viola's school in Holland Park presided over by Miss Tulse. Viola's great friends were Gwen and Joan Williams, whose brother Orlo[1] was also in attendance from Eton. In those days Orlo Williams was extremely shy and stammered badly. I count Orlo Williams among the best minds with whom I have come into contact and I have had a lifetime's admiration and respect for his judgment of music, literature and the fine arts. That meeting was to have a profound influence on my future. One day Orlo would be responsible for my getting to Gallipoli. Moreover, when my sister went to stay with his sisters at Taynton near Burford she met there my future brother-in-law, Christopher Stone, who was in College with Orlo Williams at Eton, and later on Christopher, a freshman at the House, would call on me, a freshman at Magdalen. Finally it was that visit to Taynton which made Christopher familiar with Burford

[1] Dr Orlo Williams, C.B., D.C.L.

and led to our both taking a cottage there in 1904. Orlo Williams was a son of Orlando Cyprian Williams, the distinguished barrister who wrote Williams on Real Property, a classic work of law. His mother was a gifted painter and, in spite of being stone deaf, one of the most acute and entertaining women I have known.

The nineteenth century went out on New Year's Eve in the south of England to a savage gale, so savage that one of the megaliths of Stonehenge was blown down upon that night; I have always felt this was an omen of how much of the past the twentieth century would destroy.

Of stage plays I saw that January I recall my aunt Kate Compton as Lady Huntworth in her husband's play *Lady Huntworth's Experiment*, but the Cartons were still on their dignity in The Red Lodge at Acton and a reconciliation with them would not come for another two or three years. Then there was *Mr and Mrs Daventry* at the Royalty, in which Fred Kerr gave a remarkable performance of brutish love-making to Mrs Patrick Campbell. How much of this play was Oscar Wilde, how much Frank Harris remains uncertain to this day. Anyway, the play itself is not worth arguing about.

Some time in the middle of the month I went up to stay with the Duncans. Ever since I parted with Norah and Myra in Grindelwald we had been exchanging long letters, and I had met them again staying at an hotel in Oxford Street when they came back from Lake Maggiore in the autumn. I must have spent my eighteenth birthday in Glasgow with the Duncans in their large, comfortable and cosy flat in Huntley Gardens on Kelvinside.

Entry into my nineteenth year was marked by an amusing experience I had in the train on the way back to London.

And if I had not contrived that nervous breakdown a year ago I might still have been going back to school.

EIGHTEEN YEARS OLD: 1901

I HAD a wonderful time in Glasgow. Dance after dance, at one of which the famous Iff's band played, and a rugger match in which Glasgow Academicals beat Edinburgh Academicals. I seem to recall the victory bringing much pleasure to Norah and Myra Duncan because they were interested in one of the Glasgow halves or three-quarters who scored a couple of tries. On the only Sunday of my fortnight I had the unique experience in my life of attending a Church of Scotland service. I was impressed by the comfort of the pew and the way the congregation leaned over during extempore prayers instead of kneeling. The sermon was very long but admirably delivered.

It was a Saturday afternoon when I drove in a cab to St Enoch station, and Glasgow on a Saturday afternoon in the first January of this century was a sight completely incredible to-day. Once we had emerged from the respectable surroundings of Kelvinside the streets became a phantasmagoria of drunkenness. Many men and even a few women were lying blind drunk in the gutters; others were staggering about singing; some were fighting. I suppose the same scene might have been witnessed in the Old Town of Edinburgh at this date.

There was only one other passenger in the third-class compartment; corridors had not yet been started. My companion had a wall eye with which he kept staring at me and when we reached Carlisle I had a mind to get out and go to another carriage in case I was shut in with a madman. However, I felt it would be unworthy of one of Her Majesty's second-lieutenants to show nervousness and I remained where I was. Another hour or so passed in silence, the wall-eyed man still staring at me. At last he spoke.

"Young man," he said in a strong Lancashire accent, "I've been looking at you."

"I know you have."

"Can you understand what I've been doing all this while? I've been watching your soul, lad. Ay, watching your soul. It's been fluttering round this compartment and it's just fluttered out of window like a butterfly. You're an atheist."

"I'm not an atheist," I asserted indignantly.

"Oh yes, you are, lad. You've got the same look in your eye as a brother of mine has, and he's an atheist."

"Well, I'm not."

"It's not a bit of use your arguing about it, young man. You're an atheist. I've been listening to Dr Torrey and Mr Alexander all this week."

Dr Torrey and Mr Alexander were a couple of American revivalists, successors of Moody and Sankey and precursors of Billy Graham. They would return at intervals to Great Britain for the next four years with as little permanent effect as revivalists always have, but skilful at whipping up popular emotion for the moment and no doubt perfectly sincere in believing they had a divine message for humanity.

"Yes, I've been listening to Dr Torrey and Mr Alexander. Eh, lad, it was champion. I could see souls all around me being washed in the blood of the Lamb, souls that had been looking for Jesus all their lives and finding him at last. But you wouldn't understand what I'm talking about. You can't grasp the power of the Lord because you're an atheist."

"I am not an atheist."

"It's no good your telling me that. You've got the same look in your eyes as that poor brother of mine who lives in Wigan. Eh, we're coming into Preston. I'll tell you what I'll do, young man, I'll send a telegram to my brother to come along to Wigan station and you'll see for yourself the same look in his eyes as what you have."

Presently the train stopped at Preston and the wall-eyed man hurried out of the carriage to telegraph to his brother. When he was gone I again debated with myself the advisability of finding another compartment but in the end decided to stay where I was. The wall-eyed man soon came back.

"I've sent off telegram, and I hope my brother will be waiting for us on platform at Wigan." What the wall-eyed man had failed to realize was that the train's next stop was Crewe not Wigan.

"Eh, this is too bad," he exclaimed as the train slowed down to pass through Wigan without stopping. "Train's not going to stop. Never mind, lad. There's atheist!"

He pulled me to the window of the compartment and on that wet January evening I saw a solitary figure gazing at the passing train in obvious bewilderment.

"Can tha see atheist?" the wall-eyed man shouted. "Can tha see look in his eyes?"

A moment or two later the train had passed through Wigan, leaving that solitary figure to wonder why he had been summoned on a wet wintry night to meet a train that did not stop.

"I did my best, lad," said the wall-eyed man sadly. "But the ways of the Lord are not for us to question. Some shall be taken and others left, and you'll just have to remain an atheist till the Lord has mercy on you and shows you the path of salvation."

"I wish you wouldn't keep on supposing I'm an atheist. I happen to be a Catholic, not a Roman Catholic but an Anglo-Catholic."

"Well, that's pretty nearly as bad, isn't it? Still, I'm not going to say it is quite as bad. And I'm very tolerant myself. My wife and I have a little maid down in Cardiff where we're living now, and she's a Roman Catholic. Every Sunday morning I go along at six o'clock and rap at her door and say 'Get up, lass, and be off to that mass of yours you're supposed to attend.' Oh yes, I'm very tolerant."

And for the rest of the journey we chatted amicably. At Euston he urged me if ever I were in Cardiff to call upon him. "You'll always be welcome, lad, and the wife will always be glad to give you a cup of tea." With this the wall-eyed man gave me his card, which has long ago vanished.

Out in the Euston Road the paper-men were calling out the grave news from Osborne whither the Royal Family was being summoned.

On January 22nd Queen Victoria died. Two or three days later I was commanding my half-company when the Ware company reinforced the two Hertford companies to line the square in front of the town hall for the proclamation of King Edward VII's accession. The chief inspector of police, full of his own importance to the occasion, started to order my men about as if they were part of the crowd. I, wearing for the first time my dress-tunic with silver lace and white metal buttons, was not inclined to put up with any interference from the police and told the chief inspector to attend to his own business and leave the military to carry out their own orders. My chaps were delighted to hear the police being ordered about by their young commander.

"That was just what those bluebottles were asking for," my trusty colour-sergeant observed, and after the bugles had sounded and Edward VII had been proclaimed King and Emperor by the grace of God, one of the jolly McMullens who commanded a Hertford company told me that Colonel Longmore had been pleased by the way I had held my ground with the police. I was naturally gratified and hoped optimistically that I might be one of the subalterns chosen for the mixed company of the 1st V.B. (Herts) of the Bedfordshire Regiment which would go to London and line some fifty yards of the route of the funeral procession on February 2nd. I need hardly add that I was being much too optimistic for a very junior subaltern.

Although throughout my life I have avoided all kinds of public ceremonies, I felt that this was not merely the passing of a Queen but the passing of an epoch, and I thought it would be wrong to be absent at such a portentous moment of history. So I bicycled up to London on the day before and arranged to call for Dick Hewlett in his digs at 144 Finborough Road, which overlooked Brompton Cemetery.

That Candlemas of 1901 was completely still as if the very weather itself was holding its breath. All traffic stopped at Sloane Street and under that silvery-grey sky, which seemed not so much clouded as misted over, Dick and I walked along till we came close to Hyde Park Gate somewhere near where to-day the traffic swirls around in every direction. We gradually reached the front of a waiting crowd, all dressed in the darkest clothes they had, all silent. Some cleversticks had climbed up a plane-tree to get a better view, but when he had reached the branch that was to give him a perfect view of the procession he found himself sitting on it with his back to the prospect he had climbed up to attain. Every time he tried to work himself round the bough he was sitting on, it crackled and creaked, causing the crowd to growl angrily at the disturbance he was making. When the strains of Chopin's Funeral March were heard floating up from Constitution Hill the cleversticks made a renewed effort to turn round, but the growling of the spectators below became more menacing and in the end he had to stay still and instead of seeing the procession all he saw was the trunk of the plane-tree round which he had to put his arms in order not to fall.

When the head of the procession passed through Hyde Park Gate the music stopped and I hear now from that still, grey morning of long ago the clatter of the hooves of the horses ridden by the kings and princes of Europe behind the bier. I am almost sure the Kaiser was riding a white horse. Then as the first band reached the Marble Arch the muffled drums of Handel's Dead March from *Saul* could be heard faintly as the procession moved on toward Paddington, and the spectators in Hyde Park dispersed. Dick Hewlett and I stayed behind to watch the descent of the cleversticks from the plane-trees and presently we saw another ludicrous sight. A young couple were sitting on the next bench arguing about something. Presently they both jumped up and walked away toward the Park entrance. The argument turned to a quarrel; they whirled round and walked away from one another in opposite directions, and both of them, presumably to avoid the temptation to look at the other and appear to weaken, went into the lavatory at Hyde Park Corner, neither seeing the other go into the Gentlemen or the Ladies. After each of them had waited long enough to give the other an opportunity to be out of sight before he or she emerged they both, unfortunately for the dignity of their parting, emerged simultaneously and came face to face. Alas, they did not laugh and kiss and make it up; both of them flounced round and walked away in opposite directions without looking back.

I think it would be true to claim that I had a vague feeling of relief upon that February day, but it is only now in old age that I have come to think what a pity it was Queen Victoria did not die soon after her Golden Jubilee. If King Edward VII had ascended the throne in 1887 I believe that the break up of Europe and the break up of the British Empire might not have happened. Queen Victoria was an obstacle as much to our conduct of foreign affairs as to social progress. The insensate imperialism of the 'nineties to which she lent the support of her prestige might have been checked. The long hostility between ourselves and France might not have had to wait for the Entente Cordiale to die down; I refuse to withhold from Edward VII one tittle of the credit for that Entente Cordiale and award it instead to British 'statesmanship'. That such an Entente came too late to avoid the catastrophe of 1914 was due to the prolonged reign of Victoria. That women were refused the vote, that democratic progress was impeded, that the wisdom of Gladstone was continually flouted, that Ireland was refused Home Rule, all of these various failures of insight and foresight must be charged against those last thirteen years of Queen Victoria's reign. How empty today appears the pageant of the Diamond Jubilee!

But I must get back to High Cross in the Spring and Summer of 1901. Eric D— who had been a fellow pupil with me when I first came to the Vicarage had now left. I remember him as an early example of the self-pity so prevalent among the literary young of today. He and I had got on quite well because I have always had an unenviable capacity for being sympathetic when I should have been more sensible and more practically useful by being unsympathetic. I recognize this as a weakness, but I have never been able to overcome it. Poor Eric D— was convinced that Mrs Overton was for ever saying or doing something with no other purpose in view than to upset the feelings or spoil the comfort of Eric D—. Even the obligation to attend the Vicar's very short morning service in the church at eight o'clock was believed by Eric D— to be a device by Mrs Overton to make him get up in the morning. As I remember, he had an unhappy home life and I used to listen to long complaints about the unreasonable behaviour of his father; but I lacked the strength of mind to tell him that his father's behaviour to him was probably his own fault.

Francis Underhill, a pink-faced young man with fair curly hair, came to stay at the Vicarage for a few days sometime in that autumn. He was just down from Exeter and was a student of Cuddesdon Theological College. He and I became intimate friends immediately, and that friendship would last for over forty years: from the time he was a theological student until he died as Bishop of Bath and Wells. Francis Underhill had called Eric D— an impossible young man and protested against Mrs Overton's spoiling of him.

"You really must not be so kind, Mum, to impossible young men."

Mrs Overton's favourite pupils called her 'Mum' and Francis Underhill did not consider that Eric D— was entitled to such familiarity.

I went up to Oxford to pass my matriculation for Magdalen in April and was duly notified that I had been accepted as an undergraduate of the College and would take up residence in October in St Swithun's Quadrangle 3 2 p.r., in other words staircase three, two pairs up on the right. Coming away from the examination, I found myself in the company of a tall good-looking Harrovian called Pirie-Gordon. He became a friend of mine from that first encounter and in my third year I should share rooms with him at 43 High Street. Much more of him later.

Francis Underhill came into Oxford from Cuddesdon and we bicycled down to Beech. On the first day we rode through Wantage and up over the Berkshire Downs to reach Newbury at twilight, but pressed on to Highclere where we stayed for the night at a small inn. I recall sitting on a hill near by next morning to watch the hares gambolling below as if the madness of March was still over them. Francis Underhill always spoke of people of whom he approved intellectually as 'interior': this must have been the fashionable word for awhile among the 'aesthetes' at Oxford; when I went up, it had vanished, although 'aesthete' was still the current way of describing any undergraduate who had a mind above sport.

As Spring ripened to Summer I became more and more completely concentrated upon poetry and spent most of the day in the garden summer-house at High Cross Vicarage writing verses, none of which shall I inflict upon the gentle readers, as they were still being called, of *My Life and Times*, although I did inflict them at the time on Mrs Overton, who always generously encouraged me. When I was not writing poetry I was usually in the company of Ted and Tom exploring the countryside, both of whom were outrageously disagreeable to the two new pupils who had arrived after Eric D— left. S— was a dull youth, with the face of an amiable sheep and a bubbly way of talking, who was for ever complaining about the privileges I seemed to be enjoying over him. The fact was that Mr Overton had to keep him hard at it if there was to be any chance of his passing Responsions in the following autumn. The other new pupil C— was the son of the owner of a big hotel near Victoria, with too much pocket-money and a meagre allowance of brain. He, too, had to be kept hard at it if he was to reach Oxford.

At a village called Puckeridge some two or three miles further along the old North Road the Reverend William Crofton was the Perpetual Curate. Mr Crofton was a cyclomaniac. He treated his three bicycles like favourite horses, and indeed with his little moustache, tight trousers clipped round the ankle and black cricketing-cap he was much more like a groom than a parson.

"Looking at my cap, eh?" he would say. "Don't think I'm fool enough to waste valuable time chasing a parson's extinguisher blown off when I'm riding."

Mr Crofton had two rooms in a small house in the middle of the village. Here he stabled two bicycles in the hall, and another, his favourite, in the sitting-room. If he could have taken this jewel, as he called it, up the narrow staircase to his bedroom every night, I have no doubt he would have done so. One of these bicycles was kept for his parochial rounds, one for shopping in Hertford or visits in the neighbourhood, and the jewel for expeditions further afield.

One of the latter was an expedition to Epping Forest on which S—, C—, and I accompanied him. He never allowed us to rest anywhere except half-an-hour for tea at an Epping inn. "There is no need to ride fast so long as you keep in the saddle. I don't object even to walking up a steep hill so long as you keep walking and don't stop for the excuse of looking at the view. It is the way people will stop to look at views which spoils the time. And these new-fangled free-wheels are a menace. They're bound to make people dawdle."

When we got back from that expedition to Epping he adjured us all before we flung ourselves down in comfortable armchairs to groom our bicycles thoroughly. "Nothing exasperates me more than to see cyclists leave their bicycles ungroomed after a long ride. It's so ungrateful. You must realize that a bicycle responds to considerate treatment in the same way as a horse."

"You ought to found a society for the prevention of cruelty to bicycles, Mr Crofton," I told him.

"Not a bad idea," he said. "Not a bad idea at all. I sometimes wish the safety bicycle had never been invented. Cycling in the old days, ah, that *was* cycling. But I mustn't hurt the feelings of my three beauties of to-day," he added quickly, patting the saddle of his favourite as if it was the neck of a well-loved horse on which he had just won a steeplechase.

Canon Lyttelton, the headmaster of Haileybury, called one afternoon at the Vicarage. He had just earned renown by caning every boy in the school for some misdemeanour in which they were all involved. I always forget to ask Lord Attlee whether he remembers being caned on that occasion. It must have been a pretty tiring task even for a Lyttelton. One day thirteen years hence when Canon Lyttelton was headmaster of Eton he would write a letter to *The Times* damning books which were undermining the very foundations of our English public schools, and the book he meant was *Sinister Street*, though he did not mention it by name. I do not feel that on that early summer's afternoon I struck him across his cup of tea as a menace in the future.

Another visitor was Andrew Lang, who was staying with Mr Pullar, the local squire, for a few days of trout fishing. He talked with that irritating drawl which certain Scotsmen affect to disguise a Scottish accent. I was more than ready to admire him for his Jacobite writings; yet he was so languid and condescending that I took a dislike to him. It is hardly fair to judge a man from a single meeting, but I suspect that Andrew Lang lacked humour.

Almost every week during that Spring and Summer I was kept busy as a Volunteer. Once the battalion was reviewed in the park at Panshanger; more exciting than that was a field-day in the country round High Cross, when the Ware and Hoddesdon companies were called upon to repel an invasion by the two Hertford companies reinforced by the Haileybury Cadet Corps, which was attached to the battalion. Ted and Tom Overton were in an ecstasy of excitement and both of them depressed by my inability to let them go rushing off to spy out the enemy. Fortunately for my reputation with them they were not around when I was captured by the enemy. I had walked down a lane to see if I could spot any hostile redcoats through my glasses when round the corner of it rushed four small Haileybury boys who with fixed bayonets called on me in squeaky voices to surrender as their prisoner. There was nothing for it, and I surrendered my sword with good grace, asking what they intended to do with me.

"There's a barn close by, sir," said one of them. "I think we'd better take you to this barn." So we retired to the barn and sitting down on a bundle of straw I took out a packet of cigarettes.

"Cigarette?" I asked.

"Oh, thank you, sir. Rather!"

In those days I always smoked Brazilian cigarettes which were wrapped in maize and cost sixpence for a packet of twenty. Presently I noticed that my four captors were in difficulty with the strong dark tobacco of which Brazilian cigarettes were made.

"They taste awfully funny, sir," one of them said.

"Yes, I expect they do," I agreed. "Chuck them away if you don't like the taste." I was tactful enough not to suggest that the tobacco was too strong for them and they quickly tossed away their cigarettes, stamping them out on the floor of the barn. It was lucky I did so. Soon afterwards a sergeant or corporal of the Cadet Corps came in.

"What are you kids doing in here?" he demanded.

"We have taken prisoner this enemy officer," he was proudly informed.

Corporal or Sergeant Attlee pulled himself together and saluted me. Then he told me that the rival forces were being mustered to hear the verdict of the umpires on the performance of the two sides.

"Your sword, sir," he said. I buckled it on, and we all went along to hear the verdict.

In honesty I must admit that Lord Attlee denies he was ever a corporal or a sergeant in the Haileybury Cadet Corps and insists that he remained a private. However, he certainly must have been at that field day, and I shall continue to believe against the evidence that it *was* Sergeant Attlee who came into that barn sixty-three years ago as I tell this tale.

A third son was born to Mrs Overton that summer. I forget who his godfathers were but neither of them was able to be present and I made by proxy the promises a godfather makes at a baptism. I think the baby was christened Mark.

One last memory before I leave High Cross. In those days I always slept with a window wide open; indeed, I did not give up that foolish habit until Norman Douglas persuaded me of its folly nearly thirty years later; since when I never open my window at night and sleep perfectly in consequence with hardly ever a waking dream, my deep sleep preoccupied with whatever I am writing at the moment. Owing to my still keeping the window open my sleep was disturbed night after night that Spring by a nightingale's song from a hawthorn tree on the lawn just outside my room. That bird was as grimly determined to sing as an amateur soprano who had brought her music with her to an At Home.

It was no use leaning out of the window and clapping my hands; the nightingale thought I was applauding. One night I was driven by exasperation into flinging my pillow at the bird; it merely stopped for a moment and then continued to sing 'of summer with full-throated ease'. Moreover, I had to go downstairs and out into the garden to rescue my pillow.

At July's end the time came for me to leave High Cross, where I had spent so many happy months. To my pride and joy I had been given the job of taking a mixed company to Aldershot a day or two ahead of the main body of the battalion in order to pitch our camp, with the rest of the Home Counties Brigade, for a week of summer manoeuvres at the beginning of August.

My trusty and well-beloved colour-sergeant was with me on that cross country journey from Hertford to Aldershot with two changes of stations on the way. We marched through Aldershot bound for Scroggs' Bottom where our tents were to be pitched. I was continually giving 'eyes right' or 'eyes left' to saluting sentries as we passed various barracks. At last after a long tramp we reached Scroggs' Bottom where my colour-sergeant suggested it would be a good idea to let the men fall out for a minute or two in order as he put it to relieve themselves. I gave the order and the men started to relieve themselves with a will. In the middle of the performance a subaltern of the Oxford Light Infantry, whose volunteer battalion was brigaded with ours, came rushing along to me, a monocle in his eye which he dropped in consternation.

"Don't you realise, sir, that your men are pumping ship exactly where we are going to pitch our mess-tent?" he asked indignantly.

"I'm very sorry, sir; naturally I didn't know."

"Well, can't you do something about it, sir?"

I could have given the order to cease fire, but I was at a loss how to give an order to cease pumping ship, and their performance on the ground of the Oxford Light Infantry's mess-tent was carried through to its conclusion accompanied by profound apologies from myself.

In those days the famous 43rd Foot or Oxford Light Infantry had not been amalgamated with the equally famous 52nd Foot to become the Oxford and Bucks Light Infantry. To this day the 52nd Foot cannot tolerate being a second battalion and are offended if addressed as the 2nd Oxford and Bucks Light Infantry. When my brother was gazetted to the 1st Royal Inniskilling Fusiliers I was warned always to address him as F. S. Mackenzie Esq, Royal Inniskilling Fusiliers, 27th of the Line. The 1st Battalion was not prepared to recognize the 2nd Battalion which had once been the Hundredth and something Foot. I do not know how far these old regimental prejudices have survived since Division worship started in the Second World War and was fostered when F. M. Montgomery was C.I.G.S. It is not for me or any amateur soldier who remembers when the Royal Army Service Corps was the A.S.C. and known as Ally Sloper's Cavalry to express an opinion about the advantages or disadvantages of amalgamating famous regiments, the Royal Scots Fusiliers with the Highland Light Infantry or the Seaforth with the Cameron Highlanders, under a new name.

That subaltern in the Oxford Light Infantry put up his monocle and watched with a baleful eye my company move on to their appointed camping ground. I had the satisfaction of being congratulated by Colonel Longmore when the rest of the battalion arrived on our camp, congratulations which had been entirely earned by the non-commissioned officers who treated me like a favourite son.

That was indeed a memorable week for me, with only one very brief mortification) which was when Captain Kendall, the adjutant, told me that my hair should be cut shorter and I re-appeared looking like a convict, but approved by bullet-headed Captain Kendall, who was an Inniskilling Fusilier temporarily attached to a volunteer battalion. I do not think I went to my tent before three o'clock on any night, and reveillé was at six. As the junior subaltern it was for me to respond at dinner to the mess-president's, 'Mr Vice, the King,' and rising at the other end of the table to say 'Gentlemen, the King'. I was always nervous that I might say 'Gentlemen, the Queen' in a moment of aberration but luckily I never did commit such a *gaffe*; it was still difficult to realise that Q.C.'s were now

K.C.'s and that there was a King again upon the Throne, a royal figure beyond the memory of anybody taking part in those manoeuvres. I recall as a topic of mess conversation at the time the trial of Lord Russell in the House of Lords for bigamy, because he had married a barmaid called Molly Cook after a Reno divorce. He was sentenced, as I remember, to three months at Brixton in the First Division.

After dinner when the senior officers retired to play whist or this new-fangled game of bridge there was much horseplay in the ante-room. One game was for two subalterns to be blindfolded and lie down beside each other with their heads in the opposite direction; both were armed with a rolled up *Graphic* or *Illustrated London News*. Then one of them would have to say something and try to roll out of reach of the other before he was caught a whack on the head. Another game was squatting with a stick under one's legs and trying to charge down one's opponent. I think this was called 'frog-hopping'. Finally there was tilting, when two of us were mounted on two others and tried to unhorse each other. Guest-night was a great occasion with the gold-lace of the Horse Gunners and so many other splendid mess-uniforms. I am glad I have a picture in my mind's eye of what a guest-night at Aldershot looked like once upon a time.

Henry Croft, who commanded the Ware right half-company, was always very pleasant in spite of being now in his third year at Trinity Hall. His elder brother had won the Colquhoun Sculls but his rowing career had been cut short by losing both legs in South Africa. Henry Croft had been at Eton and then for some mysterious reason had been sent to Shrewsbury. He still considered himself an Old Etonian and I remember going with him late one afternoon to visit some of his former contemporaries in camp with a Buckinghamshire volunteer battalion. As I remember, they were brigaded with us and not with the other school cadet-corps, among which our own Haileybury Cadet Corps found itself.

I see Henry Croft now, tall and slim with a beaky nose, in blue undress with his swagger cane under his arm at the correct angle as we walked away from the Eton Cadet Corps, and hear him say: "Not as bad as I expected. I was afraid they might have gone back since I left Eton. However, they are quite a likely lot."

Henry Croft had as much serene self-confidence as anybody I ever met. Ten years later he would be member for Christchurch in Hampshire, and when war broke out in 1914 he was commanding the 1st Herts Territorial Battalion with distinction. It is not surprising they were brigaded with the Guards; no War Office mandarin would have ventured to brigade a battalion commanded by Henry Croft anywhere else.

In 1919 he became member for Bournemouth, where he found the ideal background for his true-blue (I almost wrote blue-nosed) conservatism. He became Prior of the Primose League, and when the Second World War started he was already a baronet, to become a peer in 1940 and Under-Secretary of State for War. He will be remembered for his advice to the Home Guard to arm themselves with pikes until rifles were available.

One of our majors was Hoare, who was a master at Haileybury where he commanded the Cadet Corps. Major Hoare was an elderly man who was inclined to treat us subalterns as if we were under him at Haileybury. He was full of instructions and always trying to make us answer military problems set by himself. I recall his taking me aside on one occasion and presenting me with a diagram drawn by himself.

"Here's a hill strongly occupied by the enemy, but you are unaware of this until the enemy opens fire at your men as they are reaching the top of the hill. How would you handle such a situation?"

"I should probably be killed, Major, before I had had time to know what I should do. But if I wasn't killed I should order my men to get back down the hill as fast as possible and take any cover they could find at the bottom."

Major Hoare shook his head over a pupil's stupidity and proceeded to give me a long lecture on what I ought to do and what orders I ought to give should I ever be caught in such a situation. "You must remember that as you would be using blanks the umpires would have to imagine whether you'd been killed or not. Meanwhile, they would expect you to grapple with the situation and I do not think any umpire would give you good marks for running away down hill."

This was only one of many little problems with which he used to buttonhole myself and other junior subalterns.

The most remarkable day of that week was the great sham battle on Laffan's Plain, in which 30,000 troops were to be engaged, the largest number at that date ever gathered for a sham fight. We were away by half-past six on a blazing August morning in full marching equipment which, unnecessarily as it seemed to us, included greatcoats slung round our red tunics. Red sounds very hot, but in point of fact the red coats were cooler, or rather not quite so hot as the grey coats. I had often wondered how on earth our redcoats stood the heat of India and now I understood that in fact the colour helped them. Still, by Jove, it was hot enough in that English August. We spent about eight hours marching here, marching there, lying down here, lying down there without a sight of the enemy. In those days the lesson of the South African War had made close formation almost a capital crime, subalterns and sergeants spent their time running up and down to keep the rank and file in fully extended order, that is with at least a couple of yards between every man. So subalterns and sergeants were twice as tired as the men when a half-company was spread out for at least a hundred yards. Phew!

I have sometimes wondered whether on the extreme left flank of our army I may not have been personally responsible for the two armies missing one another by giving the order for a half-left turn when I should have kept straight on. Anyway, the two armies did miss one another and the great sham battle never really took place at all.

It was about two o'clock and we were lying down in extended order when my colour-sergeant came along and asked if I thought it was enemy cavalry we could see moving along the ridge of a low hill in front of us.

"It might be, colour-sergeant."

"If I was you, sir, I'd say it was, and I think it would cheer up the lads if they could have a bit of a blaze at them. They haven't fired a single blank all day and they're a bit disappointed."

"All right, colour-sergeant. I'll give the order."

I stood up and in my most imperious voice shouted: "Left half-company! Enemy at 800 yards! Rapid fire!" And my half-company blazed away with enthusiasm as fast as they could shoot.

Presently one of the enemy cavalry came galloping down the hill and across the ground between us, my men firing all the time more enthusiastically than ever. At last a captain with a red and blue brassard reached our position.

"Who is in command here?" he demanded.

"I am, sir," I replied, saluting.

"Do you know your men are firing at the umpires? Order 'cease fire' immediately."

"It would have been a bit awkward, sir, if the cartridges hadn't have been blank," said my colour-sergeant with a grin as the mounted captain went galloping back to join the other umpires.

Some twenty-five years later I was telling the story at the late Lord Sackville's house in Guernsey of which he was then Lieutenant-Governor.

"That's a perfectly true story, Monty," said His Excellency. "And I happen to know because I was that umpire."

Just after this incident the battle was declared over and we gathered at the edge of a coppice to hear the pow-wow. After the final salute with drawn swords we enquired eagerly when lunch would be ready. We did ourselves well in the 1st Herts and knew it would be a jolly good one. We felt the tiring day would have been worth while if we were fortified for the march back of over ten miles to our camp. And then to our dismay we saw the mess-stewards start to pack up the crockery spread in a shady green glade. The tragic news was broken to us. The men's lunch had not arrived and was not likely to arrive because apparently it had been taken some miles in the wrong direction. So of course we could not eat our lunch, and the order was given to move from camp.

What a march that was in the grilling heat of that August afternoon! Luckily our band was with us and nobly did they blow away to keep our spirits up. I can see them now when we reached a horse-trough beside the road in a village and a halt was called at that moment. Down went their instruments on the village green and they rushed to plunge their heads into the trough water and gulp it thirstily down. It was late afternoon when we got back to our camp and not a man of that battalion 900 strong had fallen out. Later when we were enjoying iced drinks in deck chairs outside our mess-tent we watched, with self-esteem and an awareness of our own superiority as a battalion, stragglers from the 2nd Herts limping back in their grey uniforms. They were still limping back after mess that night.

"Poor old Second Herts," said somebody with condescending compassion. "Of course, they haven't got the officers."

Next day the manoeuvres were over. I obtained leave to quit the battalion and go straight back to Alton some twelve or thirteen miles away. I reached Beech early in the afternoon, undressed, got into pyjamas and was asleep instantly. When I woke up it was twelve o'clock next day. I had slept twenty-two hours without turning.

About a week later I went to stay with Harry Pirie-Gordon at Gwernvale, the Pirie-Gordons' house a mile or so beyond Crickhowell in the lovely valley of the Usk. The station was Abergavenny, where in this very year of 1963 I was entertained to lunch at the

Angel by the Chairman of the Monmouthshire County Council, Alderman Bevan, a cousin of my dearly loved and still sorely missed Nye. The young Mayor of Abergavenny was also present and it was good to know that at last Monmouthshire, which for so long had been excluded from Wales, was no longer an English county. The last time I had visited Abergavenny had been sixty years ago. Yet I could recall vividly the drive to Gwernvale in a dogcart and seeing the Usk flowing along on the left of the road and the hills of Brecon rising above the valley beyond.

Mr Pirie-Gordon was an Aberdeenshire laird, and Harry his only son, younger of Buthlaw, steeped in heraldry and Scotland's romantic past was in perfect accord with my own dreams of that Scottish past. Mrs Pirie-Gordon was a woman of tremendous personality, a matriarch in the grand tradition who ruled Gwernvale, strongly outspoken and as I remember usually right in her judgment of mice and men. Two girls were staying with the Pirie-Gordons, a Forbes-Robertson whose Christian name I have forgotten and Violet whose surname I have forgotten. Harry was very mildly enamoured of the former and I was much attracted to Violet, who appropriately for her name had eyes the colour of Parma violets.

I must have been a guest at Gwernvale for about a month, and as I look back it seems a month of unbroken enjoyment—garden-parties galore, drives in a wagonette to dances twenty miles away, walking round the walled fruit-gardens of Gwernvale to pick and eat pears, plums, nectarines and peaches. I think it was at a garden-party given by Sir Shirley Salt that Tempe Crawshay, a pioneer of the strong-minded young women who were emerging at last from Victorian convention said to me: "That Cupid's bow of yours is a ridiculous mouth for a boy; it's a perfect mouth for a girl."

At eighteen to have one's mouth called girlish was an insult beyond bearing. "Are you suggesting that I look effeminate?" I demanded furiously.

"No, no, but you must admit it is a bit of a handicap for any boy to have a complexion like yours and that pretty mouth."

Soon after this, Tempe Crawshay and I were opponents at croquet and never did I enjoy so much that rule of once upon a time which allowed one to put a foot on one's own ball and hit one's opponent's ball off the lawn. I can see now Tempe Crawshay's ball disappearing in a thicket of rhododendrons from the ferocious stroke of my mallet.

Sometimes we at Gwernvale would have long walks among the

hills behind and not long after I arrived there Violet and I were caught in a sudden thick mist. We wandered about hopelessly lost until at last we found a shepherd's hut in which we took shelter. There we sat for half a summer's day, the world without obliterated and only the far away baa of a sheep to remind us that the world without was still alive. This was a time for kisses and kiss the time away we did until at last the mist cleared and we could find again the path down the mountainside to home.

The time came to leave Gwernvale after a month of enchantment. I should stay there again with Harry Pirie-Gordon once or twice during the next two years and on a later occasion we had amateur theatricals in Abergavenny. I do not remember what the play was or what was the part I played, but I remember that beautiful Jenny Monsell was the star of the performance.

Back at Beech in that September of 1901 I found to my amazement that my mother had introduced Nanny to the bungalow. I suppose she had grown tired of the incompetent nursery-governesses who succeeded Miss Stanwell and felt it was convenient to have somebody there all the time who would preserve economy. Perhaps she found in old Annie Curry a sentimental link with the early days of her married life, although I never discovered in my mother any more signs of sentimentality than I perceive in myself. Anyway, there she was, and I told Hammond our gardener how ill pleased I was to find her there.

"Do you think she has a bit of Chinese in her?" he asked.

"Chinese?" I exclaimed. "What on earth makes you think that?"

"Haven't you noticed the way she rubs up the end of her nose when she's feeling annoyed about something?" Hammond imitated the gesture with the palm of his hand.

"I never heard that was a particularly Chinese habit."

"Yes, yes, oh yes, there was a Chinaman who used to come to my shop in Maidstone and if ever he saw me cut him a chop he didn't like the look of he would rub the end of his nose just the way she does."

I had my last battle with Nanny soon after this ethnical observation of Hammond's.

I had left a copy of Pierre Loüys' *Aphrodite* beside my bed and when I could not find it I asked Nanny where it was.

"I burnt it," she told me.

"You did what?" I exclaimed.

"I burnt it. Can't have a book with pictures like that lying about."

I cannot remember what I said to Nanny but whatever it was it made no impression on her as she stood in wrinkled unreasonableness, rubbing the end of her nose in 'Chinese' disapproval. It was not until my mother told her coldly that if she ever did such a thing again she would have to go back to Catford, whence my mother had brought her down to Beech, that Nanny's obstinate noddle surrendered and she promised never to do such a thing again. However, I think it was my sister Fay, seven years old in that September, who finally convinced Nanny that her tyranny over childhood was now with the snows of yester year.

A week or two before I went up to Oxford I heard from Harry Pirie-Gordon that he would not be coming up himself until the beginning of the next term, as he was going to Constantinople.

Magdalen College in the first year of this century believed that any undergraduate who loyally regarded his own college as the one of which he was proud to be a member would always say that, if he wasn't at Oriel or Trinity or whatever other college was his, he would like to be a Magdalen man. Perhaps I should except Balliol and New College men from this claim; they could not imagine themselves ever being at any other college, even Magdalen. Earlier in the 'nineties the wise men of the Junior Common Room had considered it advisable to break up a tendency for the members of the College to form cliques by always breakfasting together. This was done by instituting breakfast in the J.C.R., which was served every morning from eight to ten o'clock. Then every Sunday night after dinner in hall people sat round the two long tables in the J.C.R. to drink port or burgundy or sherry, which was followed by what was called an 'after'. This was held in one of the big rooms in Cloisters lent for the occasion by its resident and subscribed for in turn by three or four senior men, who provided whisky, lemon squash, and cigarettes for the guests, always Turkish or Egyptian cigarettes, never Virginian. It was a miniature smoking-concert at which various undergraduates performed, with occasionally a visit from some professional comedian from London. I have evoked in *Sinister Street* the atmosphere of Magdalen at this date and I am not going to attempt to re-write it with elegant variation. I have already made it clear that, however much I have used a certain amount of my life's experience for the story of Michael Fane, he is not myself and his story is not my story.

I hate repeating myself and therefore I shall not attempt to take some of Michael Fane's first day at Oxford to describe my own, while admitting that in fact some of it was very like my own. I did write a pink cheque for five pounds at the London and Counties Bank (the Westminster Bank of to-day) and was suitably impressed by seeing my signature *E. M. C. Mackenzie* written on a cheque for the first time. My allowance was £250 a year at first but this was raised in the following year to £300, which was what most undergraduates at Magdalen were given. It may have been possible to live at some of the less fashionable colleges for £200 a year at this date, and even at Magdalen the 'Demys', as our Scholars were called, and some of what Gunstone, the steward of the J.C.R., called the 'quiet men' may have had to manage with less than £250, but they kept to themselves mostly. The origin of the word 'Demy' is the £80 a year that was half the value of a fellowship once upon a time.

Tommy Bouch, who came up in my year from Cheltenham with a History demyship, brought with him a couple of horses for hunting, and this shook the dons so much that he was asked to resign his demyship, which he did with relief. Tommy Bouch was, and still remains, a remarkable personality. He published a book of poems at Oxford from which he went on to join the 10th Hussars and later became Master, first of the Galway Blazers and then of the Belvoir. He has managed more successfully than anybody I have known to live to-day the life of a country squire before 1914.

With the five pounds jingling in my pocket I went to a picture shop in the Cornmarket and bought an autotype of the Mona Lisa which still hangs in my Edinburgh bedroom. I bought at the same time a small copperplate reproduction of the Primavera for two guineas. Then I went to Colin Lunn's tobacconist shop in the High and bought an obese tobacco jar which is still beside my chair; it was not blazoned with the College arms like Michael Fane's, but like him I did buy a miniature five-barred gate for a pipe-rack; the hookah he bought on his first day would not be bought by me for another two years.

My rooms were two pairs up on the right of Staircase III in St Swithun's Quadrangle. I still have the Inventory Valuation of £31-4-3, for which the Home Bursar requests payment within three weeks to the late occupant; the items have a period flavour:

Sitting Room. Set Fire Irons. Bordered Carpet. Rug. Set ash dining tables. Ash Chiffonier. Easy chair. Study chair. 4 Cane seat chairs. Roller blind. Brass Window Poles. pr. Chenille curtains. Brass Rod and Tapestry Curtains in recess. Wicker chair. Settee in cretonne. Bamboo table. Chimney Shelf. 2 Rods and 2 Curtains over doors. Walnut writing table.

Bed-room. Bedstead. Matting palliasse. Mattress. Bolster and Pillow. 2 Blankets and Quilt. Polpine Chest of Drawers. Washstand. Dressing Glass. Blind. Horse. 4 pieces ware. Waste pail.

Stamp and Fee 12/6+repairs to bedding 14/3.

(signed)
John A. Bridgnall
Appraiser.

My sitting-room looked out on the High, from which came hardly more noise in those days than was made by the occasional rumble of a green horse-drawn tram. To-day the noise in that sitting-room must be deafening.

My bedroom looked out across the President's garden to the Deer Park and New Buildings; Swither's, as it was called, was a very much newer building of which Bodley was the architect. It was not strictly a quadrangle, being open in front, and beyond the gateway was the Old Grammar Hall, the most ancient building in the college. There were no baths in those days but a row of water-closets at the end of the right angle of St Swithun's quad, these water-closets equipped with prodigal rolls of toilet-paper. I still look back regretfully to the bath-tub in one's own bedroom which one's scout filled with the hot water that was such a joy after the mud of a rugger match. On the ground-floor the rooms on the right housed 'Crack' or 'Harky' Rose, an uncle of Peter and Ian Fleming; on the left was Andrew or 'Dan' Pope, a gentle Harrovian. Above him was Miller, a rather tiresome Wykehamist, who was always blowing a coach-horn; above Rose was Raymond Wavell, a first cousin of Archie Wavell then at Sandhurst, who had been in Fort's House at Winchester when his cousin was in College. Opposite me was a little German named Oppenheim of a rich banking family. Oppenheim left after a term and to my great pleasure Harry Pirie-Gordon got his room.

Raymond Wavell became one of my most intimate friends. He was still five months away from eighteen in that October; his elder brother Arthur was in the Welch Fusiliers. Arthur Wavell was home on leave from South Africa that autumn after being wounded. One day Raymond asked myself and one or two other freshmen to lunch because his brother was coming.

"You won't mind, will you? He's rather an extraordinary chap. He hardly ever says anything."

We agreed to overlook such eccentricity and kept the conversation going as well as we could at lunch, through which Arthur Wavell sat as silent as his brother had warned us he would. This habit of

Viola with Charlie and Claudia Danforth at Charnay, July 1900. Taken with a 5″ × 4″ Kodak

Magdalen College

silence seems to overtake all Wavells sooner or later. When I met Major Archibald Wavell in 1916 he was almost as talkative as I am myself; presently he became 'guinea a word Archie'. His son Archie John was quite as talkative as I am. I suppose he would have become silent if the world had not lost somebody with the making of a great man by his death in action. Arthur Wavell, whose taciturnity we young freshmen agreed so kindly to overlook, was to have a remarkable career. After the South African war he went to Somaliland and wrote a fascinating book about a daring visit to Mecca. When war came in 1914 he raised a force of Somalis and was killed leading them against an overwhelming German force in East Africa. There is a statue to him at Mombasa.

Underhill the Senior Tutor, known as Squish on account of some reported connection of his with marmalade (not Cooper's Oxford Marmalade), did not interview me about my scholastic future; he left it to Christopher Cookson the Dean, who had been master of the Upper Eighth during my first term at St Paul's in 1894.

Cookson was an admirable Dean; I only once recall his being completely exasperated by undergraduate behaviour. He had a slightly sardonic way of speaking and a stiff-necked walk. Later in life that stiff neck of his would become a goitre and I have heard that his old age was not happy, and that he was treated ungenerously by the College he served so well.

Nearly all the dons had rooms on the first floor in New Buildings, the back of which looked out on the Deer Park. That fine Palladian edifice, built in 1735, was intended to form one side of a great Italian quadrangle, the completion of which would have involved the destruction of the Cloisters, a piece of vandalism mercifully never accomplished. Such vandalism was reserved for the Magdalen dons of the mid-twentieth century who erected that ghastly new building on the other side of the road.

"You'll be taking Honour Moderations five terms hence," said Cookson.

"But, Mr Dean, I gave up Classics and was in the History Eighth."

"One would not suppose you had given up Classics from that Latin Prose you wrote in your Matriculation papers."

"I want to take Pass Mods," I insisted, "and after that to read History."

"Well, I can't compel you to take Honour Moderations," said Cookson. "Unfortunately," he added, eyeing me with a sardonic glance.

So Pass Mods it was to be, and in those days Pass Moderations were not taken until one's first summer term. I forget which Latin book of Cicero was set; Plato's *Apologia* was the Greek book. Greene, known as Grugger, a plump lazy amiable don who could only pronounce his R's by taking them down to the back of his throat, lectured on Cicero. Bee-neck or P. V. Benecke, a great nephew of Mendelssohn, was responsible for our Platonic studies. A. D. Godley, that witty writer of light verse, had the task of expounding Jevons' Logic, a task that might have driven anybody mad except a quiet humorist like Godley. Besides Pass Mods in the following June we were supposed to satisfy the examiners in Divinity at the end of the Hilary term. To get through Divvers first time was regarded as a breach of decorum and we were in honour bound to fail. The Dean of Divinity was the Rev. C. R. Carter, who had succeeded Cosmo Gordon Lang when the latter left Magdalen to become Vicar of Portsea on his way up to end in Lambeth Palace.

At the time of the Abdication the Archbishop of Canterbury was being dined at various clubs in London, before the crisis, in order to impress his personality on select public opinion. Among others he was entertained at the Savile and when I was presented to him he murmured with a perfectly staged smile, "Ah, Magdalen. I always say that Balliol was my revered Alma Mater and All Souls my loving wife and that my years at Magdalen were years spent in the arms of a beautiful mistress."

Indeed, no other college in Oxford or Cambridge can compete with Magdalen in beauty. Antony Wood called it "the most noble and rich structure in the learned world," and declared what was later to be known as Addison's Walk round the water-meadows of the Cherwell "as delectable as the banks of Eurotas where Apollo himself was wont to walk."

William of Wayneflete, the founder, was headmaster of Winchester before he became the first headmaster of Henry VI's new foundation of Eton. It was for that reason the lilies of Eton were incorporated in his arms and therefore in the arms of Magdalen. Dean Colet, the founder of St Paul's School, was at Magdalen, and so was William Lily the first High Master, who compiled a Latin Grammar that was to last for over 300 years in the schools of England and was finally incorporated in the Public School Latin Primer which was still being used in the mid 'nineties of the last century until it was supplanted by Kennedy's Revised Latin Primer. Another Magdalen lily was Lyly, the Elizabethan Euphuist who wrote 'Cupid and my Campaspe played at cards for kisses.'

In 1901 Magdalen was a college of 160 undergraduates of whom about half were Etonians and more than another quarter Wykehamists, Harrovians or Carthusians. One of those Wykehamists was Johnny Bramston who had been runner up in the Amateur Golf Championship, a fantastic achievement for a twenty-year-old in his second year at Oxford. He had not forgotten his promise to Dolling and in the lodge on that very first day he asked how I was getting on and told me to consult him if there was anything I wanted to know. I see him now in that lodge with his red curly hair. With him was a handsome dark undergraduate who gave me his blessing at the same time. This was Richard Graves, an elder half-brother of Robert Graves, a third-year man from Haileybury.

Johnny Bramston would die of what used to be called a galloping consumption some three years later. Dick Graves would have a distinguished career in the Egyptian Civil Service and become an intimate and dearly loved friend of mine much later in life, when he retired from service in the Levant to become one of the pillars of the Savile Club.

At this date, although golf was rapidly becoming more and more important in the athletic life of the University, it was still regarded by many as a threat to cricket, and rightly, for the decline of amateur cricket would be started by golf.

Our chief aspiration at Magdalen was the headship of the river, competing for it in my time with New College and Univ; as I remember, Christ Church was almost at the bottom of the Second Division when Third and Fourth and Fifth Divisions were undreamed of. Our second aspiration was to win the soccer cup, for which Oriel was our great rival and in my time always successful. The great rugger college was Trinity. We were not distinguished for rugger at Magdalen, which may explain why I was in the Fifteen, playing left wing three-quarter with Parsons, a future Bishop of Manchester, and Kenneth Fisher, a future great headmaster of Oundle and father of ornithological James, in the centre.

The grossly swollen Magdalen of to-day competes with Balliol itself for Firsts in the almost numberless Honour schools that have been invented during this century, but it has fallen from first, second or third place on the river after remaining in one or other of them for over sixty years. That one day Keble or St Edmund's Hall would be head of the river would have seemed to us in 1901 a far more fantastic vision of the future than anything in Jules Verne or H. G. Wells. I remember our being drawn against Keble in a soccer cup-tie and hiring a coach and four to watch the match because we thought the Keble ground was somewhere out in the country.

I was tempted to write a footnote to *Sinister Street* after the Second World War and call it *Pink Flows the Don*; all the dons then did seem as pink as a schoolgirl's cheeks. There was a silly breach with Eton in a flutter of egalitarian anxiety. Scouts no longer waited at the tables in hall, which became a cafeteria for Prince Rupert to gaze down at. There was a similar turn over of opinion after the Reformation, when a President of Magdalen was so afraid of Popery that he would not even wear his academic robes and was chaffed by Queen Elizabeth who, whatever else my prejudice may deny her, cannot be accused of not having a sense of humour.

Herbert Warren, the President, had been a young Fellow when elected in 1886. Dr Routh, the last President but one had been elected in 1791, he and his successor Dr Bulley lived to 99 and 100 respectively. Warren, who was the son of a Bristol chemist, had won a scholarship in the first examination for scholarships at newly founded Clifton College of which Dr Symonds, the father of John Addington and a cousin of my grandfather, Henry Compton, was a Governor. The other Governors were against awarding scholarships to the sons of Bristol tradesmen; Symonds, who had much influence, said that if such a rule were made he should resign as a Governor. So Herbert Warren was admitted to Clifton and from there went on to a brilliant university career at Balliol from which he was elected to a fellowship at Magdalen. He has become in legend the great Oxford snob, as Oscar Browning was at Cambridge. It was a harmless romantic snobbery and when he had his drawing-room in the Founder's Tower decorated with the arms of William de Warenne I doubt if he believed any more than anybody else did that he really was descended from him. Apocryphal tales about him abounded. He was supposed to have always introduced his wife, dear kind Mrs Warren, when they were first married, as the daughter of Sir Benjamin Brodie, Bart. It is true that when he welcomed the freshmen each year at the President's Lodgings a card of greeting from Lord Wantage was stuck in the portrait on the right of the door through which we took our leave, and that when the speech he had made and would make to freshmen for many years to come was over, the card was removed and put away for a future occasion. Without doubt he was gratified, even thrilled, when Magdalen was chosen as the college for the Prince of Wales, but so would have been most other heads of houses. I do not recall hearing of any display of disagreeable snobbishness by failure to interest himself in the future of some demy of humble birth. He was a graceful minor poet of conventional sentiment, and he felt strongly about the ungentlemanliness of realism in a novel or in a play. I sent him an inscribed copy of *Carnival* when it came out, and when he wrote to thank me he added that he feared from what he had read of the reviews it would not be a book he should take any pleasure in reading. His dark beard and toothy smile were never seen except above a tailcoat and a white silk knotted tie. He was a notably efficient Vice-Chancellor and his Presidency of Magdalen was of the greatest help to the College.

Christopher Stone was known to his contemporaries at Eton as 'Polly' Stone, because one day πολύστονος occurred in a construe. πολύστονος means 'full of sighs' and Christopher was far from that. However, Polly Stonos served schoolboy wit. He came along to call soon after I reached Oxford and invited me to breakfast. What we at Magdalen considered the barbarous habit of inviting people to breakfast at eight o'clock still obtained in other colleges. We did not think breakfast a sociable occasion as we sat in the J.C.R. and frowned over our morning papers at anybody who tried to start a conversation. We all had to feel that it was not the thing to talk at breakfast. The only time we breakfasted out was on Sunday after chapel, when those of us who belonged to the O.U.D.S. or the Grid set forth in dark suits and bowler hats, carrying a pair of kid gloves but not a cane, to enjoy that late breakfast: the O.U.D.S. Sunday breakfast was considered the best obtainable in Oxford, but dinner at the Grid was usually better than dinner at the O.U.D.S.

Christopher's rooms were in Meadows, that agreeable secluded little quad far from the whip-cracking inhabitants of Peckwater. In Meadows were to be found all the holders of the close scholarships from Westminster, and indeed most of the House men who came to Oxford to work, instead of hunting with the Heythrop, the Bicester or the Vale of the White Horse packs; or to wear a grey bowler hat with the blue Bullingdon ribbon round it. On that autumn morning I may have met Wilfred Greene, a future Master of the Rolls, or George Bell, a future Bishop of Chichester, for they were both close friends of Christopher. I remember thinking that the 'quiet men' at the House were much more tolerant of the bloods than the 'quiet men' at Magdalen were. Very early in that first term I was at a gathering on the top floor of New Buildings, where most of them lived, and made up my mind that they were all suffering from what would one day be called an inferiority complex and was irritated by their assumption that because I had not been at Eton I ought to turn up my nose at the most civilized school in England. There is only one thing as tiresome as the snobbery of the *nouveaux riches* and that is the inverted snobbery of envious egalitarians, so much encouraged by the popular Press nowadays.

The president of the J.C.R. during my first year was Sir Randolf Baker, who was an impressive figure to us freshmen. At one of the 'afters' in the middle of that first term a professional comedian had been brought from London to amuse us, and thought the way to do it was by telling smutty stories, which embarrassed his audience because in those days it was considered bad form to tell a smutty story except in a very small intimate circle. Presently Randolf Baker got up and walked out, saying as he left the room that he was afraid it was no place for him, yet saying it with a smile that took away the faintest suggestion of priggishness. This will sound like an example of Victorian prudery: that may be so, but it is also an example of good manners.

I had an experience that term which has never happened to me since. I received a letter from Violet to say that she was going to be married to some clergyman and that she hoped I regretted as much as she did our behaviour at Gwernvale in the summer. I wrote back to say I never regretted past pleasures and thought it was a mistake for her to do so.

The end of that first Michaelmas term came half way through December and I reflect, with an apology for the recording of so much that will seem trivial to others, that during that first term of mine at Oxford the Twentieth Century was enjoying its first term. During it the first submarine was launched, the first navigable balloon was flown by Santos-Dumont, and Marconi received the first wireless signals across the Atlantic, from Newfoundland to Poldhu on the west coast of the Lizard peninsula in Cornwall.

After such a momentous trio of events it does seem a little ridiculous to record that I went to the University rugger match at Queen's Club in pouring rain and was warmed by an Oxford victory. The top-hats of the previous decade were fast disappearing as the correct attire for a University match at Queen's Club; most of the spectators wore bowlers by now. When the match was over I walked along to West Kensington station (there was no Baron's Court station then) and instead of turning to the left toward Avonmore Road took the train to Earl's Court. We had left 54 Avonmore Road; the fifteen years of my boyhood there were a thing of the past. My father had sold Number 54 for £600, which was £400 less than he had paid for it in 1886, and bought 1 Nevern Square for £2000, which was to be our home until he died in 1918 when my mother sold it for £2500. 1 Nevern Square no longer exists; it was blown to pieces during the Second World War.

I saw very little of the new house that vac because I had agreed to go with Harry Pirie-Gordon on a month's tour in Spain and Morocco. The circular ticket cost £14, 10s, second class in train and first class in boat, and we calculated that £15, 10s. each would pay our living expenses. In those days a journey to Spain was a very rare adventure indeed for youth. Hardly anybody in Great Britain, old or young, visited Spain as a tourist.

We left Victoria on Boxing Day, crossing by Newhaven to Dieppe, which was a little cheaper than crossing by Dover or Folkestone. We were much impressed by our passports in which the Marquess of Lansdowne, the Secretary of State for Foreign Affairs, invited all and sundry to come to our help, almost it sounded as a personal favour to himself. A passport then was a large engraved quarto that crackled like a five-pound note. Passports were essential for Russia and Turkey and considered advisable for Spain; in fact ours remained folded up in our waistcoat-pockets throughout the tour. For some reason or other we each had to leave a deposit of ten shillings with Cook's in Paris. We were annoyed about this at the time; we should be grateful for that deposit a month hence. I have never revisited Spain because I have not wanted to confuse Spain as it was, not yet three years after the war with the United States, with the Spain of to-day cluttered with tourists in search of a cheap part of Bikiniland. To be sure, Harry and I were only able to make that trip because the peseta was at 36 to the pound, which was like getting 36 shillings for a pound; all the other exchanges in Europe then were at par.

We boarded the Sud Express to Madrid at the Gare d'Orleans by the Quai d'Orsay, and the first thing I remember is waking up before we reached St Jean de Luz to see an incredibly blue and incredibly calm Atlantic. There was one other occupant of our second class compartment. This was a brother of Captain Machell, King Edward's trainer at Newmarket, a distinguished-looking man with greying hair who was affable to two undergraduates and whom we were sorry to see leave us at St Jean de Luz. The only advice I recall was to carry our own bags when we changed trains at the frontier. This we did when we reached Irun and left behind the blue and red French soldiers to find ourselves among the black and green Spanish soldiers. Nobody asked to see our passports and the customs examination was the merest formality. I did not even bother to declare my revolver, that decorative weapon I had won at the Actors' Orphanage Garden Party with the 17 ticket Ben Greet had given me nearly five years ago. The reason we had to walk about a hundred yards from one train to another was the different gauge.

At Miranda we got out to have dinner in the station buffet and I was so much captivated by the glances of a beautiful señorita travelling with a grim duenna that I lingered on in the restaurant till the train was on the point of moving and left behind me on the table our Spanish-English conversation-manual.

"We'll have to get another in Madrid," said Harry. I agreed, but although we tried several shops in Madrid we could not find even a Spanish-English dictionary.

It was dark when we reached the only big hotel in the Puerta del Sol, much the most expensive hotel we stayed in on our tour, the charge for full pension amounting to just over ten shillings a day. I insisted that I must have a bath, which I was told would cost me five pesetas. This seemed an excessive amount until I found what it involved in preparation. Various members of the hotel staff would come up at intervals to assure me that the bath was almost ready; when after nearly an hour it was announced to be ready, I was led down staircases along corridors to a kind of large vault in the middle of which stood a porcelain bath, the bottom and sides of which were concealed by a sheet. I lacked the Spanish to ask what the sheet was for but supposed it might be to prevent what the Italians call an offence against *pudore* by wrapping myself in it when one of the staff came in to enquire if the bath was behaving properly. Never mind. The water was warm and plentiful. I got rid of the effects of the long train journey, and considered that five pesetas was a small fee to charge for such a bath.

Next day we sat at breakfast, drinking our thick chocolate and goat's milk, with the December sun warm upon the window-pane. A girl was guiding a flock of turkeys across what was the Piccadilly of Madrid. This was my first experience of southern Europe as it can be on some halcyon December morning; it was at that moment I decided to live by the Mediterranean one day and never again go to Switzerland. I had made up my mind when reading about the Hessian troops in the '45 and the behaviour of the Hanoverian kings never to put foot in Germany. And I never have.

The first thing we visited in Madrid was the Royal Palace, and as we were walking along one of the corridors a boy came bounding down some steps and nearly landed on my toes. With him was a grandee with upturned grey moustachios who raised his finger in rebuke of such impetuosity.

"I'm awfully sorry," said the boy. "Did I step on your toe? I say, would you like to see the Armoury?"

And we were taken to the Armoury by Alfonso XIII, the King of Spain, who was still a month or so away from his sixteenth birthday. That unexpected encounter is a happy memory.

That evening Harry was engaged on working out some genealogy and I decided to go out and explore Madrid by night. A tout came up and asked me in English if I would like to meet nice girl. He was as full of four-letter words as Lady Chatterley's lover and proud of having learnt them at the Glasgow Exhibition of 1900. I was bored by his pertinacity and to get rid of him turned into a tiny little theatre called the Teatro Japonese. There I saw some marvellous dancing and was so thrilled by the castanets that I felt like imitating enthusiastic members of the audience by throwing my own hat on the stage; I felt my Trilby would look ridiculous among all those splendid sombreros and restrained myself.

The next day was wet. Harry and I decided this was the very day to visit the Prado. When we reached the finest picture gallery in Europe we found it closed and asked the janitor why it was closed. He spoke French and was able to explain to us that it was because it was raining. We suggested this was the very time for a picture gallery to be open.

"What!" he exclaimed. "And have to clean up all the mud people bring in with them on a wet day?" Then seeing our disappointment he said that the Director was in his office and that if we gave him our cards he would probably allow us to go round the gallery. "And put a peseta under each card when you give them to him." I wonder what Sir Kenneth Clarke would have said if a tourist had offered him his card with sixpence underneath it to go round the National Gallery when it was closed.

What an experience it was to walk round that glorious gallery with nobody else in it! I see now those mighty pictures of Rubens hung high in those days. I hold my breath again as I walk into that small room which holds *Las Meniñas* of Velasquez. I pity those who see for the first time that miraculous group of maids of honour round the little Infanta Margarita Maria, jostled by gaping tourists. I remember being bewitched by the portrait of a monk painted by Zurbaran, and by the El Grecos and Goyas, all seen for the first time in a sublime silence. It was one of my life's great occasions.

We had planned to go to Toledo next day, return that evening and leave for Granada that night. There were only two trains in the day from Madrid to Toledo. One left at 8 a.m. and the other at 8.15 a.m. We arrived at the railway-station with twenty minutes in hand for the first train and gave over our two bags to a porter to be put in the left-luggage cloakroom until we returned from Toledo and collected them for the journey to Granada that night. The porter took them along to a weighing-machine and started to weigh them. We tried to explain that we were not taking our luggage to Toledo, but our Spanish was not up to explaining as much and all we could do was to take our bags off the weighing-machine as fast as the porter put them on it. He called another porter but the newcomer was no better able to grasp what we wanted.

In our agitation we even forgot what was the Spanish for "to-night" and all we could say was,

"Granada, Granada, Granada ce soir."

At last one of the porters led us to a flower-stall and one of the now interested spectators managed to make us grasp that a señorita would be arriving at 8 o'clock to open the stall and that this señorita spoke French. So we decided to abandon the idea of catching the 8 a.m. train to Toledo and go by the 8.15 a.m. Alas for our hopes! The señorita had not arrived by 8.10 and we made one more desperate effort to explain what we wanted to do with our bags. It was no use; back they went on the weighing-machine. We gave up in despair and the 8.15 steamed out of the station to Toledo, leaving us on the platform.

While we waited for the arrival of the señorita, Harry with admirable self-control abstained from reproaching me for leaving that conversation-manual at Miranda. She reached her stall at last, only twenty-five minutes late, which for Spain was almost an exaggerated punctuality. The señorita was charming. She explained that in Spain it is customary to weigh luggage left in the cloak-room and that the two porters had not supposed we wanted to take it with us to Toledo. Furthermore, when she looked at our tickets, she discovered that we were setting out on our circular tour the wrong way round and that instead of going to Granada to-night we should be going to Seville at six o'clock next morning. So that misunderstanding about the luggage had really been a piece of good fortune. I bought a bunch of carnations from that heaven-sent señorita, who had saved us from what would have been the expensive complication of going to Granada when our circular tickets provided for us to go to Seville. Not only did I buy that bunch of carnations but I learned that the Spanish for carnations was *clavelitos*. The señorita advised us to be at the station by four o'clock next morning at latest, because it would be the only train to Seville until the day after to-morrow.

We decided it would be an unnecessary expense to take the luggage back to an hotel in Madrid and we saw it weighed and put in the cloakroom. All I remember of that long day in Madrid is walking about in the Park with a bunch of carnations. By midnight we were sitting in the waiting-room and at three a.m. when we found that the train for Seville was in we got our bags taken to an empty second-class compartment, stretched ourselves out at full length on either side of it and fell instantly fast asleep. When we woke it was broad daylight. The train was jogging along on its way to Seville and on the floor of the compartment were seated half a dozen fellow-travellers, men and women, who preferred to sit thus uncomfortably rather than disturb the two sleeping English señores. The racks above us were full of bundles, a couple of live turkeys, and three ducks.

Harry and I jumped up full of apologies and although we were passionately urged to lie down again we finally did persuade our fellow-travellers to take their seats. Food was soon produced and pressed upon us with such obvious hospitality that we could not have refused it without giving offence. With the help of my facile gesticulation I was able to express our appreciation of those sausages and the red wine drunk from a skin. One of Harry's very few lacks as a travelling companion was that he did not smoke and so in the darkness of that Madrid railway-station on New Year's Eve he had got us into a compartment which was not *para fumadores*. However, one of the advantages of travelling in Spain or Italy was that nobody paid attention to petty rules and regulations. Mussolini and Franco were still gloomy shapes of things to come. So presently I took out my pipe and asked with as eloquent a gesture as I could manage if I might smoke. One of the men with an equally elegant gesture seemed to suggest I must put away my pipe. This was not to prevent my smoking but in order, with marvellous grace and dexterity, to roll a cigarette with one hand and offer it to me to lick and light.

A railway-journey through Spain in the winter of 1901-2 was a slow but continuously fascinating progress. At every station all the men got out and strolled up and down till the train started again, when they would board it almost it seemed as an afterthought. Tickets were examined from time to time by inspectors ho made their way along the outside of the train to enter the various compartments. I remember once when Harry and I were the only two occupants a ticket-inspector suddenly appearing in the middle of a long dark tunnel.

There were four classes, but nobody except extremely poor beggars travelled third class, and fourth class nobody except blind beggars who believed they were travelling third.

We stayed at the Hotel Roma in Seville, where we were charged seven pesetas a day for generous board and a delightful lodging in rooms that looked across a *plaza* full of palms and orange trees. 3s 6d a day with as much wine as we could drink and a glass of brandy with our coffee! I wonder if they still serve the fish between the entrée and the roast, and soup at the end instead of at the beginning of dinner. I doubt if such an order of service has held its own against the surge of tourists in the Spain of to-day. I still think that the proper place for soup is at the end of a meal but I have not been able to convince others of this. I do not remember whether it was on that New Year's Day or on the eve of the Epiphany five days later that our waiter gave us, according to custom, a present of eight cigars, Harry's being luckily for me lost on him. Those cigars were Cabanas of the last crop before that wretched war with the United States would lead to the hygienic and mechanical production of the cigars we smoke to-day, when the rising cost of them coincides with the deterioration in quality and with *colorado* cigars being completely ousted by *claros*. Oh, for those large Manilla cheroots which mercifully I was still able to smoke during my time at Oxford; they cost 2d each and I was never without a box of a hundred. I should not taste a really good cheroot again until I went to Burma in 1947. That does not mean we can get a really good Burma cheroot anywhere in Britain to-day; the pygmies we import and sell to-day at a preposterous price are hardly worth smoking.

I must not claim that on the edge of nineteen I was able to appreciate those Cabanas of the last crop before the war of 1898 as much as they would have been appreciated by an older man with a longer experience of cigars, but I did luxuriate in every puff.

The first thing we did in Seville was to ascend the Giralda tower of Seville Cathedral, that masterpiece of Moorish architecture which allowed one to ride nearly to the top of it along a bridle-path. I recall dismounting to climb the steps that led out to a great balcony and looking down at Seville above the clanging of the great bells just below. I seem to recall that we could see those great bells swing into view but this may be a deceitful trick of memory.

One of my ambitions was to hear Mass according to the Mozarabic rite, which could be heard only in Seville anywhere in Christendom. To my surprise this Mass was said in an eighteenth-century side-chapel, the one comparatively modern side-chapel. To wander over the roof of that vast Cathedral and sit there in that azure winter weather dreaming on the sun-warmed stone of its innumerable undulations was to hold the world in one's lap.

We went to High Mass on the feast of the Epiphany and saw that famous dance before the altar performed by about a dozen small boys in crimson and gold tunicles, under the direction of a clean-shaven middle-aged master in black silk coat and knee breeches with a powdered wig and a white wand. We also heard a sermon from the Cardinal Lord Archbishop of Seville. I see him now in his pulpit round the bottom of which, squatting on the stone floor, are a bunch of church-fowls in black mantillas; and as he preaches he clears his throat from time to time and spits a substantial gobbet of saliva and phlegm right over the heads of the pious women on to a flagstone some three yards beyond them. It was the finest piece of spitting marksmanship I have ever seen or am ever likely to see.

It may have been when the bells were ringing on that Epiphany morning in 1902 that I saw ripe oranges fall from the trees in the plaza of the Cathedral, oranges rung down by the clangour, and a lot of little boys running to pick them up, scrambling and pushing one another, and quarrelling about whose orange had been seized first by whom.

I do not remember how it was that Harry and I managed to find ourselves in the Alcazar garden without any other visitors in it. It must have been closed and I suppose with a peseta we had persuaded the janitor to let us in. I forget which King Philip it was who had the walls round the garden of this Moorish relic painted with scenes of Spanish military prowess, for I was more interested in the garden itself than the pictorial decoration of its walls. There was a delightful old gardener in charge to whose good will I found the magic key by telling him how lovely his carnations were. I blessed that señorita in the Madrid railway-station for teaching me to say *clavelitos*. Don Blas Toro was his name and for many years I had his card thus inscribed. Indeed, I may yet find it again in some forgotten envelope. Don Blas Toro took us along every one of the tiled paths of that enchanting garden and then as a final favour he turned on the fountain, showing us where to stand to avoid being caught in the fountain which was the largest and tallest I ever saw, spouts coming up from the tiled paths all over the garden to form a kind of huge cupola of water. I have asked many people who have been to Seville whether they saw this immense fountain but nobody I have asked has; I wonder whether it is no longer working.

What else do I remember from those days in Seville? Walking along the banks of the Guadalquivir and seeing the cigarette-girls come laughing out of the factory like so many Carmens. There was no toreador for them to acclaim because the bull-ring was closed during the winter. This was a relief to me because I should have felt bound to go and I should certainly not have enjoyed it. Every night I went somewhere to see dancing. I was intoxicated by it, but I felt I could not afford at this stage of our tour to invest in a Spanish cloak and a sombrero, for the pleasure of flinging my hat on the stage to show my admiration of whatever bolero or fandango had been danced. I cannot bring myself to go back to Seville and see motor-cars driving through the narrow streets along which bullock-carts used to rumble. My last memory of Seville shall be the delightful love-affair I had *in camera* with the black-eyed chambermaid who looked after my room.

From Seville we went to Cadiz to catch a boat for Tangier. At this date the famous port seemed derelict and it was here that I first realized what that war with the United States had done to Spain. The harbour was a desert of empty wharves and quays. Cadiz in spite of the people that still thronged its picturesque streets seemed as dead as the remains of Roman empire. I cannot understand why historians never present the Spanish-American war and the South African war as parallel examples of aggressive imperialism. We are both of us still paying for those wars, the U.S.A. in Cuba today, ourselves in South Africa. Yet to-day the U.S.A. has made Cadiz its central naval base in Europe.

It must have been in Cadiz that I first tasted the dry sherry Spaniards drink themselves. I brought back to Oxford the news of this discovery, only to be told that it could not possibly have been sherry; twenty years must have gone by before dry sherry became popular in England. What did the sack that Falstaff drank so heartily taste like? I think it must have been fortified sweet sherry.

And the malmsey from Greece in which Clarence was drowned: that also was probably a sweet heady wine.

There was an amusing incident at the Cadiz railway-station before the train started to go round a big bay and comparatively narrow breakwater which, as I remember it, seemed to enclose the roadstead in a huge white horn. Harry had put our bags one on top of another against the door of the carriage from which when it was suddenly opened by a very fat priest they fell on top of him. He fancied it was an anti-clerical demonstration and shouted for the police to come to his help. However, as all the onlookers laughed, the police did not arrest us, and we reached the steamer for Tangier without any trouble.

It was a calm blue day. So I was not seasick and was able to look with respect at Cape St Vincent and ponder on the scene of Trafalgar over the waters of which we were passing. In those days steamers could not come alongside in the harbour of Tangier; the noise and confusion of getting off into small boats to be rowed ashore was terrific and just as terrific was the confusion and noise of handing over the passengers' luggage to be fought for by the porters yelling along the quay. However, at last we reached the Hotel Cecil, the only European hotel with any pretensions to Europe in the whole of Morocco. Its owner was a Levantine Englishman with a strong accent, whose great pride was a water-closet he had recently installed. As soon as he had shown us up to our rooms he took us along to look at the chef-d'oeuvre of his career as an hôtelier.

"I think you say this is vairy good, yes?" He pointed to the seat as if he was showing us the throne of Solomon. A placard hung on the wall above it on which was scrawled in large untidy capitals:

Wisitors shall be prayers
Not to stand on the seat.

I asked if he was afraid of visitors hurting themselves.

"They can hurt themselves what they will," he replied indignantly. "But they must not hurt my seat." He then pulled up the plug, and pushed it down again.

"Doulton you see. Very good. I am patriotic Englishman."

Tangier was for me Baghdad during the reign of the Caliph Haroun al-Raschid. The crowded bazaars, the craftsmen working away in their dim shops cross-legged, the camels, the mules, the whining monotones of the blind or mutilated beggars, the heady perfume of the East. I just wandered along through narrow street after narrow street in a dream. I recall one incident. A Moorish policeman was leading a very fat old Jewish woman to prison in the Kasbah. When they reached the narrow entrance between high walls he unlocked the gate and told her to get in. She was so fat that she found it hard to move as fast as he wanted. He lifted his leg, planted his foot against the woman's behind and with a kick sent her sprawling headlong into the festering courtyard crowded with miserable debtors, whose misery was lightened for a moment by the sight of this fat old woman lying on her back with her legs in the air.

Harry and I had planned to ride to Fez, a seven days' journey there and back, but we were told by the British Consul that such a journey was out of the question in the present disturbed state of the country, and we decided to make the forty-odd miles journey to Tetuan instead. Even for that it would be necessary for us to have a Moorish soldier as escort, not to mention a dragoman.

I have forgotten the name of that extremely competent, excitable and entertaining Spanish dragoman. I will call him Don Tomás. We set out for Tetuan at sunrise, and I recall seeing tall Sir Arthur Nicolson, our Minister to the Court of the Sultan, walking along a field beyond a thicket of prickly pears with two others, probably members of the Legation staff.

The fields were white with tazetta narcissus threaded with the blue of *iris alata*, but I do not recall seeing any of Tangier's own iris, *tingitana*; probably it was a week or two early for it. When we stopped at a caravanserai to eat and rest, our Moorish escort could not eat because it was the middle of the rigid fast of Ramadan. Dusk was falling as we drew near to Tetuan and I can see now a Riff with his rifle watching us in the twilight, a sinister figure. We were tired and saddle-sore when we reached the gates of Tetuan, only to find them shut. We banged and banged without any response from the gate keeper. The prospect of camping outside the high walls of Tetuan was not agreeable. There might be other Riffs about with rifles who would shoot us in the hope of plunder. It was nearly dark by now as we went on banging at that great closed door. At last the gate keeper put his head out of one of the towers beside the door to ask what we wanted. There was a stream of Arabic from our escort and Don Tomás. The argument continued for a good five minutes. At last Don Tomás told the gate keeper that Harry and I were two personal friends of Queen Victoria, who would be furious when she heard of the way we had been treated and would make a complaint to the Sultan, which would mean a bad end for the gate keeper. Don Tomás's argument prevailed. The gate keeper came down from the tower and unbarred the great door. We rode through and along a road between the outer and the inner walls of Tetuan, figures huddled against them in the hope of sleep that night, to reach the only European inn, a squalid affair with some high-sounding name like Excelsior. Our bedroom was full of bugs which attacked us in force as soon as the candles were blown out. I had never met bugs before and did not realise when I started scratching the back of my neck that this was always the first warning of an attack by bugs. Neither Harry nor myself was skilled in the tactics to be used in a bug-war. We had a tin of Keating's powder; it seemed as innocuous to bugs as talcum powder to one's cheeks after a shave. Finally we discovered that the only thing to do was to keep the candles alight and try to sleep in chairs. The following night we insisted on our beds being taken up on the roof of the inn where we slept comfortably enough.

Next morning we went to the market-place and sat drinking glasses of mint-flavoured tea. I thought this was really the best tea I had ever drunk. When we finished our refreshment we decided to call on the British Vice-Consul, who was what used to be called a trading consul. Do trading consuls still exist or has the immense expansion of the foreign service done away with them? As we were setting off we heard the noise of a furious argument between Don Tomás and the man who had served us with tea. We asked him what the row had been about and he told us that the swindler had tried to charge us what was the equivalent of three-farthings in our money instead of the halfpenny to which he was entitled.

"He must be a very clever man who can get too much money out of Don Tomás," he said, shaking his head in self-congratulation.

The Vice-Consul lived in an attractive small house in a lovely small garden which even in January seemed full of flowers. He was excellent company after he had eased himself of the grievances which consuls always used to have against embassies and legations. In the foreign service now you can be a consul one day and a secretary of embassy the next; consulitis is no longer a virulent complaint. The Vice-Consul also had a grievance against Kew; he had been asked to produce for them berries of the golden mistletoe. "Which as you may know is the origin of the golden apples of the Hesperides," he said. "Well, it was quite a job to get berries of that golden mistletoe. I knew where it was to be found, but the country's in a very touchy state just now. With some difficulty, and without making too much of a song about it you could say at the risk of my own life, and after an argument with one of those poshed up secretaries at the Legation, I managed to get off a packet of those golden berries in the Legation bag. And I haven't had a word of thanks from Kew or even a word to say whether they had got the berries."

"Surely they must have got them, if they were in an official bag," I said.

"Of course they must," said the Vice-Consul bitterly. "And I suppose one of those leather-bottomed wallahs at the Foreign Office got the acknowledgment from Kew without thinking it worth while sending it on to me. Oh, no, I'm just a vice-consul. I'm not in the diplomatic service."

The Vice-Consul soon forgot his grievances and was a generous host to us while we were in Tetuan. He helped Harry to secure a Moorish rig-out in which he proposed to ride back to Tangier in advance of Don Tomás, who wanted an extra day to finish a bargain he was making over a donkey the cheapening of which would take a little time. He was to come back with the donkey with Harry's European clothes on his mule.

Meanwhile I had taken a fancy, a perfectly respectable fancy, to a little Moorish girl of eleven who was owned by two old Jewesses from whom I offered to buy her. While Don Tomás was bargaining about a donkey and Harry was bargaining about his Moorish costume I was bargaining with the little girl's mistresses and we finally agreed on her price, around ten pounds of English money. So I arranged that Don Tomás should bring her with Harry's European clothes and the mule to Tangier, but I said nothing to Harry because I thought he might object to Fatima's company for the rest of the tour and desired to make that company a *fait accompli*. Then the two old Jewesses refused to let Fatima go until they had the money for her in hard cash. So I arranged with Don Tomás that he would get the money from me in Tangier and go back to fetch Fatima from Tetuan.

Harry and I set off next day, Harry in his white robes looking like a sultan. It was twilight when we reached the outskirts of Tangier and as we were passing a thicket of prickly pears three large dogs rushed out from a neighbouring house and attacked us savagely. This was the long awaited moment for my revolver. I fired at one of the dogs and Harry's horse shied into the middle of the cactus bushes. The dogs fled but when Harry emerged his Moorish robes had been ripped down on each side of him. Luckily it was dark by the time we were in the town, but Harry had to retire to his room until Don

Tomás should arrive with his clothes and for that he had to wait all next day. Moreover, when Don Tomás did arrive with them they had to be dried before he could put them on because Don Tomás's donkey had walked into a river with them.

Meanwhile I asked the hotel-keeper to cash me a cheque for ten pounds in Moorish currency, and foolishly told him about Fatima. Of course he gossiped about my purchase and that afternoon I received a note to say that the Minister would like to see me. I was asked about Fatima and when I told him what I had done I think he found it hard to be grave when he enquired if I was unaware that it was not legal for a British subject to buy a slave.

"And what on earth were you proposing to do with this girl?"

"I was going to take her back with me to Oxford, sir."

"Well, I think it will save you from being sent down if your purchase remains in Tetuan."

I must be frank and admit that by this time I was quite glad to be relieved of the responsibility of Fatima. Already, even in Tangier, she was beginning to seem rather a problem.

I bought a crimson and white silk Moorish caftan instead, and used it as a dressing-gown in Oxford instead of keeping Fatima there as Monte Cristo kept Haidée, the beautiful Greek, in Paris.

We were to return to Spain by way of Algeciras in a packet boat which we were told had once been a royal yacht. A south-west gale was blowing from the Atlantic and a ferocious sea was running in the straits of Gibraltar. I have been very sea-sick many times in my life but I have never been so sea-sick as I was on that accursed crossing. Writing now with octogenarian equanimity I cannot evoke the full horror of it; freedom from sea-sickness is old age's greatest boon. To-day the stormiest blast leaves me imperturbable and as I sit down on board ship to eat anything put before me I wonder why the dining-saloon is so empty. I should have to wait until my beard was white before I was liberated from sea-sickness; I believe all such victims have to wait until that moment. I do not remember seeing a white beard leaning over a ship's side in misery. A sea-sick white-beard must be as rare as once upon a time, according to Sam Weller, was a white horse crossing Westminster Bridge.

I seem to remember, humiliating though the memory be, that on that ghastly crossing I lay on the floor of the cabin wishing the ship would go down with all hands. When we mercifully reached Algeciras at last, even the prospect of the tranquil passage in the ferry to Gibraltar filled me with dismay. I recall absolutely nothing of

Gibraltar except the rather dreary little bedroom I had in a rather dreary little hotel. Next morning we had to be up and away on our journey to Granada before dawn. Even after a night's sleep my mind was still clouded by the sickness of yesterday; when I packed my bag I forgot to pack my revolver and left that gilded weapon in the top left-hand drawer of the rickety little chest of drawers in my bedroom.

The railway-journey to Granada took all day and my mind must have remained clouded, for I cannot recall a single incident, but only a long wait at the junction of Bobadilla where we had had an equally long wait on the journey to Seville. Bobadilla may be a thriving town to-day for all I know; in 1901 it was just a railway-junction in the middle of an empty countryside. After a night in the Granada hotel I was my ebullient self again on the edge of nineteen.

To expatiate on the beauty of the Alhambra is not an impertinence in which I shall indulge. It is enough to say that Harry and I were granted a privilege few can have enjoyed to-day of wandering under a cloudless sky about its courts and gardens without another tourist to break the silence with so much as the click of a camera. We were accompanied by a thirteen-year-old boy who had attached himself to us as guide, but we hushed his voluble informativeness, and he followed us round, puzzled and depressed by our indifference to his knowledge.

Pedro cheered up after we left the Alhambra when I accepted his invitation to let him take me to see what he promised in much broken English should be the best display of flamenco dancing in all Granada. I see now the eager expression on his face as I came out from dinner and found him waiting in the hall of the hotel. Harry, as usual, declined to accompany me on one of these nocturnal expeditions, preferring to occupy himself with his insatiable passion for heraldic research and go to bed early.

Pedro and I walked in the frosty moonlight through a maze of narrow streets, to be received by an effusive gypsy hostess jingling with necklaces and bracelets. The dancer, who was a rather more than buxom girl, was presented to us and we drank wine together. Presently the guitarist came in and the dancer retired to strip for the performance. When she came back she was wearing nothing but a woollen vest. This shocked Pedro's notion of propriety and there was an angry argument between him and the hostess. I asked him what was the matter and he told me indignantly that the dancer was asking permission to keep her vest on because it was such a cold night. I told him that of course the girl must be allowed to keep her vest on and the dance began. As she displayed the mobility of her muscles in front and behind Pedro sat scowling at her performance. He obviously felt that her performance of these wriggles in a woollen vest was a reflection upon his competence as a guide to flamenco dancing. His client was being cheated and he was responsible. He suddenly jumped up and smacked the dancer's behind as hard as he could. The girl gave a yell. The hostess turned on Pedro with a torrent of abuse. Three or four other girls appeared and after being shown by the dancer the crimson mark of Pedro's hand on her behind the other girls added their stream of abuse to the torrent of the hostess. Only the guitarist kept out of it all; he just put down his guitar and laughed.

I held up my hand for silence.

"You had no right to do that, Pedro," I told him. "Tell them we must all sit down and have some wine and tell the poor girl to get some clothes on."

After a bit Pedro's ruffled dignity as a guide was soothed and the evening went well, with us all sitting round amicably over the wine and singing flamenco songs.

Pedro was inclined to argue about the bill when it was presented. The slur on his reputation made by that woollen vest was beginning to anger him again. I insisted that I had not been in the least disappointed by the evening and added an extra 25 pesetas for the dancer herself.

When we left the house I told Pedro I should like to go to a place where I could look at the Alhambra by moonlight. He cheered up at this. He knew better than any guide the very spot to make for. And indeed, he did. After a steep climb we came to a bench on which we sat; the Alhambra spread out below in a radiance of frozen moonshine. While we sat there Pedro told me what his ambition was for the future. He would go to the Argentine and make a fortune. I asked him in what business. He shrugged his shoulders. He was not yet sure exactly how the fortune would be made; he was only sure that somehow it would be made. I like to fancy that at this moment there is a rich man in his 75th year who arrived in Buenos Aires to make his fortune and succeeded.

In one of the main streets of Granada a tramway line had been laid but as yet there was no sign of a tram. A number of old Moorish houses had been pulled down to widen the street for the new traffic and the doors of those ancient houses were leaning against what must have been the scaffolding of the new houses that were to be built. They like the trams were waiting for *mañana*. These doors were immense, with wonderful carving and huge latches in which were stuck keys a foot long. I asked what was going to be done with these magnificent doors and was told they were being sold for firewood. I asked the price and was told that an offer of 1000 pesetas would probably secure the lot. I had dreamed of taking them to England and making a huge profit by selling them over there for the panelling of the country houses being built for the *nouveaux riches*, but when I found that it would cost at least £400 to transport them to England my dream faded. I was told in Morocco that some of the Moors there still had the keys which used to open the doors of their ancestors' houses in Spain. I regret those glorious doors that opened to the patios of long ago. I still see them leaning against the scaffolding of houses not yet built in that widened street where the tram-lines had been laid but the trams had not yet started to run.

I have a notion that my nineteenth birthday came when we were in Granada but I cannot be sure of this. We went from Granada to Madrid, another long railway-journey, with no doubt another long wait at Bobadilla. This time on the day after we arrived we did catch the 8 a.m. train to Toledo and spent a wonderful day there. Toledo seemed almost forbidding on that grey January day after the warmth and gaiety of Seville and the blue sky above Granada. The gothic bridge over the gorge of the Tagus and the glorious cathedral inspired awe. In the sacristy of that cathedral I saw what must be the finest collection of vestments in the world. As the sacristan pulled out wide shallow drawer after drawer, cope after cope and chasuble after chasuble were produced, each more richly embroidered than the last.

We went to the famous steel foundry where I bought a swordstick with a Toledo blade for 50 pesetas. To show its quality the salesman pierced a soldo with it. I kept that swordstick until my house in Athens was sacked in December 1916. My last memory of Toledo is of sitting in a café drinking chocolate before it was time to drive to the station to catch the train back to Madrid, and of seeing groups of Spaniards all in sombreros and wrapped round in their black cloaks with an oblong of red plush in front to keep them from slipping from the shoulders. They looked like a bunch of conspirators; no doubt they were merely retailing the gossip of the day.

The next day we were off to another early start, bound for Barcelona and the journey home. It must have been about half-past six when, as the train was coming into Barcelona, a police official entered our compartment with the ticket-inspector.

"You will not be remaining in Barcelona to-night?" the police official asked us in French.

We told him we intended to stay two nights at whatever hotel it was we were bound for. He shook his head.

"You cannot stay in Barcelona. There is a great strike and much disorder. You must drive to the station for Toulouse as soon as you arrive and take the train there."

It was evidently idle to protest. As soon as the train stopped the police official conducted us to a fiacre outside the station, and getting in with us he ordered the driver to go to whatever the name of the other station was as quickly as possible. On our way we passed one street in which the barricades were up with bonfires burning along both of them, but there was no shooting.

When we reached the other station the police official took us to the train bound for Toulouse, saw us safely in to a second-class compartment and waited till the train steamed out with us.

"He must think we're anarchists," I said. "But I wish he'd let us wait until we'd had dinner. I'm pretty hungry." At the first station we stopped at in France I urged Harry to get out and forage for some sandwiches.

"I haven't got any money left," said Harry.

"You haven't what?" I gasped. "But damn it, I haven't got any money. You were in charge of the funds after we paid our hotel bill in Madrid. I told you then I was cleaned out by buying that sword-stick and you said you had enough to last us till we got back our deposit at Cook's in Paris."

"I miscalculated."

I felt like running Harry through with my swordstick, but one could not be angry with him for long.

"I'll eat the biggest breakfast of my life when we get to Paris to-morrow morning," I vowed.

"We shan't get to Paris to-morrow morning," said Harry with one of those deep chuckles at something he found funny but which nobody else did. "This train stops at Toulouse. We get there at one o'clock."

So at one in the morning we were dumped at Toulouse, where even if the buffet had been open we could not have bought anything to eat, because we had no money. We drowsed and shivered away the time on the hard seats in the waiting-room, until at long weary last the train for Paris appeared somewhere round about eight o'clock. I watched with hungry eyes and a rumbling inside passengers lapping up bowls of café-au-lait until the train started and the sight of other people filling themselves up no longer tantalized me. It may have been at Cahors that a Frenchman got into our compartment with a luncheon-basket which he put down on the seat opposite myself. In spite of the gnawing pangs of hunger I could not help being entranced by the beauty of the countryside through which we were travelling. The train stopped at one small station after another and at one place —ending of course with 'ac'—a steep conical wooded hill with a château on the top of it rose half a mile or so from the station.

"I must come back to this country one day," I said to myself.

Just over sixty years were to pass before that resolution was fulfilled, and now in that entrancing countryside I sit writing these words. I have not yet discovered the railway-station where I made that resolution, but when I do I shall scribble in the dust of the road outside it *hoc erat in votis*.

We were well into the Limousin when the Frenchman opened his basket and started to eat his lunch. I believe I should have asked to pick his chicken-bone if he had not gnawed it first himself. At last he finished, leaving uneaten two of those almond-shaped sweets which always used to accompany a railway luncheon-basket in France and probably still do. I wanted to say "If you're not going to eat those sweets, monsieur, do you mind if I eat them?" I thought of those Spanish peasants who shared their food and wine with Harry and myself on the way to Seville, but thinking about those sausages made the pangs of hunger almost unbearable.

At Limoges the Frenchman got out to buy a paper, and as I saw him walking away from the carriage I leaned across, opened the lid of that luncheon basket, took out the two sweets, and ate them, the first morsel I had eaten since this time yesterday. I was glad that when the Frenchman returned with a paper he did not lift the lid of the basket.

When we reached what was then the Gare d'Orleans I told Harry firmly that we were going to stay at the Palais d'Orsay hotel whatever it cost, and that he would have to get up early next morning to recover our deposit from Cook's with which to pay the bill. We had to carry our own bags across to the hotel, having no money to tip a porter.

We had a glorious dinner that night and a comfortable double room in which to sleep off the effects of that journey from Madrid to Paris. Next morning while I was drinking my café-au-lait in bed I hustled Harry out to walk to Cook's and redeem our deposit in French money. When we had paid for our bed and our board for a night at the Palais d'Orsay hotel we had four francs left, which paid for a fiacre to the Gare du Nord. We had some difficulty in keeping our bags out of the hands of eager porters whom we should have been unable to tip, and equal difficulty with stewards on the boat from Dieppe and the porters at Newhaven. However, we reached Victoria that evening and drove in a hansom to 1 Nevern Square to find my mother was out at one of her charitable functions. So I borrowed two shillings from our parlour-maid to pay the cabby his fare and give him what was then the very generous tip of sixpence.

"The mistress will be in by seven," the parlour-maid told me. "And dinner will be at half-past."

I was ravenous again after a day on café-au-lait and a couple of rolls and asked if there was any cake. "There's a Genoa cake," I was told.

"Would you like some cake?" I asked Harry, who had begun that deep chuckle of his at a private joke. He shook his head. When the parlour-maid went off to fetch the cake he asked me if I could guess what he was laughing at.

"I've no idea."

"Well, the joke is that I had some money all the time but I had a complete collection of current notes, coins and stamps and I didn't want to spoil it." And he went back to that low rumbling chuckle of his.

NINETEEN YEARS OLD: 1902

LITTLE Oppenheim had gone by the beginning of that Hilary term, and I was glad to have Harry Pirie-Gordon in the rooms opposite to me. He was regarded at first by many of the freshmen as almost impossibly eccentric; they could not understand a man who covered the walls of his sitter with small heraldic shields. I had already shocked them by hanging Mona Lisa and the Primavera on the walls of my sitter instead of Thorburn's studies of grouse, and with having Boccaccio, Rabelais and Cervantes on my shelves instead of Jorrocks. However, either because I amused them or because I obviously thought any failure to amuse them would be their fault not mine, the general opinion was that in spite of the handicap of being at a day-school I was a good egg, and by now I had become 'Monty'. Yet even in my third year I was still a bit of a puzzle to those contemporaries of mine. In the sitting-room at 43 High which Harry Pirie-Gordon and I shared in our third year was an Arundel print of the Primavera, and I can see now Kenneth Carlisle, the Captain of the University cricket eleven, gazing at it in perplexity.

"I say, Monty," exclaimed 'Salt' Carlisle, whose nickname dated from his Harrow days when one of the masters had referred to him as the salt of the earth, "you don't really *like* looking at those frightful women, do you?"

My friendship with Harry Pirie-Gordon was regarded at first as a deliberate display of nonconformity. The other freshmen could not understand what I found to talk to him about. This was because Harry himself never took the faintest trouble even to appear interested by anybody who was not interested in what interested him, and he declined to surrender to a single convention of a College the pattern of whose behaviour was rigid. A Magdalen freshman who found that his title was prefixed to his name in the list of names at the bottom of every staircase at once ordered it to be deleted. The Christ Church custom of advertizing such titles was considered all very well for the House but not at all the thing for Magdalen. If a Magdalen man was elected to the Bullingdon he was expected to decline. It was considered unnecessary for a Magdalen man to join the Union; those who did were presumed to have done so because they found themselves superfluous in Magdalen. The wearing of a black and white College tie or the College crest on a blazer was regarded as the equivalent of wearing a made-up tie or buttoning the bottom button of one's waistcoat. Members of the College Eight wore the wide scarlet ribbon with the lilies round their straw hats during the summer term. Straw hats, be it noted, not 'boaters'. It was Noel Coward who first disseminated the belief that a period atmosphere could be created by calling straw hats 'boaters'. The word was unheard of at this date, except perhaps in the catalogue of some second-rate women's outfitters. Canes and walking-sticks were never carried except by a few House men. I was unwilling to yield to what I thought was a foolishly uncomfortable convention and always used a walking-stick when I took an afternoon off from football.

The freshmen's tables in Hall were on either side of the entrance. The second-year men's tables were side by side in the middle. Beyond our table on the right of the entrance sat the demys. At the head of our table was Claude Kirby, who had had Luxmoore as his tutor at Eton, where without either athletic or scholastic prowess he had been regarded as insignificant. Now with his deep voice and completely self-assured manner he immediately became a personality. It was the duty of the head of the table to sconce anybody who talked shop or bawdy, who swore even as mildly as a 'damn', or who made any remark considered out of keeping with manners at table. I recall being sconced once for saying, when a favourite savoury of the college cook called "green butter" was put before us, that I wished they wouldn't be sick so often in the kitchen. A 'sconce' was half-a-crown, and at the end of the term the sum total of sconces collected paid for wine all round at the last dinner. As freshmen we were proud of incurring enough sconces to make the wine served at the end of that term champagne.

I was strongly supported by Claude Kirby in my determination to follow my own taste in pictures and books, and he who had been encouraged at Eton by his tutor Luxmoore was now an 'aesthete' unashamed, with the Hermes of Praxitiles and the Naples Narcissus on either side of his chimney shelf.

One had to keep three roll-calls a week at eight o'clock on Monday, Wednesday and Friday. If one fell behind in the first part of the week it involved Chapel on Thursday or Saturday, and how often Friday as well when rushing along to keep a roll-call the clock would start striking before one could reach Hall and one made for one's stall in Chapel, which was nearer for us in Swither's.

Most colleges at this date had a gate-bill, which meant that undergraduates paid a rising charge for coming into college from 9.15 p.m. up to midnight. At Magdalen we had no gate bill, though one's time of coming back into college was entered by the head-porter or his assistant. Kingston, our head-porter, was a Dickensian figure of monumental pomposity with a 'nice derangement of epitaphs' like Mrs Malaprop. That once upon a time he had been a trooper in a Hussar regiment we found incredible, but it was true.

The outstanding event of that term for me was the O.U.D.S. production, *By permission of the Vice-Chancellor and the Right Worshipful the Mayor*, of Shakespeare's Comedy *The Two Gentlemen of Verona* on Wednesday February 5th till Tuesday February 11th with matinées on the Saturday and Monday.

The O.U.D.S. club rooms were over a Freeman, Hardy and Willis boot-shop at the corner of George Street, the big bay-window of what to-day would be called the lounge looking out immediately at the Norman tower of St Michael's Church and beyond it up the Broad. The walls of the club-room, the dining-room and the committee-room were hung with large souvenirs of previous productions in which every member of the cast had his photograph in costume, the latest being last year's production of *Much Ado About Nothing* in which H. M. Tennent had scored a great success as Benedick and G. P. Langton an equally great success as Dogberry. Harry Tennent had gone down, but Philip Langton was still up at New College and a member of the Committee. He was not acting this year on account of Schools. Yet he was still playing with the notion of making the stage his profession. In the end he decided upon the Law and would one day become Sir George Langton, President of the Court of Admiralty and Divorce.

I had persuaded Harry Pirie-Gordon to join the O.U.D.S. at the beginning of the term and he appeared as an outlaw; so did Raymond Wavell and Dan Pope; I was cast for the Duke of Milan. Staircase III in St Swithun's was well represented.

In Fort's House at Winchester B. Forsyth had inspired the other men to go in for amateur theatricals, and naturally Raymond Wavell was eager to join the O.U.D.S. Bertie Forsyth was a mass of nerves but a first rate actor; he had a notable career with the O.U.D.S. When he went down from Oxford he became a professional, but some years later in one of his recurrent fits of melancholy he took his own life in New York. In *The Two Gentlemen of Verona* he gave an admirable performance as Sir Thurio. He occupied the office of Dramatic

Treasurer, which was abolished in a shake up of the Club the following year when the office of President was created. At present the equivalent of President was the Secretary. This office was held by A. T. Loyd, who would one day inherit the Wantage estate; Tommy Loyd of Hertford was good-looking, and popular throughout the University.

Oxford and Cambridge had different rules about women acting. Oxford insisted that women's parts should always be played by women, Cambridge on the other hand insisted that they should be played by men; this applied equally to the Amateur Dramatic Club, better known as the A.D.C. and to the Footlights D.C. which went in for musicals. The proliferation of dramatic clubs in the two Universities that is a feature of to-day would have been unimaginable in 1902.

The O.U.D.S. productions while I was up were in the hands of G. R. Foss as director. With a nose that would have done credit to a Roman dictator, and a resonant bass voice, he was able in barely a fortnight of rehearsals to bring out of all of us as much as we were capable of giving. During that fortnight we lived either in Verona or Milan even when we were entertaining the ladies to lunch or going to tea with them in Paradise Square.

The Two Gentlemen of Verona is one of Shakespeare's least attractive plays on the stage, and in that cold wet February weather the amount taken did not reach £250, which meant a fairly heavy loss for the O.U.D.S. The only outstandingly successful scene was the serenade by Sir Thurio of the Duke's daughter Silvia, when Schubert's exquisite setting of that exquisite lyric 'Who is Silvia?' sung by W. L. Greenlees of Magdalen captivated the audience. The two clowns, Launce and Speed, were played by Viscount Tiverton,[1] of New College and Kennedy-Cox[2] of Hertford. Tivvy was a remarkable personality. He was in the New College Eight, then head of the river, and at the same time was a friend of 'aesthetes' like Eric Maclagan[3] and Archibald Russell.[4]

The last night of an O.U.D.S. show was always a great occasion. After playing to a genially obstreperous house speeches were made at the end of the play and after bouquets had been handed up for the ladies various toys were presented to the men. Tivvy as Launce

[1] The late Earl of Halsbury.
[2] Sir Reginald Kennedy-Cox, C.B.E.
[3] The late Sir Eric Maclagan.
[4] The late Sir Archibald Russell.

received at least half-a-dozen toy-dogs. My prizes were four wooden toy-engines. This was an allusion to the Duke of Milan's line to Valentine when he snatches from under his cloak the rope-ladder by which he was proposing that his daughter Silvia should elope from the palace. 'And here an engine fit for thy proceeding.'

It must have been before the end of this term that I managed to persuade seven other undergraduates, all of them except Harry Pirie-Gordon and Claude Kirby third-year men in Univ. and Trinity to invest £5 each in founding a bi-terminal shilling review to be called *The Oxford Point of View* and edited by myself. As the first number would appear at the beginning of May, the project must have been debated before the Easter vac. I confess I am still baffled to know how I did it. When I look back at this term I seem to have spent every single evening except when the O.U.D.S. show was on playing bridge, and on Sundays after a lunch of which mulled claret in a silver jug was always a feature four of us would sit down and play all through the afternoon.

On Sunday evening there was wine after hall in the J.C.R. followed by the 'after' at which we drank whisky and soda or lemon squash. In the morning there were lectures and on most afternoons I was playing rugger. I really do not know when I found the time or the opportunity to inspire those third-year men to support my project. I think it must have been Lance Andrewes of Univ. who did the missionary work. He was on the Committee of the O.U.D.S., an elegant enthusiast for any project that caught his fancy for the moment but inclined to let one enthusiasm be blown away by the next that took its place. He was a member of the High Tory Strafford Club, for which he proposed Harry Pirie-Gordon and myself and to which we were both elected. The most distinguished member of it in my time was the late Sir Richard Livingstone, that great President of Corpus. We used to meet for an occasional wine and listen to a paper read by one of the members. We had a ramshorn of snuff set in silver dating back to the time of Charles II. The membership was small, hardly more than a dozen.

I spent most of that Easter Vacation in London. George Alexander had put on *Paolo and Francesca* at the St James's and critics were acclaiming Stephen Philips as the long awaited genius who was to restore to life poetic drama upon the English stage. For the part of Paolo, Alexander had discovered a handsome young provincial actor of twenty-three with a rich voice called Henry Ainley. Dick Hewlett was engaged at a guinea a week to walk across the stage in one scene as Dante and undoubtedly he did manage to convey exactly the impression we all have of what Dante looked like. At the bar of that public house behind the theatre where the male members of the cast used to foregather after the show Dick Hewlett introduced me to Henry Ainley who invited both of us to have a drink.

"A French and Italian vermouth, " I said.

"The same, please," Dick Hewlett said.

Ainley looked at us both, consternation upon his noble young brow.

"Good god, boys, if you start drinking that kind of stuff at your age where do you think you will both end?"

I protested that I had been drinking French and Italian vermouth for a couple of years and considered it as harmless a drink as one could find.

"Harmless!" Ainley ejaculated. "Well, I'm not going to be the one to encourage you to drink such poisonous stuff." Then as if he were delivering a sonorous line by Stephen Philips, he declaimed to the barmaid in his richest voice "Three ports, miss. Three glasses of your Offley's 1880." The three glasses were placed upon the counter.

"That's better for you than that foreign muck you think its clever to pretend you enjoy. What was it called?" Ainley asked.

"Vermouth."

"Vermouth indeed!" he boomed contemptuously, and raising his glass of port he added, "Here's to wishing you a little more common sense in the future!"

Alas, poor Harry Ainley himself would one day spoil the career of a fine actor by losing much of his own common sense through drink. At this date he was still a completely unsophisticated young man from Yorkshire, engaged to a young woman as simple as himself. It was inevitable that he should be bewildered by his projection into fame and he was studying anxiously a part he had probably never expected to play, a part much more difficult than Paolo. I always hesitate to criticize those who without any background of the arts find themselves suddenly famous as novelists or actors or film stars or television personalities. I realize how much easier it has always been for me to take success for granted if it came and never to worry myself about criticism or resent it.

George Alexander may have felt that Ainley's success in *Paolo and Francesca* was not quite what he had intended when he brought him to the St James's. Nor had he allowed for the skill with which Suzanne Sheldon would teach Ainley how to improve his acting. Suzanne

Sheldon as well as being a fine actress herself was a woman of dominant personality. She was a sister of Edward Sheldon, an American playwright of great talent, and of Eleanor Sheldon who was married to Anthony Hope.

So when Alexander produced a play about François Villon called *If I Were King* Ainley was given a part from which not even Suzanne Sheldon could extract a success for the man with whom she was now in love, and whom she would marry a year hence.

I shall run ahead of this Easter vac to that production of *If I Were King* in which the four *filles de joie* were played by Jean MacKinlay, May Saker, Dorothy Scott and Auriol Lee.

"You're a friend of Auriol Lee's, aren't you?" Ainley said to me. "Do tell her not to wear that flashy red coat she's always about in. It makes her look cheap, and no girl can afford to look cheap, can she? I ran against her in Piccadilly yesterday and with that eyeglass of hers and that dreadful red coat I was quite embarrassed when she walked along with me all the way to the theatre."

Auriol was the elder daughter of old Dr Lee, who lived at a corner house in Gunterstone Road where Trevanion Road runs off it into Edith Road. My first sight of her had been years ago when she was at Scott's school in North End Road and looked at me through her monocle, which she wore not from affectation but because she was extremely short-sighted. Later, after she left Scott's, we became great friends.

Dr Lee was a pioneer of to-day when Queen Victoria was on the throne. He was regarded by the rest of West Kensington as almost more than eccentric; yet most of his opinions and habits are commonplace to-day. Perhaps even to-day it might be thought a little odd to send one's daughter to be the only girl in a boys' prep school, but Dartingtons were not then available. His wife was supposed to have gypsy blood but this may merely have been an attempt by West Kensington to explain her bohemianism. Anyway, she was a very voluble and very entertaining woman of boundless hospitality. Her younger daughter Esmée was now about twelve. She was an enchanting little girl who would one day marry St J. Field, an undergraduate of Balliol at this date who sported the heaviest moustache in the University; their daughter Virginia Field would be a film star of the 'thirties.

It was at the Lees' house that I met George Moore just before he forsook what he called the Brixton Empire, sickened by the Jingoism of the South African War, and went to live in Dublin there to write that incomparable trio, *Ave*, *Salve* and *Vale*. I had not yet read *Evelyn Innes* when I was presented to George Moore and thought him rather a ridiculous figure, with what seemed then his air of an outdated masher. He looked like the man in the moon with a heavy drooping moustache and tried to kiss Auriol's pretty maid in the hall.

Auriol was a wonderful confidante, and her keen enthusiasms were so many that she always encouraged mine. I recall one of mine she supported when nobody else did. It was some time in this year that walking along Pall Mall I saw in the window of an estate-agent the announcement of an island for sale in the Bay of Panama for £2000. On making enquiries I found that this was one of the Islas Perlas or Pearl Islands, an archipelago covering about 450 square miles, called as I seem to remember San Paolo but of this I am far from being certain. It was 14 miles long and 7 wide with two or three indigo plantations worked by negroes and some coconut groves. The pearl fishing was exhausted. There were other details which I have forgotten. It seemed to me that the value of such an island would be immensely increased if and when the Panama Canal was made and I was fired by the notion of acquiring it. I asked my father if he would put up the necessary money.

"What on earth will you be asking for next?"

"But when the Panama Canal is made. . . ."

"Ah, *when* the Panama Canal is made."

And that accentuated 'when' was the reply of everybody I approached for that £2000.

Auriol agreed with me about the value of such an island in the future and tried to enlist the interest of some of her rich friends who liked investing in musical shows. If there had been groves of chorus girls on that island instead of coconuts she might have been successful.

Nine years later that island was sold for £99,000. I cannot remember how I heard about this; I have a vague idea that it was bought by the American Government. When the news came I was entirely preoccupied with the corps de ballet of the Alhambra and the prospect of my first novel's being published at last.

When Auriol Lee was playing in *If I Were King* she read somewhere about prostitutes in gaol being branded on the arm with a fleur de lys.

"I'm going to add a touch of realism to our scene, old son," she said to me. "I'm going to make up my arm with a fleur de lys."

She practised for about a week until she had a fleur de lys that satisfied her and then one evening she tried it on an audience. Unfortunately for Auriol she chose an evening when Mrs George

Alexander was in the box she occupied occasionally in order to report to her husband on the way the show was going; when the curtain came down on that act Mrs Alexander sent this note to Miss Auriol Lee:

Mrs Alexander was surprised to see that Miss Lee had not covered the vaccination marks on her arm. Will Miss Lee please be careful about this in future.

Auriol Lee married the popular actor, Frederick Lloyd, but they were separated later. Auriol became a great friend of Air Chief Marshal Sir Geoffrey Salmond, who in 1933 was killed in that dreadful disaster to the R 101 dirigible balloon, a tragedy which saddened the end of her life.

Mention of Gunterstone Road reminds me that I forgot to recall in my previous Octave another resident of Gunterstone Road who played a part in my youthful education. One evening, when I was looking through the second-hand books outside one of the shops in the terrace before Addison Bridge, a rugged man with a white beard and a game leg got into conversation with me and on finding out who I was told me he had known the young Comptons in Stamford Road thirty years ago.

"I remember Emmie particularly. She was a very pretty little girl and a great tomboy. And I remember your grandfather's getting a job for Henry and Percy Compton with Barry Sullivan and their being sent back to Kensington almost at once because one of them had bet the other that when he had to say in *Richard III* "Stand by and let the coffin pass' he wouldn't say 'Stand by and let the parson cough'. And by George, he did, and Barry Sullivan was so angry he turned them both out of his Company immediately."

This was Sydney Whiteford who called himself the last of the pre-Raphaelites; when he invited me to come and look at his pictures in Gunterstone Road I accepted with alacrity.

Those visits to Sydney Whiteford were for me a never failing romantic thrill. He lived alone with an elderly housekeeper who treated him like a spoilt child and indulged his bohemian habits. The house was crowded with pictures, books and nicknacks of every kind from attic to basement, and I never tired of wandering round with him and listening to the history of them all or his reminiscences of Rossetti, William Morris, Holman Hunt, Ford Madox Brown and the rest of them. Suddenly, whatever the time, he would ask me if I felt hungry and before I had time to answer would bellow down to his housekeeper to make us a Welsh rarebit which he would eat in whatever room we happened to be in at the moment, whether it was on a table in the studio littered with paints and palettes or on our knees in his 'den' seated on either side of the fire in high-backed gilded Venetian chairs.

To come back to that Easter vac of 1902. Dick Hewlett was finding that the guinea a week he was being paid for walking across the stage of the St James's Theatre as Dante was getting him into arrears with his landlady, and he asked me to come down with him to Addington, where his mother and sister were living, in order that I might paint to his mother such a vivid picture of his penury that she would persuade his brother Maurice to let him have £25.

"After all, Maurice has his salary as Keeper of the Crown Records and he's doing jolly well out of his novels. I can't ask my parson brother to lend me money, poor chap. They'll be sending out some musical comedy tours in the autumn and I shall easily get a job in the chorus."

I must have been sufficiently eloquent about Dick's prospects and sufficiently heartrending about his poverty for Mrs Hewlett to write to her eldest son, because soon after our visit to Addington Maurice did send him a cheque for £25 with a brief note pinned to it.

'This *is* the *last* time.'

I wrote some nonsense rhymes based on compound animals and birds and suggested that Dick should set them to music and that one of the penurious artists we knew should illustrate them. I have lost the rhymes I wrote long ago, but by chance I came across the names of some of those compound animals and birds scrawled on an old scrap of paper among the drafts of poems I wrote at High Cross, some of which appeared in a volume of poems that Blackwell would publish five years hence. I copy them out now: The Kangarooraldean, The Fountain Penguin, The Caterpillar-box, The Omnibustard,

> The Antimacassowary,
> '*which lives in corners of the room*
> *shedding an atmosphere of gloom*',

The Panthermometer, The Marmosettee, The Camelectric, The Dromedarimaid, The Shoehornet.

I think it was some time in this spring that Robbie Ross opened his Carfax Gallery in Ryder Street. There is a preposterous attempt to present a picture of Robbie Ross by Rupert Croft-Cooke in his life of

Lord Alfred Douglas which he calls *Bosie*. It is as much like Robert Ross as one of those compound creatures above. The book was published too late for me to rebut in my previous Octave some of the statements; having known Ross, Turner and Lord Alfred Douglas in 1899, when Oscar Wilde was still alive, I am not aware of anybody else who can claim as much to-day and I consider I am better entitled to judge between Ross and Douglas than my friend Croft-Cooke, who only knew Douglas when he was an old man embittered by the failure he had made of his life and offering to the young people who would listen to him a completely imaginary portrait of himself. No amount of whitewash can hide the fact that Douglas was primarily responsible for that insane libel action started against Lord Queensberry, and no kind of extenuation can be found for Douglas's base partnership with the unspeakable Crosland.

Back at Oxford I was absorbed in the task of bringing out in May the first number of *The Oxford Point of View*. The great moment when I went into old Mr Alden's office at the Boccardo Press in the Cornmarket seems but yesterday. There he sat in his stained and faded navy-blue tail-suit, his long greying beard yellowish below his mouth with the last remnants of what once must have been a golden beard, the baldness of his domed head covered by a dark-blue cricketing cap.

"A letter has arrived for the editor from Dr Bridges," he announced as he handed me a long letter from the great poet on the proper pronunciation of Latin:

Dear Mr Editor,

Among the myriad interesting topics which lie appealingly before you, and concerning which the world at large will, to judge by my own feelings, be dying to know "*the Oxford Point of View*", *there can scarcely be one more worthy of your attention than the pronunciation of Latin, as at present practised in England. I am therefore emboldened to write to you, Sir, to ask you to tell us who are severed from our Alma Mater, and out of hearing of her sweet accents, what the actual condition of things at Oxford is, and what class of person or notions is now the chief obstacle to radical reform.*

Then for five pages the poet went on to plead for what to-day is the recognized way of pronouncing Latin, a plea which would be answered sympathetically by Robinson Ellis, the Corpus Professor of Latin, in the October number of *The Oxford Point of View*.

Robert Bridges wound up at the end of the six pages his letter occupied in print:

I must not trespass further upon your space. The object of my letter is to elicit opinions. . . . You will be able to tell us what the Oxford Point of View *is. I know that in the matter of opinions the University is very like a tin of mixed biscuits; but one kind is at one time preponderating or fashionable, another at another. I shall be much disappointed if it does not prove on enquiry that science and common-sense have already struck their indomitable alliance, and have only to show their flag and walk over.*

With best wishes for your literary welfare.

I remain,

Yours faithfully,

Robert Bridges

No doubt the reform of Latin pronunciation would have been brought about in due course and the pronunciation of the modern Latin languages made easier for Englishmen in consequence, but there is no doubt that Robert Bridges hastened the reform with that letter. For me the value of that letter were the visits from time to time which the great poet paid my rooms both in College and later at 43 High, and the visits I was privileged to pay him on Boar's Hill.

Bridges was in a ferment of anxiety over the reception of his attack on the current mode of Latin pronunciation. He used to bicycle down from Boar's Hill that summer term, wearing grey-striped white flannel trousers, patent-leather shoes, a flowered silk waistcoat of eighteenth century brocade, a crimson silk tie pulled through a cameo ring, and to crown everything a yachting cap. He was a superb figure of a great poet who believed he had successfully disguised himself as a man of the world in order to find out how the obscurantists of Dondom were standing his cuts and thrusts. Once in the middle of a tirade against the imbecility and illogicality of the old public-school Latin Primer pronunciation he picked up a volume of Herrick which was lying on my table.

"Why do you read this r-rot?" he growled with that slight stutter of his.

"Because he is almost my favourite poet," I declared.

He opened the volume haphazard and read:

"Her eyes the g-glow-worm l-lend thee,
The shooting s-stars attend thee."

Then he shut the volume with a snap and tossed it to the other end of the room. "R-rot!" he growled. "What eyes has a g-glow-worm g-got to l-lend anybody?"

Once up on Boar's Hill I saw him pitch a volume of Courthope's *History of English Literature* to the other end of his room in a similar spasm. "This fellow is the most abominable charlatan alive," he declared.

Great poets are apt to find pedantic professors irritating. When I was asked by the President of Magdalen to meet Professor Churton Collins at lunch I remembered that Tennyson had called him a louse upon the locks of literature because he had written a painstaking article tracing the derivatives from earlier poets in some of Tennyson's best lines. I was inclined to agree with Tennyson when I listened at lunch to Churton Collins's pedantic condescension and professorial complacency.

On another occasion at Boar's Hill Bridges asked: "Have you ever heard of a fellow called George Bernard Shaw? I've just been reading some p-plays by him, and they're not at all b-bad, you know. He's a clever fellow, I tell you. You ought to r-read him. They're called *P-plays P-pleasant and Unp-pleasant*."

Legend related that Bridges had never read any of Keats until he was asked to write an introduction for the edition of his poetry in the Muses' Library, after which he produced the finest piece of poetic criticism in the English language. When he was made Poet Laureate in 1913 the popular Press discovered that he had practised medicine once upon a time and always alluded to him as Dr Bridges, implying by that prefix a censure of him for not responding in verse to the pulse of the popular Press when it was beating fast in one of its periodic fevers.

Bridges was always a poet severely aloof from popularity; yet in 1929 at the age of 85, a year before his death, his long poem *The Testament of Beauty*, which was a poetic summary of progress as he had viewed it through a long life, went into fourteen editions in a year. That of course made the *précieux ridicules* of contemporary criticism doubt whether Bridges was so great a poet after all.

Every number of *The Oxford Point of View* began with a series of paragraphs called 'Through Oxford Glasses'. In the first three numbers these were written by Desmond F. T. Coke of Univ., who a couple of years hence would write a farcical Oxford novel called *Sandford of Merton*, but whose brilliant early promise somehow petered out. He was one of the third-year men bewitched into putting up his £5 for me to edit a paper. It may have been Coke or it may have been Hugh de Sélincourt, another backer from Univ., who suggested asking a hard-working undergraduate at Univ. from Glasgow University to write an article. This was A. D. Lindsay, a future Master of Balliol, and I see him now in a small room two pairs up as he tells me with Scottish gravity that he will write an article on 'The Liberal Outlook'. Here is his final sentence: "We may expect to see after the conclusion of peace the belated revival of the Liberal Party owing to the way in which the Government has revived the old question from which the old Liberal Party won its strength. It will be interesting to see if adversity has given it wisdom to deal with the new questions of the day."

Might not those very words be written about the Liberal Party to-day?

I wish that Clement Attlee, another Univ. freshman, had been noted down to discuss the outlook for Labour, or that Philip Lloyd-Graeme,[1] yet another Univ. freshman and a great friend of mine, had been picked by me to write about the outlook for Conservatism.

The Rhodes bequest had just been announced that April and naturally our first number carried an article which doubted the value of the American scholarships and thought that the interests of the Empire would have been better served by giving these to India.

The larger Press received the 68 pages of that first number with a seriousness which we found most gratifying and which we assumed, perhaps correctly, marked the interest that the rest of the country was taking in the direction along which the first young men of the twentieth century were moving. Indeed, we had gone so far in a preliminary announcement as to take a phrase from one of Ibsen's plays and proclaim ourselves to be those who were coming after and who were already knocking at the door. That a University review costing a shilling, slightly priggish and absurdly solemn, should sell 1500 copies of its first number was an indication of the interest it aroused outside Oxford, for the support of the University itself was but a poor fraction of this. Alas, I did not keep a letter from Franklin D. Rooseveldt, the editor of the Harvard *Crimson*, suggesting we should exchange our papers.

In Univ. they were all much too preoccupied with the prospect of depriving New College of the headship of the river when Eights Week arrived to be much interested in *The Oxford Point of View*, notwithstanding that three of its promotors came from their own College. And indeed Univ. did displace New College on the second day.

For the second number of *The Oxford Point of View* in that June I wrote a brief obituary of Robert Radclyffe Dolling whom I had known since childhood as Uncle Robert.

[1] The Earl of Swinton.

'Had Father Dolling lived, in these pages where now stands his obituary notice there would have appeared an article by himself. He was too ill to write for the first number: alas! he cannot now write for this.

'Possibly nowhere has his death been so much felt as in Oxford, the place which after Winchester he loved best in the world.

'Many fine eulogies were penned on his death, in the journals of every denomination, and it is pleasant to think how much those who entirely disagreed with his religious teaching appreciated his devoted life. Truly he was a great man. His power of organization was marvellous; added to this, he had a boundless compassion for the sick in body or soul. He seemed to have stepped from the ranks of the early Franciscans, for like them his first thought was for the poor and unhappy; yet strangely enough he had no sympathy with religious orders.

'His endurance was extraordinary; when we think of him toiling through that last weary Lent to get the necessary money to carry on the work of the Poplar Mission we can only wonder at his strength of mind. His name will go down the ages as a noble gentleman and a splendid Christian. R.I.P.'

I attended Dolling's funeral at Brookwood. The train from Oxford reached Paddington exactly 20 minutes before the train to Brookwood was due to leave Waterloo. I offered the cabby ten shillings if he could make it, and he made it in 16 minutes, the fastest drive I ever had in a hansom cab, the traffic thick all the way.

The O.U.D.S. had decided to make an effort to recoup itself for some of the financial loss incurred by *The Two Gentlemen of Verona* by putting on a pastoral of *Twelfth Night* in the lovely garden of Worcester College, and as that bleak and rainy May moved on toward Eights week, we became apprehensive about the success of such an innovation, to extract permission for which from the Vice-Chancellor had been quite a business. However, the clouds cleared away for our first night and we had perfect weather for our three evening performances and one matinée. Harry Tennent had managed to get himself invited to produce the play. This would not have mattered if he had not tried to manage the club as well. That he had been Secretary in 1900-1 did not seem to some of us a good reason why he should indulge in undergraduate club politics when he was no longer an undergraduate. The man who has recently gone down but persists in haunting his university has always been a feature of both English and Scottish universities. Tennent himself had been at Wadham but he had made a point of making friends in the more fashionable colleges of the period and was a resolute climber with a keen eye for those boughs which might be of help to him in the future. He was a deservedly popular performer at smoking-concerts, when he sang light and amusing songs to his own accompaniment, but he was too much about the place during those two first years of mine. I did not dislike him personally, but I did disapprove strongly of his almost feminine manner of intrigue. For instance, Jack Gilliat, who was an outstanding personality in his own right, allowed himself to be worked upon by Harry Tennent to suspect a deliberate plot against his position in the O.U.D.S. because by a printer's error the venerable *Oxford Magazine* in its criticism of *Twelfth Night* had in the *dramatis personae* attributed the performance of Orsino to A. P. Boissier (Balliol) and Sebastian to J. F. G. Gilliat (University).

"Good god, Jack, you really are being ridiculous," I told him. "The *Mag.* said in the criticism that you were an impressive and dignified Duke with admirable enunciation. What more do you want?"

"But that chap Boissier who lives in Wellington Square and was rotten as Sebastian probably thought it would be a way of scoring off me because Henry Tennent told him he was tight at one of the rehearsals."

It is true that Paul Boissier was a failure as Sebastian and that his digs in unfashionable Wellington Square were the headquarters of a tribe disapproved of by the rest of Basutoland as we used to call Balliol; but he was a good comic actor, and much more important, a first-rate mathematician; he would one day be headmaster of Harrow.

Viola was played by Beryl Faber, a sister of the cricketer and actor Aubrey Smith. She was married to Cosmo Hamilton, an elder brother of the late Sir Philip Gibbs. Cosmo, who was then writing amusing articles every week for the *World*, was one of the great romancers, great enough to figure in that book I shall never write called *Great Liars I Have Known*. In years to come Americans would ask me with reverence if I had ever seen Cosmo Hamilton's ancestral home at Uxbridge. "It must be a wonderful place. I sure would like to see it. It's fine the way he comes over to the States and lectures to get the money to keep it up."

In fact, Cosmo's ancestral home at Uxbridge consisted of two rooms over a chemist's shop where he entertained all who visited him as lavishly as if he really were a country squire. The lovable thing about dear Cosmo was that so many of his improvisations were inspired by good-will towards his friends. I recall meeting him once in 1911 when I was turning out of the Adelphi into the Strand. At this time Lord Howard de Walden was trying to bring the British drama to life by going one better than Vedrenne and Granville Barker at the Court Theatre with expensive productions at the Haymarket.

"Monty!" Cosmo exclaimed. "Why, isn't this extraordinary? I was talking to Howard this morning and he asked me if I could suggest somebody who would make a tour of the States lecturing on what he's doing at the Haymarket. 'You can offer £4000, Cosmo, to the right young man,' he told me. And here you are, the very man for the job. Would you like it?"

"I certainly would," I answered, knowing perfectly well that Cosmo had just been thinking as he walked along the Strand how jolly it would be if Howard de Walden said to him just what he had told me and that I was the first friend he happened to meet.

To return to *Twelfth Night*, Bertie Forsyth played Malvolio, Alban Hood was Sir Andrew Aguecheek, Raymond Wavell was Fabian, and I played Sir Toby Belch. Jessie Ferrar was our sparkling Maria. Alban Hood from Bradfield was a fellow freshman at Magdalen, and one of my most intimate friends. He had rooms in Chaplain's Quad with a grand piano on which he played exquisitely. Much against his will he abandoned music as a profession and took a job with the Burma Teak Company, to spend the years before the First World War with elephants in tropical forests. He was badly wounded and died not long after the war was over.

I had a notion for a rag late that term in which a greased pig was to be introduced into College under the notion that it would give us a wonderful run before we caught it. It was voted a good idea and the money having been subscribed I set out in a hansom to buy a pig in Iffley, which I duly did, bringing the pig back with me on the splash board of the hansom. From time to time the pig would grunt its protest at being bound up in a sack, and when the hansom slowed down in the traffic passers by would eye the sack, evidently under the impression that I was a kidnapper. The problem of getting the pig into college was solved by hauling it up on a rope through the window of Alban Hood's rooms which looked down on the banks of the Cherwell flowing through Magdalen Bridge. With Alban's grand piano and the pig his sitter looked pretty full, but we greased the animal well and somehow persuaded it to go down the staircase and out into Chaplain's Quad where we tried to make it run and afford us the amusement of trying to catch it. This, according to my reading, had been a favourite pastime at country fairs in days gone by. The pig refused to run and there is not much fun in catching a pig, however well greased, if the pig simply lies down and grunts. After a while I had to admit the rag was a complete fiasco, and we all retired to our rooms, leaving the pig to wander about until it made its way into the deer-park where one of the gardeners found it next morning and took possession of it to supply him with bacon for a long time to come.

At the matinée of *Twelfth Night* on Saturday Bertie Forsyth was driven nearly as mad as Malvolio himself. Our dressing-room was in the cricket-pavilion, some fifty odd yards away from the scene of the pastoral, along a narrow path between thick shrubs. Sir Andrew, Fabian and myself had retired to powder our faces for our next entrance and hurrying back we heard what we thought was our cue; coming on too soon, we cut Malvolio out of most of his best scene. The cup of Bertie Forsyth's fury overflowed when Raymond Wavell, in an attempt to console him, suggested that probably the audience would not have noticed the cut.

But for me the most momentous event of our pastoral of *Twelfth Night* was that the part of Olivia was played by Rachel Daniel, the elder daughter of the Revd. C. H. O. Daniel, the Bursar of Worcester College and creator of the famous Daniel Press. Not long after the pastoral I was attending a garden fête in aid of some charity held in the grounds of Headington Hall. Rachel introduced me to Mrs Daniel, who had a jumble stall, and then to her younger sister Ruth, with whom I fell in love at first sight. She was just nineteen, and I see her now as I saw her first upon that sunlit day in June exactly sixty-one years ago as I write these words. She was wearing an organdie dress patterned with small pink flowers. Her light brown hair was drawn back over a pompadour, and when we looked at one another the roses of her face deepened to a blush, and her momentary embarrassment set her off talking what seemed to me the most bewitching nonsense I had ever heard. A year would pass before I told her of that love and heard from her that she too had loved me at first sight and that I also had blushed. It was indeed the most deeply moving moment I had lived since I had that experience we call conversion on the cliffs of Swanage which I related in the previous Octave. I must have been afraid of destroying the magic of that moment by letting it turn into another of those brief flirtations along the primrose path of youth's dalliance, for I locked that moment away in a secret place of the heart.

Meanwhile, before that fateful garden fête, peace in South Africa had at last been achieved and on another glorious First of June we celebrated it with the greatest rag since the Prince of Wales had opened the new Folly Bridge in 1896. On that occasion the Oxford municipal authorities had made the mistake of importing police from London to reinforce the local police who, believing rightly that they were better able to handle excited undergraduates and resenting the importation of police from London, stood by and watched some of those bold fellows being thrown over Folly Bridge into the Isis without lifting a finger to help them. The municipal authorities of Oxford did not repeat their mistake on this present riotous occasion.

At Magdalen we raised £88 to buy fireworks and had a rich variety stored in one of the rooms in Cloisters, where eight of us arranged for a supper of dressed crab with plenty of champagne to fortify us when we returned to College at midnight as a preliminary to the firework display. Meanwhile, we sallied forth to celebrate the signing of peace.

I see myself standing on the sloping sill of one of the bay-windows of the O.U.D.S. and delivering a patriotic speech to a crowd of townees swaying backwards and forwards from the Corn Exchange to St Giles, prevented from falling headlong on top of them by the miraculous immunity which can be conferred by champagne. While I am spouting away I see A. F. Matthew of Wadham in a fisticuff encounter with a townee in the little churchyard of St Michael's, to which nobody is paying the least attention. Matthew, known affectionately as Martha, would become a distinguished member of the Sudan Civil Service. Probably piqued by failing to collect an attentive group of listeners to my fervid eloquence, I decided to pique the crowd by aiming O.U.D.S. postcards at them. I was successful in cutting several townees with the sharp edges and presently a lot of them tried to break in to the Club through the narrow entrance in George Street. We held the staircase as stoutly as Horatius held the bridge against the ranks of Tuscany and the assault was repelled. The next thing I remember is being knocked through the plate-glass window of an ironmonger's shop at the opposite corner of George Street, but again thanks to that miraculous immunity conferred by champagne without a single cut. I seized the first weapon that came to hand, a frying-pan, and emerging with this into the Corn I brought it down on the head of the nearest townee in reach.

News came that the Magdalen dons had decided to leave the gate of the lodge open, no doubt to avoid possible damage from revellers coming back after midnight. From the confusion of the next hours all I can recall is the magnificent blaze made by the burning cab-shelter in the Broad outside Trinity. It was after three o'clock when we gathered in that room in Cloisters to enjoy our dressed crab and still more champagne. By the time we had finished the sun of that glorious First of June had risen. Somebody said we should have to postpone the fireworks until the evening. I opposed this suggestion and with what seemed the deadly logic champagne can inspire I argued that unless the fireworks were let off at once the £88 we had subscribed would be wasted. My deadly logic prevailed and it was decided that the fireworks must be let off on the lawn in front of New Buildings without paying any attention to that bland sun shining down on us from the other side of Addison's Walk, or Adders as we called it then.

So Roman candles, rockets, maroons and golden rain did their best to compete with the sun, and the sun, though it might spoil the colours of the Roman candles and rockets, could do nothing to diminish the bangs. Among those bangs some of the loudest were made by large Chinese crackers, over a foot high, which had cost us four shillings each. Three of these crackers we had tied to the Dean's oak (his outer door) and having lighted the long fuses we had hurried down the staircase on to the lawn. As we reached it the Dean's window was opened and leaning out of it in his pyjamas he was saying, "Mr Mackenzie, Mr Wavell, Mr Rose, and the rest of you gentlemen, if you don't go to bed at once you will all of you be sent down tomorrow" when there was a really superb bang which put his oak out of order until a locksmith could come and release him.

We were not sent down next day but about half a dozen of us were fined £5 each.

On the following Saturday I went to Cambridge to represent the O.U.D.S. at the Footlights supper after the musical show. I was staggered to find that in Tabland they even went to the theatre in their caps and much more voluminous gowns than ours: this seemed to me an almost slavish attitude to the Proctors. It was a wearisome journey to Cambridge in those days, with never less than an hour's wait at Bletchley Junction.

In spite of so many various occupations during that summer term of 1902, which included a certain amount of attention to getting through Pass Mods, I managed to bring out the second number of *The Oxford Point of View* and received an encouraging letter from the Pre. as we called the President of Magdalen.

This number seems full of good stuff. . . . Materially, it's one of the handsomest magazines Oxford has ever produced. I hope it's not ruinous. It's certainly attractive.

The notice of *Twelfth Night* was written by Harold F. Davidson, and I am puzzling my brain to remember how I met that clerical figure more fantastic than the most fantastic clown ever created by Shakespeare. Some will remember the case of the Rector of Stiffkey in Suffolk who was unfrocked, as I thought and still think on insufficient evidence, for misbehaviour with young women. After his deprivation Davidson toured the country performing various eccentric acts at fairs, ending up with trying to emulate Daniel by sitting in a cage with a lion, and less fortunate than Daniel being killed by that lion at Blackpool.

I have a notion that the introduction of Davidson was by Kennedy-Cox, who had played Feste in the pastoral as well as I ever saw Feste played. Davidson, who was not much more than five feet tall with a remorseless voice of maddening timbre, and an unsquashable determination to do and say what he wanted to do or say at the moment, was looking after another fantastic creature called Masterman in Walton Street digs, as unfashionable a quarter for digs as Wellington Square.

C. M. Masterman and Kennedy-Cox brought out a book of nonsense verse, published no doubt at Cox's expense by Alden. I never detected a vestige of humour in Masterman who was a kind of poor imitation of Baron Corvo. Harry Pirie-Gordon with his passion for oddity was inclined to fall for Masterman, as one day to the disadvantage of his pocket he fell for the unspeakable Corvo, for whose cult I have no patience. Masterman, another small man, with a black waxed moustache, believed himself to be a serious poet and spent most of his time in bed, while little Davidson fussed over him and took him out for walks at night. The problem uppermost in those squalid Walton Street digs was how Masterman was to be got back to the continent.

"He has a fatal fascination for the sea," Davidson explained. "When he crossed over from Calais last year it was all I could do to prevent him from throwing himself overboard. I assure you I had to cling on to him all the way to Dover."

"That is true," said Masterman, his dark eyes gleaming. "And yet I must return to Europe. I cannot stand life on this bourgeois island. But I warn you, Davidson, that you will not prevent me from throwing myself into the sea next time. There is only one way to get me back to Europe. I must be taken back in a coffin."

Some months later Davidson told Harry Pirie-Gordon and myself that he had in fact taken Masterman back to Calais in a coffin.

"But wasn't there any difficulty with the customs?" we asked.

"None at all. Of course, we opened the coffin as soon as the luggage was landed, and as he had his ticket to Paris we just got on the train. We gave the coffin to the porters."

I never heard what ultimately became of Masterman.

We all dutifully failed in Divvers at the end of the term; it was not considered the thing to pass in Divvers at a first attempt. However, Pass Mods. were negotiated successfully by all the freshmen who took that not very arduous examination. Yet already progressive young dons were agitating for the abolition of Greek in Pass Mods as an unfair demand upon the brains of youth.

Toward the end of that first summer term some of us freshmen were beginning to venture into Gunner's little office when there were no seniors about, but we should have to wait until autumn before as second-year men we should be able fully to enjoy that atmosphere of security without which a club, unlike an orchard, never tastes sweet.

At this point I must quote from *Sinister Street* because Gunner's was such a vital part of Magdalen before that damnable war which took away so many lives and obliterated so many customs that I cannot exclude Gunner's from any tale of my life. In *Sinister Street* Gunstone is called Venables and Gunner's becomes Venner's.

"Gunner's office was one of the small ground-floor rooms in Cloisters, but it had long ago been converted to its present use. An inner store-room, to which Gunner always retired to make a cup of squash or to open a bottle of whisky, had once been the bedroom. The office itself was not luxuriously furnished and the accommodation was small. A window seat with a view of the college kitchens, a square table and a couple of Windsor chairs were considered enough for the men who frequented Gunner's every night after Hall, and who on Sunday nights after wine in J. C. R. clustered like a swarm of bees. Gunner's own high chair stood far back in the corner behind his high sloping desk on which, always spread open, lay the great ledger of J. C. R. accounts. On the shelves above were the account books of bygone years in which were indelibly recorded the extravagances of more than thirty years of Magdalen men. Over the fireplace was a gilt mirror of Victorian design stuck round with the fixture cards of the University and the College, with notices of grinds and musical clubs and debating societies, in fact with all the printed petty news of Oxford. A few photographs of winning crews, a bookcase with stores of college stationery and a Chippendale sideboard with a glass case of priced cigars on top completed the furniture. The wall-paper above the varnished wainscot was of that indefinite brownish yellow which one found in the rooms of old-fashioned solicitors.

"The office itself, haunted though it was by the accumulated personalities of every generation at Magdalen, would scarcely have possessed the magical effect of fusion which it did possess, had not all these personalities endured in a perpetual present through the conservative force of Gunner himself. Richard Gunstone had been Steward of the Junior Common Room for 33 years but he seemed to all these young men that came within the fragrance of his charm to be as much an intrinsic part of the college as the tower itself. The bearded President, the dry-voiced dons, the deer-park, the elms, the ancient doors and traceries, the lawns and narrow entries, the groinings and the lattices, were all subordinate in the estimation of the undergraduates to Gunner. He knew the inner history of every rag; he realised why each man was popular or unpopular or merely ignored; he was a treasure-house of wise counsel and kindly advice. He was an old man with florid, clean-shaven face, a pair of benignant eyes intensely blue, a rounded nose, a gentle voice and inimitable laugh. Something there was in him of the old family butler, a little more of the yeoman farmer, a trace of the head-gamekeeper, a suspicion of the trainer of horses, but all these elements were blended to produce the effect of someone wise and saintly and simple who could trouble himself to heal the lightest wounds and could rouse with a look or a gesture undying affection.

"With such a tutelary spirit, it was not surprising the freedom of Gunner's should have been esteemed a privilege that could only be conferred by the user's consciousness of his own right. There was no formal election to Gunner's; there simply happened a moment when the Magdalen man entered unembarrassed that mellow office in that sunny effluence. In this ripe old room, generous and dry as sherry wine, how pleasant it was to sit and listen to Gunner's ripe old stories; how amazingly important seemed the trivial gossip of the college in this historic atmosphere; and what a thrill it was to come into college about half-past nine of a murky evening and stroll round Cloisters to see if there was anybody in Gunner's; sometimes the old man would be alone, the fire would be dying down and during the half-hour that remained of his duty, it would be possible to peel a large apple very slowly and extract from him more of the essence of social history than could be gained from a term's reading of great historians."

One of Gunner's applauded tricks was to attach a piece of string to the tongs for a listener to hold to his ears while Gunner struck the tongs with the poker and evoked the sound of the Magdalen chimes. A decade later Gunner was telling me about a visit King George and Queen Mary had paid to Magdalen at the time when the Prince of Wales was up.

"Oh, I liked the King very much, and he quite enjoyed Magdalen chimes. But, oh dear, I thought Queen Mary was a little ignorant. She was looking at the cigars in the glass case over there, and she asked me what all the figures were.

" 'Why, your Majesty,' I said, 'that's the different prices of the cigars.' 'Dear me, Mr Gunstone,' she said, 'I never knew cigars had different prices.' You wouldn't think anybody could be as ignorant as that, would you?"

The other day I received a letter from what is apparently now called the Manciple of the J.C.R. to say that undergraduates kept asking him if he had a copy of *Sinister Street* and could I spare one as it was not in the College library. So I sent one along, gratified, I must admit, that the frequenters of what was once Gunner's should take any interest in a book written before most of their fathers were born.

It can be imagined from what I have written about Gunner's that the election at the end of that summer term of a President of the Junior Common Room for next year was a very important event. Most of us freshmen had no doubt whatever that C. L. Macdonald would be elected easily. We could not imagine any other candidate competing with him successfully. Macdonald was a Carthusian who played back in the eleven which had only just been beaten by Oriel in the final of the soccer cup and was very popular with us freshers on account of the way he had welcomed us and given us good advice when we were still anxiously feeling our way about life in College during our first term. Macdonald had the big room on the first floor in the corner staircase of Swither's, where he was a genial host. He had three great friends: W. L. (Bill) Sampson was a brother of the famous air-ace of the R.N.A.S. who from Nieuport went on to Gallipoli; E. C. (Junks) Willoughby was an old Wellingtonian, a quiet, clumsy-looking, unassuming chap who would be killed at Gallipoli; and Oscar von Grunelius. Grunelius had come up to Magdalen in the autumn of 1900, speaking hardly any English; a year later he was speaking English with perfect fluency and without any trace of a German accent. Within my experience that linguistic feat of his has never been equalled. He was an extremely attractive personality and I have been told that he was one of the Germans whom Hitler hanged. In spite of our confidence that Macdonald would be elected he was defeated by Valentine Fleming, an old Etonian and a rowing man. 'Tammy' Fleming would be the father of Peter and Ian Fleming after marrying a sister of Harky Rose. In 1910 he would be elected as member for South Oxfordshire; seven years later, he would be killed in the war.

Macdonald's defeat broke his heart, and I believe the not particularly successful career he had was partly due to the mortification of that disappointment. I think Tammy Fleming was probably a better President of the J.C.R. than Macdonald would have been; the latter might have hesitated to imperil his popularity by taking action when action was called for; many of his second-year contemporaries may have suspected him of trying to curry favour with the freshmen.

We had one more rather good rag before we went down for the Long Vac. I discovered that if one put a stick in a roll of toilet paper and then placed the stick in one's grate one could, by sending the first dozen sheets or so up the chimney on a breezy day, unwind the whole roll. So we collected toilet-rolls from the three College lavatories and put a roll in every one of the fireplaces on the side of Cloisters that faced New Buildings; the wind being favourable, every single one of those generous rolls of long ago, each at least a hundred yards long, rejoiced in the June breeze and sent their paper up into the blue sky. As they rose into the air the perforations parted at every few pieces and the paper went fluttering about all over the city of Oxford. I reckon that we released about three dozen rolls which meant that at least two miles of toilet-paper would have shed itself over Oxford.

When we were fined for lighting the 'bonners' that were usually the climax of any rag our fines were paid in to the College Library, and it would have been poetic justice if our fines for publishing so much toilet-paper had gone towards the accumulation of more paper; but in the event nobody was fined because with every single roll of toilet-paper missing from the lavatories it was impossible for the Dean to single out culprits, however sure he may have been in his own mind who they were.

The Long Vacation was hardly a fortnight old when the country was shaken by the news that King Edward was gravely ill and that the Coronation would be postponed. The operation for appendicitis was successful and it was presently announced that the Coronation would take place in the middle of August. A Coronation in August? But London would be empty! I cannot hope to convey what a shock that announcement was; people would hardly have been more surprised if it had been announced that the Coronation would take place in the Sahara.

It was during that Long Vacation that the jolly habit began of taking our pastoral of *Twelfth Night* round to play for local good causes. As I remember, the first house which entertained us was Horrington Hall by Abbots Ripton in Huntingdonshire, where Jack Gilliat's parents entertained us lavishly. The Hall was a large house but not quite large enough to house us all; Raymond Wavell and I, with Kennedy-Cox, were put up in a cottage in the park where we would be visited at breakfast by Jack Gilliat's younger sister, a fourteen-year-old whose powers of conversation for her age remained unique until ten years later when I should spend a memorable afternoon with Daphne and Angela du Maurier who, younger than Jack Gilliat's sister, would equal her as conversationalists.

From Abbots Ripton we moved on to Hinchingbrooke. I had not then met Lord Sandwich's nephew, George Montagu, who was to become a lifelong intimate friend. 'Uncle Hinch' was a bachelor eccentric of rich late Victorian texture. The ladies of the company were sent to stay in country houses near by; only the men stayed in Hinchingbrooke itself. The great house was run by the butler whose name I have forgotten. When his lordship told a story at lunch or dinner it was the butler's duty to know when to join in the laughter or when to keep gravely silent. If he failed to laugh when his lordship thought he should have laughed he would be asked if he had no sense of humour and if he laughed when his lordship thought he should not he was told to get out of the room; I can see him now winking at us with a grin as he closed the door behind him.

Lord Sandwich had a Japanese garden in the middle of which was a miniature Fujiyama. I remember his taking me along to see an eruption of the famous volcano. The gardener was summoned and his lordship with that slight stutter of his would say:

"F-fujiyama."

Whereupon the gardener would light the fuse and presently Fujiyama would erupt for about a minute until the charge was exhausted. The gardener would then recharge the volcano in readiness for another visitor to be brought along by his lordship to see it erupt. Lord Sandwich was a devotee of croquet, such a devotee that he used to erupt himself when a partner muffed a stroke. I remember on one occasion his flinging his mallet at one of the Ailwyn Fellowes girls because she missed a hoop at a critical moment in a game.

We went on from Huntingdon to Hunstanton in Norfolk, where I was a guest of the Gurneys. Here I made friends with another little girl, Rachel Gurney, whom I should meet again in Athens in 1915 when she was the wife of Paymaster-Commander Alec Winter with the British Naval Mission.

It was probably after this pastoral tour that I went to stay with Kennedy-Cox at Brockley in Somerset where, much spoilt by his lovable parents who, let it be added, spoilt their son's guests as much as they spoilt him, he lived in a picturesque thatched house in the middle of a perfect garden. Brockley was close to Spaxton which has been in the news again sixty years later over an ecclesiastical dispute. At this date Spaxton was notorious as the scene of Smyth Pigott's Agapemone or Abode of Love, of which he was the 'Messiah'. He was a connection of the Catholic Smyth Pigotts who were squires of Brockley.

Smyth Pigott's career is worth recording. He started in the Salvation Army, and was later ordained to become a curate in a London suburb. After being entertained at lunch every Sunday by one of the churchwardens the curate received a 'revelation' of Messianic destiny and went off with his host's wife and daughter to Spaxton, from where nothing would persuade them to come back, in spite of the various other women that Smyth Pigott brought to his Abode of Love. I forget what ultimately happened to the Agapemone and Smyth Pigott but it provided titillation for the readers of the popular Press for quite a long time.

Launce and Speed of Verona, or in other words Tiverton and Kennedy-Cox, were going to share digs together in their last year in the Broad, and Kennedy-Cox has given me the following story for *My Life and Times*.

"Tivvy's father as Lord Chancellor played the chief part in the legal preliminaries of the Coronation. One day Tivvy said to me,

" 'There's a hell of a rumpus over the Coronation. It's about Queen Alexandra. Naturally she wants to look her best, but old Archbishop Temple says nothing on earth will induce him to anoint one of Clarkson's wigs. So there is a deadlock.'

"Later Tivvy said to me,

" 'It's all right. They have come to a compromise. They are going to cut a kind of little trap-door in the wig which the Archbishop will lift and pour the oil right on Queen Alexandra's head.' "

Tiverton once presented me to that great Lord Chancellor in Ennismore Gardens. He was then eighty and would live on for another eighteen years, and as a nonagenarian lead the last ditch with as much élan as Lord Russell at ninety leads the crusade for nuclear disarmament. He was sitting at his desk and I was suitably awed when I shook hands with the great little man. My awe turned to dismay when I saw Tivvy, looking twice as big as his father, produce from the tails of his coat a clown's cap which he suddenly planted on the Lord Chancellor's head. Now eighty years old myself I can reflect with pleasure that the grandson[1] and the grand-daughter[2] of that great Lord Chancellor are both dear friends of mine to-day.

After staying with Kennedy-Cox in Somerset I went on to stay with Claude Kirby in Devon where Claude's father, a successful Chancery Bar lawyer, had taken the Chichesters' country house near Barnstaple. Claude was in his artiest and craftiest mood, at work making something or other that William Morris would have commended. Working with him was Lord Gerald Wellesley[3] one of Luxmoore's pupils at Eton, who gave me a small piece of damson velvet which he cut off a larger piece of velvet that had once belonged to Rossetti of whose poetry I was a passionate admirer, I used that piece of damson velvet as a book-marker for many years until it was lost during one of the Odysseys of my library. Claude's younger brother, Alistair, still at Eton and not long hence to be President of the O.U.B.C. and row in that great Magdalen Eight which would win the Grand at Henley, was as much preoccupied as Claude Kirby and Gerald Wellesley, not with *objets d'art* but with bombs. Finally he made a time bomb to explode in the lake of the Chichester house with expensive results for his father because it blew a hole in the bottom of the lake and emptied it. Alistair Kirby's life was all too brief; he would be killed in the Great War.

I spent a certain amount of that Long Vacation in London, indulging in *vie de Bohême* with Dick Hewlett, from which two ludicrous incidents vividly remain in my memory. Dick Hewlett, once more in arrears with his landlady at 144 Finborough Road, decided to 'flit' to a room he had taken for a week or two in Lillie Road, before going on tour in the chorus of *The Country Girl*, a successful musical comedy. Dick had managed to get most of his belongings away to Lillie Road but had kept his suitcase to avoid rousing his landlady's suspicions. This he proposed to throw over the wall of the back-garden in Finborough Road into Brompton Cemetery, where I was to stand by to receive it. When I arrived at the appointed spot I found a grave-

[1] The Earl of Halsbury.
[2] Lady Flavia Anderson.
[3] The Duke of Wellington, K.G.

digger at work. Over the wall came Dick's suitcase and landed right on top of him in the half dug grave. It took all my powers of persuasion and a five-bob tip to persuade that gravedigger to let me carry Dick's suitcase to the gate of the cemetery.

Two or three days later I was sitting with Dick in his room on the ground floor when the door burst open and his new landlady entered in a state of extreme agitation.

"Mr Hewlett, Mr Hewlett, whatever shall we do? There's a baboon in the bathroom!"

"A baboon in the bathroom, Mrs X? How on earth could a baboon get into your bathroom?" we protested incredulously.

"It's no use you asking how it got there, Mr Hewlett. It's there, I tell you. A shocking great beast."

"Oh, well, I'll go up and have a look, Mrs X," said Dick in soothing tones. "I don't think it will be there now." As Dick and I went upstairs to the bathroom he asked me if I thought Mrs X was suffering from D.T. "I believe she does drink a bit," he said.

"It's obviously some kind of delusion," I agreed.

But we were doing Mrs X an injustice. Dick went into the bathroom and shot out at once, slamming the door behind him.

"My god, there *is* a baboon in there," he gasped.

"Oh, very funny, my dear Dick," I said. "But it isn't the first of April." With this I walked into the bathroom and came out again as fast as Dick. There really was a large baboon sitting at the end of the bath and showing its teeth at me.

"I hope it doesn't discover how to open the bathroom door," I said. "Monkeys are damned clever."

"Whatever are we going to do, Mr Hewlett?" his landlady wailed.

"We'll call in the nearest bobby on the beat," said Dick.

It was a job to persuade the nearest bobby that we were not trying to pull his leg, but finally we persuaded him to come up and see for himself, and when he did he shot out of that bathroom as fast as we had. In the end word reached the police that one of the baboons in the Earls Court Exhibition had escaped and must have climbed up the drain pipe to reach Mrs X's bathroom, where a posse of keepers arrived and managed to recapture the fugitive and take it back to its cage in the Exhibition.

Back at Oxford in October the story of the baboon in the bathroom was received as just one more of my amusing and improbable stories.

When we second-year men gathered in Gunner's after the first

Sunday Wine of the Michaelmas term we agreed that the freshers promised if not quite to reach the standard of our own year, at any rate not to disgrace it. We had a debating society at Magdalen called the '97, and we at once recognized that the maiden speeches of some of the newcomers were going to enliven our debates. I recall only just managing to win a motion that the House deplored the execution of Charles I because of an eloquent defence of Cromwell by St John Hutchinson of Winchester. He was a son of Dr Hutchinson who had won that Ryde bye-election for the Liberals which was the first portent of what was going to happen three years hence to the Unionists. However, Jack Hutchinson and I would find ourselves more often on the same side than in opposition, and he became a lifelong friend, one I miss as much as any of the friends who are no longer here. He would one day appear for me at the Guildhall when I was prosecuted under the Official Secrets Act over the third volume of my war memories and be junior to Sir Henry Curtis-Bennett at the Old Bailey.

Probably Norman Chamberlain was another opponent of that motion but, although he and I usually voted on different sides, he too became a great friend. He too would be killed in that accursed First World War, and his cousin Neville Chamberlain would write a very moving memoir of him for private circulation. And then there was dear Henry Lygon, with his sublime Lygon self-assurance. I can hear him now inviting E. L. Coles, Hugh Francis and myself to make up a four at bridge in his rooms, which were in Cloisters, and which again with typical self-assurance he would change next year for the only three-roomed set in Cloisters, the set that would one day be given to the Prince of Wales. We were slightly taken aback by a freshman's inviting three second-year men to play bridge with him in his first week. Coles was in the College Eight which Hugh Francis, in succession to the famous 'Cocky' Maclagan, another who was to be killed in the war and as good a cox as ever steered an Oxford Eight, would be steering presently and likewise one of the Trial Eights. In the course of the first rubber Coles made a derogatory remark about Keble.

"Steady, Coles," said Henry Lygon.

"What do you mean?" Coles asked.

"My father was one of the founders of Keble."

"Then he ought to be ashamed of himself," said Coles.

Lady Beauchamp, Henry's sister-in-law, was a sister of the Duke of Westminster, and I see now a large framed photograph on the wall of that room in Cloisters of her and her four children signed 'with love from Lettice."

Henry Lygon had ambition for a great political career, which was never to be fulfilled because he lost every parliamentary election at which he stood and never came nearer to high office than the chairmanship of the L.C.C. Fire Brigade Committee. Yet when he was elected President of the Oxford Union at the end of his second year nobody could have convinced poor Henry that he would not one day be Prime Minister. I happened to be in the lodge when Henry came back jubilantly from the declaration of the poll at the Union; as it happened Coles was there too. Henry came in, walking on his toes as he always did, and flushed with delight at his success.

"Hullo, I've just been elected President of the Union," he announced.

"What!" exclaimed Coles. "That frightful place up the Headington Road?"

Coles really did think that Henry Lygon was announcing he had something to do with the workhouse.

I recall, some seven years after this, meeting Henry Lygon in Coventry Street when people were coming away from the theatre.

"Hullo, Monty," he exclaimed. "I've just been elected to the Garrick. Come and have supper with me."

So along we went and when we entered the dining-room the long supper-table was still empty. Henry promptly took the chair at the head of it. I was aghast. Sir Henry Irving was gone, but I was sure his place at the head of that table belonged now to Sir Charles Wyndham or Sir Squire Bancroft and certainly not to a newly elected member of the Club.

"Listen, Henry," I said firmly, "if you insist on sitting at the head of this table I will not have supper with you."

"Don't be so ridiculous."

"Either you get up and take a less conspicuous place or I am leaving at once."

Seeing I meant what I said, Henry shook his head over my attitude, but he did vacate that chair. Poor Henry Lygon, life was a disappointment to him; he was stricken by disseminated sclerosis and with enduring courage suffered until he was released from pain. Henry Lygon will appear from time to time as my life goes on, and though the stories I tell of him may raise a smile they will all be told with amused affection, for our friendship was never damaged by my laughter.

Guy Bonham-Carter, 'Toad' English, Wilfred Curwen, Basil Moon, Freddy Fitzwygram, all freshmen of 1902, all friends of mine, all to be killed in that blasted war. . . .

I turn to the third number of *The Oxford Point of View* in which Professor Robinson Ellis replied to Robert Bridges. I quote some of his words:

"The strong hold which long-established practice exercises on English thought and feeling; the fear of sacrificing a tradition which coincides so nearly with the Protestant change our religion underwent in the sixteenth century; the fact that in one or two cases the altered pronunciation would not be an improvement; the difficulty of making the new style quite intelligible to those not accustomed to it; the inconsistency of changing our pronunciation of Latin and leaving unaltered our equally barbarous pronunciation of Greek; the varieties in the new mode which are taught by some schoolmasters; all these considerations more or less affect the question. . . . Not that, if asked to use the new style, students refuse to do so; on the contrary I have found my own students most ready to change; but left to themselves they resort to the old style. In this the influence of some of the large Public Schools no doubt plays an important part. I should suppose the mass of our alumni from Eton and Harrow to be more or less conservative on the point: Rugby is less so, and Marlborough is decidedly in support of the change.

"What I would urge upon the attention of those who happen to read these remarks, is that England ought to make up its mind on this subject soon. America has already discarded our pronunciation as barbarous and wrong; it is at variance with the teaching of all the Continental peoples. . . .

"Latin, we may feel sure, whatever may be the fate of Greek, must always form a part of a liberal education, as in most countries of Europe. It will doubtless be taught in Africa, as it is in India and the Colonies. How deplorable if it should be taught with all the vices of pronunciation which have clung to it from three centuries; if schoolboys should read Latin in one way, sing it in another. For my own part I cannot but hope that a move inaugurated by the greatest of our Latin scholars will not be allowed to come to nothing, and that the errors which Evelyn condemned in 1661 will cease to be heard, far less taught in 1960."

What would that great gaunt figure of Robinson Ellis have said if he had been told that, although the proper pronunciation of Latin would be secure by 1960, Latin itself would be threatened, as Greek was already threatened, by his own University and the University of Cambridge?

For that October number of *The Oxford Point of View* Robbie Ross, under the pseudonym of Philogenet, wrote a witty and amusing article called 'The Brand of Isis' from which I again quote:

"The Oxford manner is, alas! indefinable and I was going to say indefensible. Perhaps it is an attitude that finds physical expression in the voice, the gesture, the behaviour . . . without becoming personal it is not easy to discuss purely social aspects, and we must seek chiefly in literature for manifestation of the phenomenon: in the prose of Matthew Arnold for instance—in the poems of Mr Lawrence Binyon, as typical examples where every thought seems a mental reservation. Enemies rail at the voice, and the voice counts for something. Anyone having the privilege of hearing Mr Andrew Lang speak in public will know at once what I mean. . . . Though Oxford men have their Cambridge moments, and beneath their haughty exterior there sometimes beats a Cambridge heart: behind such reserve you would never suspect any passions at all save one of pride. Even frankly irreligious Oxford men acquire an ecclesiastical pre-Reformation aloofness which must have piqued Thackeray quite as much as the refusal of the City to send him to Westminster. He complains somewhere that the undergraduates wear kid gloves and drink less wine than their jolly brethren of the Cam. He was thoroughly Cambridge in his attitude towards life. How angry he becomes with the vices and corruptions of a dead past! No Oxford essayist would dream of being angry with the past. . . .

"There have been of course plenty of men unravaged by the contagion. Mr Gladstone intellectually always seemed to me a Cambridge man in his energy, his enthusiasm, his political outlook. Only in his High Church proclivities he is suspect. Mr Churton Collins again is essentially un-Oxford. . . . The poet Shelley was an obvious Cantab. He was, we are told, a man of high moral character. Well, principles and human weakness are common to all Universities, and others besides Shelley have deserted their wives, but to desert your wife on principle seems to me callous, calculating, and Cambridge like. . . .

"Oxford men are too conscious of their own superiority to be tuft-hunters, and I believe miss some of the prizes of life by their indifference towards those who have already 'arrived'; but they appear snobbish to others who have not had the benefit of a University education, and in this little essay I have endeavoured to hold up the mirror to their ill-nature—the fault to which I am unduly attached. . . . I might quote many eloquent tributes from Dryden to Wordsworth and Byron, all Cambridge men, who have felt the charm and acknowledged a weakness for the step-sister University. Cambridge has never been fortunate in having the compliment reciprocated. . . . And I, the obscurest of her children who cast this laurel on the Isis, will content myself with admitting that I sincerely believe you can obtain a cheaper and better education at Cambridge, though it has always been my ambition to be mistaken for an Oxford man. . . .

"I am not antiquarian enough to conjecture if there was ever a temple to Isis during the Roman occupation of Britain on the site of the now illustrious University; but I like to imagine that there existed a cultus of the venerable goddess in the green fields where the purple fritillaries, so reminiscent of the lotus, blossom in the early spring. In the curious formal pattern of their petals I see a symbol of the Oxford manner—something archaic, rigid, severe. The Oxford Don may well be a reversion to some earlier type, learned, mystic, and romantic as those priests of whom Herodotus has given us so vivid a picture. The worship of Apis, as Mr Frazer or Mr Lang would tell us, becomes then merely the hieroglyph for a social standard, a manner of life. This, I think, will explain the name Oxford on the Isis—the Ford of Apis, the ox-god at this one place able to pass over the benign deity. You remember, too, the horrid blasphemies of Cambyses (his very name suggests Cambridge) and the vengeance of the gods. So be it to any sacrilegious reformer who would transmute either the Oxford don or the Oxford undergraduate—the most august of human counsellors, the most delightful of friends."

To most Oxford undergraduates of to-day 'The Brand of Isis' will seem as incomprehensible as a page of Herodotus and they will probably congratulate themselves on belonging to an Oxford whose alumni are indistinguishable from the alumni of any other university in England. The only universities left in our islands where I can recapture a faint aroma of what a university once was are St Andrews and Trinity College, Dublin, and the only college left in which I can discover a vestige of the individual stamp which the colleges of Oxford could once upon a time imprint is King's College, Cambridge.

Let me quickly add that I do not suffer from nostalgia; any critic who professes to diagnose such a complaint in me will be wrong. I enjoy and appreciate the present as much as I enjoyed and appreciated the past. I should consider it a presumptuous and complacent exhibition of senescence to compare the Oxford of to-day unfavourably with the Oxford of my youth; I am merely concerned to record its difference.

Just before the first number of *The Oxford Point of View* was published *The Varsity* announced in its gossip column that there were rumours of a new University magazine which was to rekindle *The Spirit Lamp*. "We hope this is not true. We did not like *The Spirit Lamp*."

We, who were collaborating like so many Patagonian emus to hatch our egg, feared that it might be prematurely addled by such a rumour and we denied it with an indignation the memory of which reminds me with what fierceness youth revolts against the immediate past. However, any lingering smart to my own vanity was healed by *The Varsity's* notice of *Twelfth Night* in which it had "no hesitation in awarding the palm for acting to Mr Mackenzie (Magdalen) for his most laughable rendering of Sir Toby Belch." Soon after this I met the man who had founded *The Varsity*. This was G. F. Freeman, who would one day edit *The Times Educational Supplement*. Freeman was a remarkable chap now in his third year who lived in ascetic poverty in Hell Passage off Holywell; I hear that to-day it is always referred to as St Helen's Passage. He was a Pembroke man and how he managed to edit and write most of *The Varsity* every week, and at the same time read hard for a good degree, was miraculous. I found his company sane and stimulating, and used to marvel at the way he seemed in touch with every aspect of University life and yet apparently as remote from it as St Simeon Stylites on his column. He would never dine with me at the O.U.D.S. nor even drink a morning cup of coffee at Buol's; he insisted on living as frugally as those Scottish students of the past were reputed to live for a year on a sack of oatmeal. As I remember, before he went down he sold *The Varsity* to that brother of Ranger Gull I was to have met in Bournemouth.

The last faint echoes of the 'nineties at Oxford were heard in a paper called *The Broad*, which came from Exeter and had a brief life in this autumn of 1902. It was in this paper that some of the earliest verse of Alfred Noyes appeared. Noyes was born ten years too late. Granted what was almost a superabundance of melody, and able to enshrine the most fugitive moment in verse the facile accomplishment of which was almost as remarkable in its own way as Swinburne's control of metre, he had in the first rapture of his youthful singing absolutely nothing to sing about that seemed to his contemporaries momentous. By 1902 he was too late for the mood of the previous decade, and when he prolonged it he was writing in an exhausted key. I shall return to this subject when I try to explain why I abandoned verse for prose.

In the fourth number of *The Oxford Point of View* that November Desmond Coke, with the threat of Schools beginning to loom, gave up writing 'Through Oxford Glasses' and I took over from him. In my opening paragraph I wrote: "One of the Oxford papers" [I think this was *The Broad*] "is afraid that we lack the brilliance of *The Spirit Lamp* or the high romanticism of *The Germ*" [need I remind present readers that this was the organ of the pre-Raphaelites?] "and presumably is desirous that we should found a school. Yet were we to announce that in future we shall take up a firm position on immorality or invent a new cult, should we not be branded as decadent or reviled as aesthetic? It is so easy to be abnormal and original; it is so difficult to be normal and commonplace. Here in Oxford it is more difficult than anywhere. The youthful degenerate, conscious of the suspicion of the rest of the college, and weakly trying to cultivate a liking for the poems of Verlaine or the pictures of Aubrey Beardsley, forgets that many whom he regards as Philistines have a far greater knowledge of French and a far keener appreciation of good art than himself."

I feel that if I were in my second year at Oxford to-day I should write that paragraph again with different examples to illustrate the struggle to echo the *dernier cri*.

A later paragraph should have been edged with black: "The motion which proposed to do away with Greek in Responsions was thrown out by twenty-three votes and in the light of the recent clamour for a useful and unornamental education, such a small majority is woefully significant. However, notwithstanding the undoubted claims of a Sound Commercial Education to our consideration, we may humbly suggest that there are technical schools eager to teach, and that the University of Birmingham is not a very stern Alma Mater. If Greek is to be abolished, why not Latin? And if the plea of wasted time be put forward by intending scientists, surely it may be argued with equal justification that the enforced study of Euclid and Arithmetic at school is a trying ordeal for those who are not intending scientists. Apart from this utilitarian view, which really has nothing to do with the subject, it would be a pity if Oxford should cease to be conservative even of her own conservatism. Nobody, not even an intending scientist, confers a privilege upon Oxford by taking up his abode here: it is Oxford who confers the honour by allowing him to do so."

Soon after this we had a debate at the '97 at which I prophesied that if the University abandoned Greek as a compulsory subject for Responsions it would take the first step toward the decline and fall of the British Empire. Little did I realize amid the derisive laughter with which my prophecy was received that within my own lifetime I should behold not merely the decline but the very fall of that great edifice which once seemed upon the world's map a rose-red Empire 'half as old as time' to those of us who pored upon that map in childhood.

In my day those who went on the Science side at St Paul's could not get there until they had passed through the preliminary ordeal of Greek conditional sentences and learnt to distinguish between a Present or Past Particular and a Present or Past General. This seems to me an equally valuable preliminary for scientific or academic thinking. Furthermore, a knowledge of the Greek alphabet would help intending scientists to spell correctly all the chemicals and gases and diseases to which Greek names have been given and are still being given. They even have to turn to Greek to find a name for their ideal of education, and what is more with 'technology' successfully avoid barbarous hybrids between Greek and Latin like 'sociology' or 'homosexual'.

But the most damaging result of the abolition of Greek as a matter of course for schoolboys, and to-day one should add schoolgirls, was the way it begot a notion that the past did not matter. The present ignorance of and contempt for even the immediate past among young people may lead, if it continue into another generation, to the decline and fall of western civilization. But why bother? It may look like all Lombard Street against a China orange at present, but the China orange may be far more powerful than Lombard Street much less than a century hence.

I believe it was in this very November, when Congregation was obviously on the verge of surrendering to the claims of material progress, that the students of the University of Athens were rioting in protest against a decision to translate the original Greek of the Gospels into the demotic or vernacular Greek of to-day. In these riots no less than twenty students were killed or wounded. One cannot envisage the students of the University of London rioting against the recent vulgarization of the New Testament in English and that coming vulgarization of the Authorized Version of the Old Testament which will deal a death-blow to English prose.

In that summer term of our pastoral I became more and more friendly with Rachel Daniel and during that autumn term I sometimes went to Worcester House. Every time I rang the bell and waited under that Jacobean hood, gazing at the brass knocker in the shape of a dolphin, for the door to be opened, my expectation of an enchanting visit was heightened more and more. Worcester House was pulled down all but sixty years ago to make the turning from George Street into Beaumont Street easier for the growing traffic, but I never drive over the ground where it once serenely stood without feeling that I am driving through the arms of a benignant and beloved ghost. The house was papered throughout with those lovely patterns of William Morris. In the entrance hall were the little red berries and tiny black leaves and in the dining-room on the left one ate surrounded by the willow pattern. The windows of the drawing-room looked out on the garden and from them one could see the old barn in which the Bursar had his famous printing-press. The drawing-room was papered with one of Morris's larger designs, greyish-blue in shade, and from it one mounted a single step to the Bursar's small study, lined with ancient folios and quartos which had overflowed over much of the floor. The passages were carpeted with Abingdon rush-matting, and at the end of one of those narrow passages was the sitting-room of Rachel and Ruth, where the paper was Morris's green daisy pattern and the curtains were his pattern of thrushes and foliage called the strawberry-thief.

Some six years earlier, under the eyes of Lewis Carroll himself, Nigel Playfair and other undergraduates had made a pastoral of *Alice in Wonderland* in which Rachel had played Alice and Ruth had played the Dormouse at the Mad Hatter's tea-party. For me, Worcester House was Wonderland, in such a world out of this world did I seem to be living, a world in which when unwelcome visitors intruded Rachel and Ruth occasionally made short remarks to one another in a cryptic language of their own invention, by turning every consonant of the alphabet into a syllable and then spelling the word.

At this date I do not think Rachel realized I was falling more and more deeply in love with her younger sister all the time. I believe she supposed I was more interested in herself, and I fancy it was to discourage me as gently as she could that she told me of an understanding between herself and somebody who had been one of the performers in that pastoral of *Alice in Wonderland* and was now in the army. At the same time she confided in me her doubt whether she could face the prospect of being the wife of a professional soldier.

Mr and Mrs Daniel were first cousins but she was much younger than he. Mr Daniel talked little but when he did make a remark one always felt that only he could have made such a good remark, and his attitude to his wife and daughters always seemed to be that of a kindly and indulgent father toward three irresponsible children of whom Rachel was the least irresponsible. He was a handsome man of sixty-six with a full grey beard and a distinguished aquiline profile.

Mrs Daniel had a delicious sense of humour with which she bubbled over, and Ruth had inherited this from her mother. The three outstanding personalities among the Oxford wives were Mrs Morrell, the wife of the Bursar of St John's and mother of Philip Morrell who had married Lady Ottoline Cavendish-Bentinck; Mrs A. L. Smith, the wife of the next Master of Balliol, with a trail of daughters, every one of them with an exquisite complexion; and Mrs Daniel. Mrs Morrell by now was retiring from the contest and was leaving the field clear for Mrs A. L. Smith and Mrs Daniel.

I remember saying once to Mrs Daniel that to see Mrs A. L. Smith cross the Broad with her daughters was like seeing a Dorothy Perkins rambler-rose crossing the Broad.

"Yes, yes, lovely girls, lovely girls," Mrs Daniel bubbled. "I wonder who they'll all marry."

When she said that I wondered what Mrs Daniel would say if I told her that I hoped one day to marry Ruth. Would I be considered what the mothers of Oxford in those days called an eligible young man?

TWENTY YEARS OLD: 1903

FOR the Honours School of Modern History in my time we read English political and constitutional history; one of six periods of European history, each with a special subject; political economy; political science. C. R. L. Fletcher was the History tutor at Magdalen and an authority on Period 6 with the French Revolution as its special subject. As a married man he lived out of College in North Oxford; his rooms in New Buildings housed the history library which had been built up by gifts of books from the students of history when they went down. Once upon a time these rooms had been the abode of Charles Reade, who toward the end of his days became more and more eccentric. He disliked the company of others, but he disliked equally being alone and so he had had his sitting-room covered with glass to reflect himself as he moved or stood or sat. In my time there were still two panels left of that glass on either side of the fireplace in the history library; I wonder if they still survive.

I was determined not to read Period 6, for which Fletcher never forgave me, because it would mean that I should have to attend his lectures at 6 p.m. three times a week in one of the lecture-rooms in Swithers, attended only by his Magdalen pupils, when he would ascribe all the evils of to-day to the passing of the Reform Bill in 1832 and when he would always pronounce 'revenue' as 'revényue', the pronunciation in the days of Period 6. He wrote a school history of England in collaboration with Rudyard Kipling and had a passion for cats.

I hesitated for a while between Period 2 919-1273 with the First Three Crusades as its special subject and Period 4 with the Renaissance as its special subject. Finally I decided on the former, which meant that I had F. F. Urquhart of Balliol as my tutor, and I have been for ever grateful to that choice of mine because for the two last years of my academic career I enjoyed the superlative advantage of combining Balliol with Magdalen as Almae Matres, although the freedom of Balliol did not make me any less apprehensive when Magdalen for three days in the Summer Eights of 1903 barely escaped being bumped by the Balliol Eight, then fourth on the river.

The personality of Sligger, as Urquhart was known to so many generations of Balliol men, is beyond the power of my pen to evoke.

His father had been a great devotee of the Levant who had introduced the turkish-bath to England and had taught his small son to swim by throwing him at the age of three into a swimming-bath to confirm his theory that anybody could swim by instinct if he was tested early enough. Others might have to teach their offspring to swim, not Sligger's father; according to his son this theory had been proved right. He had been a friend of Edward Lear and I recall a beautiful water-colour by Lear of the blue Dead Sea which hung over the door of Sligger's sitting-room, two pairs up of that staircase in the far corner of Balliol's inmost quad.

I look back to tranquil hours in that sitting-room of Sligger's completely lined with books, leaving only enough space for that water-colour of Edward Lear over the door and as I seem to recall a looking-glass above the fireplace. Sligger's method of imparting knowledge always had a casual, almost an indolent air about it, and that manner of his was always a reproach to me when with some excuse I had failed to bring along my observations on the Cluniac reform of the Benedictine rule or whatever the subject was on which I had been told to enlarge. I did far more work for Sligger than for Fletcher, whose lectures on Constitutional History (with the ineffably boring history of Stubbs as the text-book) I cut time after time. I enjoyed enormously reading the chronicles of William of Tyre and Raimond d'Agiles in their monkish Latin, and above all the fascinating *Itinerarium Regis Ricardi*. One day I should see the mutual attitudes of the French under Philip Augustus and the English under Richard Coeur de Lion during the siege of Acre repeat itself at Gallipoli. Sligger was a devout Catholic, and therefore an invaluable guide through the early Middle Ages.[1] He had a chalet somewhere above Chamonix where during the Long Vacation he entertained reading parties. Owing to my prejudice against Switzerland at this date I never availed myself of an invitation to join one of them, a mistake I regret.

Sligger was always addressed by his nickname, and there were two other dons at Balliol with whom the undergraduates were on Christian name terms. Cyril Bailey, the authority on Lucretius, was an Old Pauline who had left before I went to St Paul's in 1894, the eldest of that athletic line of Baileys of whom I have already written. Harold Hartley,[2] the junior fellow of Balliol, was only about a couple of

[1] I realized that acutely when listening to Professor Trevor Roper's brilliantly superficial and slickly tendentious lecture on the Crusades to a television audience of Sussex students on December 3, 1963.

[2] Brigadier-General Sir Harold Hartley, G.C.V.O., F.R.S.

years older than myself. He was a chemistry tutor on the edge of a long and distinguished career in the world, and would marry Gertrude, the eldest of A. L. Smith's beautiful daughters. He is still with us as I write, and I have enjoyed sixty years of friendship with him.

Then there was J. A. Smith, a formidable and stimulating personality and one of the many Scottish scholars or philosophers for whom Balliol has been renowned. I was fortunate enough to win his approval by my knowledge of *Don Quixote*; I had mentioned *Don Quixote* when we were sitting in his room one evening.

"What do you know about Don Quixote?" he demanded in a voice of ferocious contempt. "What was the name of the enchanter who thwarted Don Quixote's attack on the windmills?"

"Pentapolin of the Naked Arm."

He gave a grunt that was half commendation, half surprise, and my number went up.

The most important literary event of my time at Oxford was the publication in 1903 of Samuel Butler's posthumous novel *The Way of All Flesh*. I do not suppose that, if *The Way of All Flesh* had never been published at all, the course of English fiction would have run differently; but there is no doubt that the younger generation did find in *The Way of All Flesh* a point of concentration for their ideas of the Victorian age which was of inestimable benefit for putting those ideas in order. Thirty years later I should ask some of my twenty-year juniors what they thought of *The Way of All Flesh* to find that it no longer made any impression on them. For them the minor horrors of the Victorian age had become something to laugh at or ignore. In 1903 we found its ruthless exposure of self-righteousness, hypocrisy, and self-deception the most tangible evidence we had that we were right in turning our backs on it and looking forward to a new and better moral approach to life. We compared *The Way of All Flesh* with the sentimental cowardice of a book like *Pendennis*; we rose from it with a dawning suspicion that Meredith might be a *faux bonhomme* of the intellect, whose elaborate tolerance and glittering liberalism might be on a level with the rest of Victorian hypocrisy. I shall not pretend that *The Way of All Flesh* was generally read when it first appeared; I do know that I myself preached its wonder on all sides and that for three or four years after I went down from Oxford more and more young people were reading it and finding it the right key to open the right door.

That such a book should have been lying in manuscript since the 'seventies amazed me at the time and still amazes me. I felt that, if it had been published earlier, the social history of the last twenty years of Queen Victoria's reign might have been altered by its exposure of human motive. It was not at this date my intention to be a novelist: I saw myself as a poet and a playwright in the future. Nevertheless, *The Way of All Flesh* certainly restored my confidence in the power of the English novel. It might be thought that *Tess of the D'Urbervilles* and *Jude the Obscure* should have done that already, but it was not until the publication of the first volume of *The Dynasts* about the same time as *The Way of All Flesh* that I began to read the novels of Thomas Hardy and by the time I had read them one after another they took the place of the red pocket-edition of George Meredith on my shelves.

I remember how shocked Tom Spring Rice[1] was when I told him I was sure that Hardy was a greater novelist than Meredith. He had to sit down at the grand piano in his Balliol rooms and play Brahms for a while to recover from it. Tom Spring Rice wanted to devote his life to music but the family tradition of diplomacy prevailed and so he never became the great pianist he might have been. Both he and Alban Hood did their best to cultivate my appreciation of chamber music but without success; that was left for the gramophone to achieve twenty-years later.

At this date the Oxford University Musical Union with its hall in Holywell and the Oxford University Musical Club were separate; they were not amalgamated till after the First World War. At the Union the members themselves performed; the Club brought professional musicians to perform, usually I seem to remember in the Balliol hall. The Club members were inclined to be rather condescending about the Union.

I recall in Eights Week of this year a lunch given by Tom Spring Rice for Donald Tovey[2], who was the guest of the O.U. Musical Club. At this date Tovey was living with two old maids at Egham where he was being cherished and coddled like a spoilt child. Tom, in his hope of bringing out my musical appreciation, which, invisible though it was to myself or anybody else, he was convinced existed and might reveal itself at the right moment, had invited me to that lunch. For some reason Raymond Wavell, who had no more appreciation of good music than I had, was also there. Raymond and I found Tovey's blah-blah voice at lunch a trial, and the way he had of as it were waving about his wide open eyes to the accompaniment of that voice

[1] Lord Monteagle of Brandon, d. 1934.
[2] The late Sir Donald Tovey.

Harry Pirie-Gordon

Raymond Wavell-Paxton

a strong irritant. When we rose from lunch and were about to leave the party Tom declared we must stay and hear Donald play. We felt it would be discourteous to hurry away after such a good lunch; reluctantly we took our seats and listened to what seemed hours and hours of Beethoven sonatas. At last we said we really must go because we wanted to see the First Division row.

"I want to see the bumps too," declared Donald Tovey, waving his eyes about with what Raymond and I considered maddening affectation. "That's excellent," said Tom. "Mackenzie and Wavell will take you with them. You'll do that, won't you, Monty?" he added, beaming at me through those kindly spectacles of his.

I could not refuse, and off we started with Donald Tovey toward the river. He was humming to himself all the way across the Broad and down the Turl. We did not mind that because at least it kept that voice of his quiet, but when we turned into the High Tovey suddenly started to hum much more loudly and to conduct an imaginary orchestra. Our embarrassment became acute, indeed agonizing. Louder and louder swelled Donald Tovey's hum, more and more vigorous became his gestures. As we were passing Queen's one of his crescendoes nearly swept a large picture-hat of the fashion from a young woman's head.

"They'll think we're the keepers of a lunatic," Raymond muttered. "I can't stand much more of this."

As we drew nearer to our own College we felt we could not face the derision of our confrères hanging about in the lodge, and when we reached the corner of Longwall I said: "I'm awfully sorry, Tovey, but Wavell and I have to go round here. We have to get dressed for the Ouds show. You'll find the barges quite easily. The Balliol barge is the first one you come to."

With that Raymond and I shot off up Longwall, leaving Donald Tovey to conduct himself and his phantom orchestra to the river. In due course, mentally exhausted, we sat back in the clubroom of the O.U.D.S. and sipped iced lemon-squash through straws until it was time to eat a light dinner and go along to the theatre to dress for the play.

Another dear friend of mine in Balliol was Malcolm Hogg[1] who was now secretary of the O.U.D.S., of which Tiverton was President. He and I were born on the same day. Malcolm was quiet, neat and completely self-possessed. Once when we were speculating what various people would do if they were debagged I said Malcolm would

[1] The late Sir Malcolm Hogg.

pick up his trousers, fold them very carefully and put them away in his chest of drawers.

It was in Malcolm's room that the expression 'hearties', to describe the sporting unintellectuals, was first coined. We were discussing on a Saturday evening the situation in the O.U.D.S., which I shall be relating presently, when as usual there were noisy cries from Trinity next door. Incidentally I was glad to read the other day that, whatever else in Oxford may have vanished, the friendly feud between Balliol and Trinity still endures. I do not recall any nearly such successful raid by Balliol on Trinity as that expedition which laid a lawn on the floor of the Trinity J.C.R.; it will take some ingenuity for Trinity to think up a really memorable reprisal for that one.

To go back to the noise in the Trinity quad on that Saturday evening in 1903. "Oh, these hearties!" I said. "Oh, these hearty Trindogs! Presently Mike Furse[1] will come out, bang their heads together and make these hearties promise to go to Matins to-morrow, and if they duly turn up he won't fine them on Monday morning." From that moment, at first as a term for Trinity men and later more generally, 'hearties' became current and is still current to-day.

Orlo Williams was another Balliol friend. It was probably in his rooms that I met the brilliant Hugh Sidgwick who as well as being a classical scholar of the first quality won the Chancellor's English Essay Prize. We were much amused when, in reading from this at the Sheldonian or wherever it is that University prizemen read their efforts, Hugh Sidgwick pronounced 'epitome' as 'epi-tōme.' Most of us at some time or other have been familiar with a word in print and pronounced it wrongly because we had never heard it actually uttered. That was Hugh Sidgwick's explanation. He wrote many ribald limericks and a magnificently bawdy epithalamium to celebrate the marriage of Cyril Bailey and Gemma Creighton. It was he too who called the intellectual mood of the Apostles of King's College, Cambridge the Higher Sodomy. From Oxford Hugh Sidgwick went on to the Education Office, and—I almost wrote of course—he was killed in the First War.

At this date Orlo Williams was resolutely overcoming that stammer of his. The method was the same as that with which King George VI fought and almost completely overcame his handicap, and consisted of blowing gently when the word would not come. During my Rectorship of Glasgow University we gave the Duke and Duchess of York, as they then were, honorary degrees. Old Sir Donald Macalister

[1] The late Bishop of St Albans, then Dean of Trinity.

the Chancellor came up from Argyll to preside over the lunch given by the Senate to their Royal Highnesses. The Duke sat on the Chancellor's right, with the Duchess on his left. Rait the Principal and Vice-Chancellor was next to the Duke; I was next to the Duchess. Sir Donald Macalister made his speech at the end of lunch to which the Duke replied:

"The Duchess and I have greatly appreciated the honour done to us by this ancient University and we wish to thank Sir Donald Mac. . . ." And then came a pause while the members of the Senate and their ladies waited with respectful attention. I remember wishing with apprehension that Sir Donald Macalister's clan did not begin with A, for I feared that clan after clan beginning with later letters of the alphabet might keep the Duke from going back to A in his effort to remember Macalister. I need not have worried. After blowing gently for a few moments 'Macalister' was said firmly and there was not even a momentary hesitation for the remainder of his speech.

One day in the summer term of that year I was lunching with Sligger in Balliol and being late almost ran through the lodge into the first quad where I met Orlo.

"Hullo, Orlo," I said, and turning to hurry on added, "Where are you going for the vac?" Orlo put out an arm to detain me.

"I'm going to. . . ." and then he stopped and still holding my arm led me back to the lodge where Hancock the porter looked rather surprised to see somebody who had just dashed through his lodge in such a hurry now strolling slowly back in the other direction.

Orlo and I crossed the Broad. I could not bring myself to run the risk of offending one for whom I had such a high regard by telling him I must hurry back to my lunch with Sligger. Nor could I make tentative guesses at where he might be going two or three weeks hence because that might deflect him from concentrating on where he was going now. By this time we were walking slowly along the Turl and just as we reached the High and I was beginning to wonder if I should ever reach Sligger's rooms at all Orlo said quietly 'Corfu' and with a wave of his arm crossed the High to reach wherever it was that he was lunching. Presently the kindly and competent Hancock looked even more surprised when he saw me rush through the lodge for the second time, by now over ten minutes late for Sligger's lunch.

Freeman had asked me to write the 'Random Notes' page in *The Varsity* for each week of that Hilary term of 1903.

Feb. 17.

"The most soothing cult yet invented by man is that of second-hand bookshops, or rather of second-hand bookstalls, where money and time can be wasted to greater profit than anywhere else. The antique scent is delightful, and the dust is cleaner than the dust avoided by scouts, but latterly I have noted with sorrow and apprehension the footprint of woman. I appreciated the feelings of Robinson Crusoe the other day when, as I took down from an old top-shelf a quaintly bound tome, a lace handkerchief fluttered to the ground. Now, the contents of that book were altogether inappropriate for female eyes.... A woman is out of place in a bookshop. Her dress, especially if she is a lady-student, consorts ill with gorgeous bindings, and her restlessness disturbs the conscientious bibliophile."

Such a paragraph will sound strange indeed to the undergraduate of to-day, but in 1903 there still lingered the last vestiges of the days when dons had to resign their fellowships if they married. We regarded with disapproval a 'womanizer'. We felt that 'does' as we called them, were out of place in College except in Eights Week or Commem. and most undergraduates regarded the members of the O.U.D.S. as chartered libertines.

That paragraph reminds me of a later experience at an Oxford bookstall. Parker's, from whom I have been buying books ever since I wrote that paragraph above, used to have a line of bookstalls at the end of New College Street during the Long Vacation to waylay tourists. When I went up for my viva after Schools in July of the following year I was looking through a threepenny row, consisting almost entirely of old volumes of sermons, when just beside me I saw a parson suddenly put down a threepenny bit and hold up the volume he had bought to show the attendant before he hurried away with it.

"My god," the young attendant exclaimed to me, "do you know what that holy Joe's just got for threepence? The first edition of *Fanny Hill*!"

"It was a volume of sermons; I saw the name," I told him.

"But you didn't see the inside, sir."

"Then what was it doing on your threepenny bookstall?"

"That's just what Mr Parker is going to ask when I tell him. Mr Parker put that book aside with orders it was to be kept locked up, and one of our chaps must have put it in with the other threepennies by mistake."

"Well, his reverence will enjoy himself this evening," I laughed.

"Not half he won't. Tut-tut. *Fanny Hill* for threepence!"

Mar. 3.

"I suppose that, when a college porter has been gored to death in his lodge, or when a don has been tossed on to one of the pinnacles of St Mary's Church, some regulation will be framed with regard to the herds of cattle which infest the High and other streets on market-days. As matters stand at present they are allowed to wander about at will; and presumably if grass grew on the streets the neighbouring farmers would turn Longwall and Holywell into a ranch. Perhaps we may look for an improvement in this direction when the stock whips of the Rhodes Scholars have become common weapons."

Harry Pirie-Gordon had spent some of the last Long Vacation at a French pension in Compiègne which he extolled as an ideal place for the Easter vacation, and when I read Madame Caron's advertisement I made up my mind that this was indeed the ideal place. Harry himself, as I remember, was going to the Levant with Lukasch of Trinity[1] who would have a remarkable career.

Here is the advertisement from *The Oxford Point of View* of a year later:

COMPIÈGNE

FOR THE VACATION

Magnificent Forest. Riding, Golf, Tennis, Polo, Stag-hunting with three Packs. Excellent roads for Bicycle and Motor-car.

MADAME C. CARON

affords unrivalled opportunities for learning conversational and literary French. Her Pension is the best appointed and most comfortable in the Town, it is opposite the Palace.
Terms from £7 to £10 per month—everything included.
One hour by rail from Paris, frequent trains.
Address: Madame C. Caron, 10 Rue d'Ulan, Compiègne (Oise)

So Guy Bonham-Carter, Arthur Asquith and I decided that the Easter vac should be spent in Compiègne, where we were made temporary members of the Société de Sport, an almost hopelessly exclusive club for Frenchmen unless they were accepted in the Faubourg St Germain. The gentlemanly status of Oxford undergraduates was presumed by M. Fournier-Salovèze, the Secretary. Fournier-Salovèze was a gloriously exuberant personality who ran what was the equivalent of a country club with perfect tact and immense practical ability. Eleven years later he would be that famous Mayor of Compiègne who defied the Germans and, after being arrested, continued to defy them even when threatened with being

[1] Sir Harry Luke, K.C.M.G.

shot. It must have been a wonderful moment for Fournier-Salovèze when he saw the Armistice signed in that railway-carriage in the forest of Compiègne; I hope he was spared the humiliation of seeing that same railway-carriage fouled by Hitler when Pétain surrendered in 1940.

Guy Bonham-Carter and 'Oc' Asquith played golf every morning on the excellent links of the Société de Sport, and they both tried patiently to turn me into a golfer. I had decided last year that golf was not my game when Raymond Wavell and I toiled round the Cowley links, taking well over 200 strokes each for the round. The Cowley links have long been buried under the Morris works; at that date they were the recognized resort for beginners before they ventured to brave the golfing heights of Hincksey. Incredible though it seems to me to-day, there was one player in the Société de Sport, whom I could beat. This was Prince Lucinge de Faucigny, who was high up in the Orleanist succession. He had a large red moustache and was delighted to find somebody with whom he could play on level terms. He insisted on backing himself every time for five francs, and of about a dozen games we played I lost only one. I feel I must be dreaming when I make that assertion but it is a fact. I see now the faintly mocking smile of that *grande dame* the Marquise d'Hautepoule, where she is sitting in the pavilion with two or three other *grandes dames*, as the Prince admits that he has been beaten again.

There were two other guests in that cosy pension opposite the Palace, which I am ashamed to remember I walked round only once. One was C. J. de Bunsen Sherringham, another Wykehamist, who was a nephew of Sir Maurice de Bunsen; the other was Jacomb who was polishing up his French before going to the University of Caen in order to get a French degree in law preparatory to entering the Egyptian Civil Service, for which one had to be versed both in English and French law as in the Channel Islands. Jacomb was earnest and solemn and inclined to confuse conversation with information.

After dinner we sipped the little glasses of cassis which Madame Caron, always followed by her little pug-bitch, used to bring into the billiards-room, and then M. Caron would guide us through the mysteries of French billiards. I see him now as he brushes back the tassel of his smoking-cap and bends over the table to demonstrate the easiness of a cannon which we should never have dreamed of attempting on an English billiards-table. Then there was a more elaborate round game in which the object was to knock down tiny skittles without hitting the *grelot*, a small bell swinging to and fro from the lamp above the table.

About nine o'clock Guy and I would decide it was time to go off to the café concert down in the town, to which Oc Asquith would never accompany us. Indeed, he definitely disapproved of our going to that café concert and did not accept our excuse of the value it was to our French. "What sort of French?" he would enquire severely.

Oc had a touch of the Puritan in him, and I am sure that without my bad example he would have been successful in keeping Guy away from that café concert. I hear from all these years away Guy saying to me, in a low gasp of genuinely shocked commiseration: "You know, it's frightful for poor Oc. His step-mother smokes."

Do not suppose that this was a piece of Wykehamist priggishness. Most young men at this date would have been embarrassed if it was known that one of their older female relations smoked. Queen Victoria had been gone only a month or two more than two years.

The great attraction of the café concert was Blanche, a tall and pretty blonde who before she took to singing in café concerts had been a chambermaid in a Boulogne hotel. I see through the fumes of *caporal* cigarettes the tall buxom figure of Blanche upon the small stage of the café, and hear above the chink of glasses her contralto singing:

> "*Assez de bicyclette, de bicyclette, de bicyclette,*
> *Moi je prefère la brouette, la brouette, la brouette,*
> *On pousse de temps en temps,*
> *C'est un mouvement épatant.*"

And I hear Guy's puzzled voice asking me what is the joke which makes the audience laugh and clap. And when I translate, 'Enough of the bicycle, I prefer a wheelbarrow, one pushes from time to time, it's a marvellous movement,' he still fails to follow the ribaldry.

She had another catching song about the flowers that befitted various professions, of which I only remember *les oeillets chez les corsetières* and *les lys chez les réactionaires. Oeillet* means carnation and also the eyes into which women put hooks; the lilies of the Bourbons were naturally a symbol of reaction.

But the great popular song of the moment was the immortal *Viens pou-poule*, and I have no sooner written 'immortal' than I realize what a ridiculous epithet it is for a song whose tune that was once hummed incessantly will mean nothing to all except a tiny few of my readers as old as myself. Never mind, with memories of Blanche singing *Viens pou-poule* in that Compiègne café, I indulge myself by repeating as much as I can remember of the words:

Le samedi soir après l'turbin
L'ouvrier parisien
Dit à sa femme 'Comme dessert
Je te paie l'café concert,
On va filer bras dessus bras dessous
Aux galèries à vingt sous,
Met vite une robe, faut dépecher
Pour être bien placés,
Car il faut, mon coco,
Entendre tous les cabots,
Ah, viens pou-poule, viens pou-poule, viens,
Quand j'entends ces chansons
Ca m'rend tout polisson,
Ah, viens, pou-poule, viens pou-poule, viens,
Souviens-toi q'c'est comme ça
Que j'suis devenu papa.

The gist of what I remember of that song is that a Parisian workman on Saturday evening after the week's grind is over tells his wife to get dressed quickly so that they may go to a café concert. "Come along, my chickabiddy. Remember these songs make me naughty and remember that's how I've become a father."

One of the male performers was annoyed with Blanche for singing what he considered was a song he should be singing himself, and there recurs the picture of Blanche. She is at our table where after drinking a *flûte* of champagne she sits moodily silent. I ask her what is the matter.

"*C'est la barbe!* Oh, it's such a bore listening to him grumbling at me because I sing *Viens pou-poule*. Does the song belong to him? *Ah, zut alors, mais non, non, non!*"

We call for three more *flûtes* and her invincible *espièglerie* re-asserts itself. "*Je m'en fous de lui,*" she declares, and is presently teasing Guy because she says like all the rest of us English he cannot pronounce B. "Why do you call me Planche? You know it isn't at all a compliment for a girl to be called a plank."

By this time Guy had fallen in love with Blanche and was much depressed when she laughed at any overtures of affection he made. "You speak French better than me, Monty. Can't you explain to her that I really am awfully keen on her?"

I tried to play Pandarus without success.

"*Mais, voyez, mon cher, il est trop petit pour moi.* To find him in bed beside me would just make me laugh and I would not like to hurt the feelings of such a good *copain*". Indeed, Blanche was at least half a head taller than Guy.

There was an English girl working in the café who was a great friend of Blanche. I say 'girl', but Nellie, whose surname I have forgotten, was well over thirty with at least ten years of cabaret life on the Continent between her and England. She was small and dark with a sharp nose but a gentle tongue. I confided in Nellie what was seeming Guy's hopeless passion for Blanche.

"Poor boy," she sighed sympathetically. "But you can easily stop him from feeling hurt. You can tell him that Blanche is going to marry Pierre and she wouldn't like to make Pierre jealous."

"Who's Pierre?"

"He's doing his military service quite close to Compiègne. Whenever he gets leave he comes to see Blanche. I don't think myself she is really in love with him, but, as she says, one has to settle down some time. And she's right. I was once engaged but I wasn't really in love and so I kept putting off getting married and now I don't suppose I'll ever get married. I'm twenty-seven, you know. Isn't it frightful?" I tried to look surprised by Nellie's age, successfully I should like to think.

"Look, I'll tell you what we'll do," she said. "We'll ask Pierre to come with us on that expedition to the castle of Pierrefonds we were planning. And then your friend will realize why Blanche can't take him as her *amant*." Thus it was arranged.

We hired a dog-cart which Blanche was to drive, Guy and I sitting in front with her, Pierre in his red and blue uniform and Nellie sitting behind. It was a lovely April day with great white cumulus sailing high above the blue sky and no sign of a shower. We drove at a spanking pace along the wide straight road to Pierrefonds. Suddenly Pierre gave an agonized gasp.

"*Mon dieu!* It's the Colonel and I've no leave from barracks." He hastily put the rug over his head and hid himself under the seat.

In front was a chaise driven by Pierre's Colonel at a sedate pace, beside him his portly wife and running behind a poodle. Blanche whipped up the horse and as we drove past the Colonel's chaise she cracked her whip over the poodle who gave a loud yelp. The chaise was out of sight before Pierre could be persuaded to emerge from the rug.

Viollet le Duc's re-creation of a mediaeval castle is sniffed at to-day, but I was mightily impressed by that first view of it, and as I have not seen it since that April of sixty years ago I can afford to be impressed by it still without bothering about the judgment of connoisseurs.

After exploring the inside of the castle we wandered round the terraces that surround it and had begun to eat our lunch when we were told by one of the gardeners that it was *defendu* to picnic where we were. If we wanted to picnic we must go to the terrace above. So we climbed up and sitting on the parapet ate our lunch. When we had finished Blanche caught sight of the gardener who had ordered us away from the lower terrace, bent over his job of bedding out plants. "*Il faut arroser les plantes*," Blanche said, and hitching up her petticoats she proceeded to water, not the plants, but the back of the gardener's neck. Then ensued a kind of early Charlie Chaplin film as the outraged gardener tried to overtake us in a chase round the terraces of Pierrefonds.

"Isn't Blanche the limit?" Nellie exclaimed when we were back where our horse was stabled and clear of the hue and cry of gardeners; from the past I hear again in Nellie's voice a wistful envy of Blanche's youth and verve.

It was soon after the expedition to Pierrefonds that a letter came from Raymond Wavell summoning Guy and me to meet him in Paris, where he was staying with his mother and sister. We caught a very early train because Guy wanted to ascend the Eiffel Tower before we collected Raymond at his hotel. It was so early that the boy had not brought up my shoes; not wanting to disturb the household in search of them I put on a pair of patent-leather shoes of which I was to be extremely tired by the time the day was over. As the morning was so cold I took my heavy greatcoat. In the previous Octave there was a photograph of my father wearing that coat as the American in Henry James's play. I had persuaded him to part with this coat, which I thought suitable for travel or sporting occasions with its double row of big buttons. That coat will have a sequel before the day is out.

In due course we picked up Raymond Wavell and as Guy and I were intending to have what might be an expensive evening we decided to eat cheaply and went to a Duval restaurant. Here to my joy I found frogs on the menu and with considerable difficulty at last persuaded Raymond to try the dish: Guy gave an adamant refusal. Presently I saw a look of utter disgust on Raymond's face.

"My god, how can you possibly eat these stinking frogs?"

"They don't stink."

"They don't stink? Smell my plate."

Raymond was right. One of the frogs served to him did stink with a ghastly mixture of bad fish and high chicken. After that whiff I could not eat any more of my own frogs, fresh though they were and delicious as I had been finding them.

In the train that morning Guy had announced to me that before he left Paris he intended to part with his virginity, though that was not the phraseology with which he expressed his resolute intention. When Raymond heard that Guy was anxious to pick up a girl he said with the confidence of a lifelong *boulevardier* that the best place to pick up a girl was at the Palais de Glace. "It's a skating-rink," he added.

I asked him if he had ever picked up a girl at the Palais de Glace. "No, of course not, you ass. I'm with my mother and sister. But a chap in the hotel told me that all the high-class tarts went to the Palais de Glace."

So off went the three of us to the Palais de Glace, unaware that in the early part of the afternoon it was the haunt of fashionable Paris and that it only became unrespectable after five o'clock. I sat watching Guy and Raymond as they skated round, smiling at girls, all of whom belonging to the *beau monde* looked at Guy and Raymond with haughty disdain.

After a while they grew discouraged by this lack of response and decided that the Palais de Glace was a failure; Raymond took us back to have tea with his mother and sister, where Guy and I left him later to get our dinner, having declined Mrs Wavell's invitation to dine at the hôtel with the excuse of having to catch the train for Compiègne. I knew that Guy was still determined to fulfill the intention with which he had come to Paris. We went to the Folies Bergères after dinner and saw Little Tich ecstatically greeted by the audience. The show came to an end with a revue called *Viens Fou-Foule*; this included a generous display of the female form which stimulated the ardour of Guy's resolve, and from the Folies Bergères we went to a café where Guy cast his eye upon a buxom *fille de joie* with whom we drank champagne and then just when I hoped all was going well, Guy muttered to me that he didn't think he wanted her after all. He repeated this performance at two more cafés and when about 2.30 in the morning we entered another café I said: "Look, Guy, I'm not going to wander around any more cafés to-night. My shoes are hurting and I'm getting fed up. Either you manage it here or we go off and find an hôtel by the Gare de l'Est where we can catch an early train back to Compiègne in the morning."

So at this café Guy took the plunge, but he had hardly retired to the *cabinet particulier* when he came out to say that she wanted more champagne and had I any money left. I gave him what I had, telling him not to spend more than he could possibly help and retaining only five francs. While Guy was away I sat on a balcony and watched the night life of Paris for an hour, having taken off those confounded patent-leather shoes. At last Guy came out to find me, his resolution fulfilled. I asked him how much money he had left.

"Not a sou," he told me.

"That means we shall have to walk to that damned station. I've only five francs. We shall have to take a double room in some small hôtel.

Near the Gare de l'Est we decided that a small rather sinister-looking hotel would be within our means and knocked on the door. It was opened by a scrofulous-looking porter with a bandage round his throat, who said we could have a double-room for four francs after I had told him he would not get a tip if he charged us five. He took us upstairs to a dingy bedroom in which was a large double-bed with a grubby pock-marked quilt. I told him we wanted to be called sharp at six to catch our train.

"*Bien. Je frapperai trois coups,*" he muttered with a cracked voice as he eased the bandage round his throat. "*Vous entendez? Trois coups. Sans quoi n'ouvrez-pas. Comme ça,*" he added, knocking on the door three times. I asked him what it mattered how many knocks he gave provided he called us in time to catch our train.

He smiled an evil and lecherous smile at my greatcoat. "*Mais, monsieur, je vous connais. J'ai déja vu votre pardessus. Vous-êtes Monsieur Vanderbildt, et voici un de vos jockeys. Je vous ai vu souvent à Chantilly. Soyez tranquille. Moi, je ne dirai rien. Trois coups comme ça.*" He knocked again three times and closed the door behind him, that lecherous smile still upon his face. Undoubtedly Guy could have passed easily for a jockey and certainly my greatcoat was more suited to the race-course than the streets of Paris.

Overcoats can deceive. Hazel Lavery once told me of an adventure of her husband caused by an overcoat. Sir John had been asked by Lord Derby to paint the Two Thousand Guineas at Newmarket. Under pressure from his wife Sir John bought a Newmarket coat with waist and skirt and thus, as she told him, was properly dressed for the occasion, Sir John went off along the course and set up his easel near the starting gate. He had no sooner done so than a policeman came along and told him roughly to move on.

"No bookies are allowed down here as you very well know."

"But Lord Derby asked me to paint the start of the race," Sir John explained.

"Oh, he did, did he? Then perhaps you'd like to paint the race down in the police-station." With this the policeman took Sir John Lavery in charge, and as nobody in the police-station would believe what he said about Lord Derby poor Sir John had to spend several hours there before he was rescued.

Oc Asquith and Guy Bonham-Carter went home a week before me, just as Osgood Mackenzie arrived to stay with Fournier-Salovèze, who invited me to dinner to meet him. The laird of Inverewe, who was now in his sixties, took a fancy to me and I could not have enough of what I found his absorbing stories of Highland life. His account of how he had made his wonderful garden at Inverewe out of a barren promontory of rocks and peat was for me an epic. It was undoubtedly he who planted in my heart the determination to span the great gap more than a century wide which lay between me and my Highland birthright, although at the moment the achievement of such a determination was nebulous as a waking dream which the busy day would dissolve. Yet Osgood Mackenzie offered me an opportunity to carry out that determination forthwith. At this date I believed that my Mackenzie descent was through the Scatwell branch, and when I told this to Osgood Mackenzie he declared that we must be cousins.

"Why don't you come to Wester Ross when you've finished with Oxford? I'll give you a good croft. You'll soon be speaking Gaelic, and you would be able to do really valuable work in Gairloch. We need youth to come to the West instead of deserting it as youth is doing to-day. You say you hope to be a writer of plays and poetry. Believe me you'll find as much material for plays and poetry in Gairloch as you'll find anywhere in the world."

I ask myself to-day whether if I had accepted that offer which Osgood Mackenzie made to me sixty years ago I should be able to call myself a poet to-day. Should I have been able to feel that I had been a steady flame in the Celtic twilight or should I feel I had been no more than a will o' the wisp? It is idle to ponder such a question. For better or for worse I did not accept Osgood Mackenzie's offer.

Yet I must not seem to suggest that when I turned my back on Gairloch I had any firm and clear notion of the course I intended to steer in writing. I had one idea in my mind which at this moment excluded all others. I must declare my love for Ruth and have her answer.

When Osgood Mackenzie made me that offer we were following

in a chaise a boar-hunt in the forest. From time to time as we drove along we would catch a glimpse of the blue liveries of the huntsmen richly laced with gold and hear the sound of their French horns; we never caught a glimpse of their quarry. A remark made by Osgood Mackenzie during that drive has stuck in my memory. He was talking about his daughter and saying he hoped she wouldn't copy Elspeth Campbell's habit of sitting about in her chemise to play the piano. A quarter of a century would pass before I met Lady Elspeth Campbell, but although we became great friends I never ventured to ask her if she remembered playing the piano in her chemise once upon a time.

That night after dinner Osgood Mackenzie told me a story he bade me hand on to a young man when I was as old as he was. When he was about five there lived in Gairloch a centenarian who told him what happened to him once when he was the same age as the laird's son. He had been standing outside the old inn at Gairloch on a beautiful April morning when a rider with his head bound with a blood-stained bandage came galloping in from the East on a pony and went into the inn. Presently a fine gentleman came out with a sheep's-head in his hand which he had been chewing. The fine gentleman hurried along to the head of the loch and waved back boats full of Mackenzies coming over from Lewis; when he had turned them back he threw down the sheep's-head and mounting a horse set off at a gallop to the East. The small boy watching him picked up the sheep's-head and was starting to chew it when the landlord of the inn came out, snatched it away from him, and nailed the sheep's-head up over the door of the inn. That fine gentleman was Seaforth himself, who was in Gairloch to gather the Mackenzies in the West and lead them to join the Prince; when that messenger brought the news of Culloden, Seaforth had to get back to Brahan as soon as he could or he would have been in trouble.

"So you see," Osgood Mackenzie concluded, "I can claim to have known somebody who must have been born five years before Culloden. I was born in 1842 and that old Gairloch crofter would have been at least 103 when he told me that story."

After that memorable week in his company I never met Osgood Mackenzie again; when I went to live in Scotland he was dead. Nor have I ever revisited Compiègne or heard that forest haunted by the hoots of motors; in my mind's ear is only the echo of a huntsman's horn.

At whatever station it was where I was to get on the train for Calais or Boulogne I opened the door of the nearest second-class compartment and asked if there was a seat left. To my surprise and pleasure I was answered by the deep voice of Claude Kirby, who was travelling with Alban Hood, and with my stories of Compiègne we had lots to laugh over until we were on board the boat where as usual I soon felt miserably sea-sick. A kindly woman passenger sitting next me on deck asked if I had ever tried to ward off sea-sickness by eating an orange. I shook my head, whereupon she peeled an orange and kept pressing slices upon me which I weakly accepted. After just managing to gulp down two of them I fled to the side and presented them to the English Channel. I can recall her exact words as I returned to my chair.

"That's very disappointing. I never knew an orange do that before."

At the end of last term it had been practically decided that the O.U.D.S. play for Eights Week should be *Henry IV Part One*, in which I should follow up Sir Toby Belch with Falstaff. When I got back to Oxford I was told by Tivvy that the play was to be *The Taming of the Shrew*. Apparently Tivvy had met during the vac an actress called Muriel Godfrey-Turner, for whom he had fallen and whom he wanted to impress with the force of his personality. This he thought he should be able to do successfully if he played Petruchio to her Katharina. There was no part in *The Taming of the Shrew* I wanted to play, least of all Gremio or Grumio of which Tivvy offered me the choice. I argued for a while but Tivvy told me that the committee had decided on *The Taming of the Shrew* and that G. R. Foss had been notified.

"All right, Tivvy, then I'll call a special meeting of the club and veto *The Taming of the Shrew*."

Tivvy grinned and told me that to form a quorum for a general meeting empowered to veto the play the rule required three-quarters of the members to be present. "And I don't think you'll find it very easy to get 75 members to a general meeting in the summer term."

However, much to Tivvy's astonishment, and indeed my own, I did succeed in gathering a quorum and persuaded that quorum to veto *The Taming of the Shrew*. Having won my point, I felt it would savour too much of personal ambition if I tried to force *Henry IV Part One* and I invited Tivvy to choose any other play of Shakespeare, promising that whatever part I should be called upon to play in it I would accept without demur.

"What about *The Merchant of Venice*? I believe Bertie Forsyth would make a splendid Shylock."

"And Jack Gilliat or Charles Maude for Bassanio, I suppose?" I asked.

"Neither of them can act this term. I shall play Bassanio and Miss Muriel Godfrey-Turner will play Portia. I suggest you play Gratiano."

Raymond Wavell was given the part of Lorenzo and except for the balcony scene in *Romeo and Juliet* the most beautiful love-scene Shakespeare wrote. I tried my hardest to make him speak his lovely lines as they should be spoken.

"Listen, Raymond. 'How sweet the moonlight sleeps upon this bank.' Do try to give the impression that you are bewitched by the moonlight. You say it as if you were trying to wake the moon with an alarm-clock. And then in a kind of ecstasy:

> '*Sit Jessica. Look, how the floor of heaven*
> *Is thick inlaid with patines of bright gold.*'

The way you say it sounds as if you were admiring somebody's new carpet."

"But I feel such an ass, Monty, spouting away at a girl like this," Raymond would keep protesting. "Why we couldn't have done Henry the Fourth and let me play Poins I don't know."

I fear that the critic in the *Isis* who said R. G. Wavell (Magdalen) had a lot to learn in the art of making love was right. I remember consoling him by saying that dramatic critics never knew anything about acting. I was feeling indignant about dramatic critics myself at the moment because *The Times*, I think it was, while saying that mine was the best performance in the play, added 'but after all the part of Gratiano, like Mercutio, is one that plays itself.' "Gratiano easy! When he's playing against the audience all the time now that Shylock is always played as a pathetic figure. Mercutio, a part that plays itself!"

Various old members of the O.U.D.S. came up to Oxford to see the matinée, among them Arthur Bourchier, one of the founders. He came round to my dressing-room and said: "Well, there's no doubt what you're going to be." I looked in surprise at the actor-manager of the Garrick Theatre.

"I mustn't interfere with your academic career but when you've taken your degree you're coming to the Garrick as my *jeune premier*. I shall want a seven-years' contract. I'll start you at £500 a year and take you to £2000 by the end of the time. Then the theatre is yours

C.M. as Phidippides in
"The Clouds"

C.M as Gratiano
O.U.D.S.

C.M. as Duke of Milan
O.U.D.S.

C.M. as Sir Toby Belch
O.U.D.S.

and you'll get all the financial backing you want as an actor-manager."

"But I don't want to go on the stage, Mr Bourchier."

"And what are you proposing to do?" he asked in astonishment.

"I think I'm going to write," I told him.

"Well, you *may* be as good a writer as you are an actor, but I think it's very improbable, indeed more than improbable, and I'm sure your father would tell you to accept my offer. I'll look forward to hearing from you soon."

I never met Arthur Bourchier again, but twenty-four years later when I was living on the island of Jethou in the Channel Islands I received a note from him which began,

'*Many years ago, more years than I care to remember, I made you an offer I never made any young man before, and indeed I don't suppose any young man ever had such an offer.... In memory of that offer wouldn't it be nice if when I came back from this tour I am making in South Africa I found you had written a play for me?*'

I wrote at once to thank him and said I should be glad to have a shot at a play for him; but before I could get down to such a play Arthur Bourchier died on that South African tour in 1927.

There had been talk already of my becoming a student at the Inner Temple, and I thought the sooner I did this the better, so that if my father heard of my rejection of Bourchier's offer I should have a good exucse for it. My mother, to whom I said nothing about Bourchier, wrote to Sir Frederick Pollock and Sir Henry Dickens, asking them to be the two necessary sponsors. I do not remember what Sir Frederick said, but I expect they were good Pollocky remarks. I remember vividly going to Sir Henry Dickens's chambers.

"I'm signing your application on my father's old desk," he said.

And I may feel that when Henry Dickens signed that paper it was not to testify to my fitness to be a student of the Inner Temple but rather a certificate of my fitness to become a novelist. Years later I would repay that signature by testifying to the fitness of Monica Dickens to be a novelist, with a confidence that has been so amply justified.

I have among many old menus of dinners the menu of the O.U.D.S. dinner on May 23rd 1903, at which I see that the toast of the ladies was proposed by E. M. C. Mackenzie and replied to by A. T. Loyd. I cannot resist playing Tantalus to my readers by giving them that menu, on which we would not have paid more than half a guinea to gorge:

Caviare

—

Clear Italian
Cucumber

—

Boiled Salmon. Hollandaise Sauce

—

Whitebait

—

Chicken Patties

—

Hind Quarter of Lamb

—

Asparagus

—

Gooseberry Fool
Maraschino Jelly

—

Plovers Eggs

—

Dessert. Ice

I was much elated that May by the *entente cordiale* achieved by King Edward VII in Paris and wrote in the fifth number of *The Oxford Point of View*:

"I am unwilling to convey a wrong impression of Oxford opinion, and I am prepared to take all the blame when I give it as *my* opinion that an alliance between Great Britain, France, and Russia is the true solution of the problem of the world's future. It seems to me that the proposed alliance between Great Britain and Germany has not proved a success, and that the spirited proclamation of the Anglo-Saxon race against the world is a windy phrase invented to justify the existence of music-halls and Mr Kipling. The policy of insular aloofness from the web of alliances may appear dignified from the point of view of the island, but from another point of view it is not unlike a child sulking in the corner."

I believe to-day that if that Triple Alliance had been effected by 1904, Germany and Austria would never have taken the course they did ten years later. That was not the Oxford point of view in 1903, and when I moved the motion in favour of that Triple Alliance at three debates that year I lost every one of them by a large majority.

On May 13th Ruth Daniel was twenty and at her birthday party she was in a bubble of excitement about 'A (perhaps) Quarterly Magazine' she was bringing out the next month called *The Sheaf*, for which I had written her an article, and because I was so anxious to make it the best article I had ever written it seemed to me the worst. She showed me a poem written by one of her girl friends which she thought so true. I was extremely depressed to read:

Happy is love expressed
But love untold
Is purer gold—
Lock fast the treasure-chest.

I brooded over this and decided that she was intending to discourage me. She must know perfectly well that I was in love with her and this wretched poem must be meant to tell me that she was not in love with me and did not want to hurt my feelings by telling me so. The production of *The Merchant of Venice* diverted my gloomy thoughts for a while; when that was over I felt I must know what Ruth felt for me whatever the pain of knowing.

At last, about a week before the end of term in that wet June, I decided one afternoon to tell Rachel I was in love with Ruth and ask her what she thought I ought to do; we were sitting in their daisied room.

"Tell her," said Rachel.

"But suppose she isn't in love with me?"

"The only way to find out is to ask her; somehow I don't think you will be disappointed."

I was amazed to hear Rachel say this. Whenever I had talked about Ruth she had always seemed to want to talk about something else.

"Rachel, do you really mean that?"

"Tell her," she said again. "She's in the drawing-room doing something or other. Why don't you go to her there?"

I walked out of the daisied room and down the narrow passage toward the drawing-room. The rain had stopped and a pale sun was shining on the garden of Worcester House. Ruth did not seem to be there, and then I saw her sitting on the step up into her father's study. Some of his folios and quartos which she had been dusting were scattered about the floor. I sat down beside her on the step, and told her that I loved her, and in a voice that seemed to come from out of this world I heard her say 'And I love you'. The cheek near to me burned with a minute crimson flame. I was so much overcome by the moment that I did not kiss her. I just sat in a trance. Suddenly I said, 'You must tell Rachel. You must tell your mother,' and getting up I hurried away from the house, and as it seemed to me but an instant later I was walking up George Street without touching the pavement, floating as one used to float in childish dreams.

The Provost of Worcester, Dr Inge, had died toward the end of May; it must have been in this week that Ruth's father was elected to succeed him. The emotion of that moment when I declared my love and heard Ruth's reply has swept from my memory whatever Mrs Daniel or Rachel said to me. All I can remember is that I was invited to stay at Worcester House in July, before the move into the Provost's Lodging took place. Even now as I seek to recapture the sequence of time I can still see nothing but Ruth sitting on that step out of the drawing-room into her father's study and that minute crimson flame upon her cheek and myself floating up George Street in a dream.

The decision we second-year men had to take at the end of the term was where we should live out of College and with whom we should share digs. Raymond Wavell, Claude Kirby and Alban Hood were going to what were then considered the outstanding digs in Oxford at 90 High, and they pressed me to make a fourth. I was tempted for a moment, but it had always been understood between Harry Pirie-Gordon and myself that he and I would share digs in our third year and I scoffed at the notion that what so many of them in Magdalen regarded as Harry's deliberate refusal to be typical would be a handicap for myself. So he and I took digs at 43 High, where we should have a sitting-room on the first floor, a dining-room above it and two bedrooms, for two guineas a week each.

Trinity term at the Temple ended on June 29th by which date those of us who were students had to eat our dinners. Before one could be called to the Bar, besides passing the three law examinations—preliminary (from which as University undergraduates we were excused), intermediate and final—one had to have eaten 36 dinners. These dinners had to be eaten in batches of three during each of the four terms, and if one of them was missed the other two were cancelled out, and the term did not count. If one ate one's three dinners regularly it meant a minimum of three years before one could be called to the Bar.

Dinner was at 6 p.m. and one was handed a gown by the Roll Keeper as one went in. A bottle of claret and a bottle of sherry were placed on the table for every four diners. We used to make up a party of five and if possible get one of us sitting with three Indian students, none of whom would be drinking wine; if we were successful in doing this we would have two bottles of claret and two bottles of sherry among the five of us. 'Any Student unrobing in Hall will not be allowed to count the day towards his Term', said the rules and again 'Newspapers are not allowed to be read in Hall during the hour of Dinner. Any Student disregarding this rule is liable not to be allowed to count the Dinner towards his Term.' I recall once losing a whole term by reading the bright pink racing final of the *Star* and on the same evening Raymond Asquith's losing his dinner by appearing from up the river in a white suit. No doubt that evening the head of the Benchers' table was a stickler for decorum, for I sometimes read a paper on other occasions. I cannot remember what annual fees were charged for dues and commons, but I know they were enough to make me feel by 1907, when I was still some way from having eaten the necessary 36 dinners, glad to be relieved of that annual payment. I never had any real intention of being called. I did not even take my Law Intermediate examination. I might have been quite a success with juries at the Old Bailey as a defending counsel, but I should have been almost always a poor prosecutor and I should have been useless to any clients at the Chancery Bar. Some fifty years later after I had followed the late Lord Birkett with a speech at some dinner he said to me, "Well, if you'd been in my profession you would have earned your £40,000 a year." I shook my head.

Among my odds and ends of papers I find the programme of a Theatrical Garden Party in aid of the Actors' Orphanage at The Elms in Avenue Road (by kind permission of Lady Augustus Harris) for the organization of which my mother was responsible. I told about the first Garden Party at The Elms in 1896 in my previous Octave. Among other entertainments on that July 10th of 1903 I read with surprise of scenes from *Twelfth Night* as a pastoral. I find that Jack Gilliat played Malvolio and that Harry Tennent played Sir Andrew Aguecheek. This I had completely forgotten and I still cannot recall a single moment of that occasion. I can only account for such obliteration of memory by my utter preoccupation with the prospect of going to Oxford about a week later to stay with the Daniels at Worcester House.

Yet two or three flashes from the end of that June and beginning of July have remained. I see myself coming out of the Temple after dinner into the bright sunlight of the Strand and going to collect Raymond Wavell at the Monico to take him to see *Old Heidelberg* at the St James's Theatre, in which Eva Moore gave a completely enchanting performance of the girl with whom the student Prince fell in love. I waited while Raymond finished his dinner, at the end of which he invited me to have a glass of Napoleon brandy. When the bill came Raymond asked the waiter what the ten shillings was for.

"The brandy, sir."

"Five shillings a glass?" he exclaimed. "Good lord, that's more than the price of a bottle of whisky!"

I see myself again with Raymond Wavell and as we turn into Bond Street my taking out a pipe and starting to fill it.

"You're not going to smoke a pipe in Bond Street?" he asks in consternation. "Look, if I buy you a cigar will you put away that pipe?" I agree and he turns into a tobacconist—I think it was Morris's shop—and buys me a shilling cigar which would have cost him at least six shillings to-day.

I recall going to Claude Kirby's house in Cromwell Road and Claude's telling me about the ball he had been to at Apsley House the night before. "The ballroom was lit entirely by candles. There must have been a thousand of them at least and I heard the King say to somebody how marvellous it was of the Duchess to keep up old times in the way she did."

My last memory of the end of that London season in 1903 is driving in a hansom down Constitution Hill and being stopped for three or four minutes by the state-coaches driving from the Mall to the Drawing-room in Buckingham Palace. I see now the Devonshire coach with the black and yellow livery of the coachman and the two footmen all with three-cornered hats, and behind the Devonshire coach the Portland coach with the coachman and two footmen in claret-coloured livery wearing tall semi-circular hats.

Some of us took a house for Henley, where we Magdalen people had the gratification of seeing our Eight win the Ladies Plate. One of the party was Medcalfe of Univ., who I remember Nigel Playfair's saying would be better when he became Medcow. I don't know what he had done to annoy Playfair on some O.U.D.S. occasion with old members, for he was a jolly chap with a temper that nobody could ruffle. One evening when Medcalfe was out on the river with a girl we thought it would be fun to have a sweep, the winner to be the first one who could make Medcalfe angry. I made an old booby trap by putting a pail of water over a door ajar, and we waited for Medcalfe to come in, I having laid a half-crown bet with each of the others that I could at least make him say 'damn!' By eleven o'clock one of the waiting audience said he was bored and was going to bed. I had to take down the pail for him to go out and set it up again. At midnight Claude Kirby said he was bored, and I had to let him out. At one o'clock two more said my booby trap was a wash out and I had to take the pail down and put it up again for them to go to bed. By this time only Raymond Wavell and I were left. At two he said he couldn't sit up any longer but just as he rose from his chair Medcalfe came in and the pail successfully emptied itself over him.

"Ha! Ha! Very funny!" he said. "But it would have been funnier if I hadn't already been soaked by falling in the river."

"You owe us all half-a-crown, Monty," said Raymond.

I had to pay up. Medcalfe's temper was still unruffled.

It must have been in the middle of July that I went to Oxford, for it was still twilight when after dinner Mrs Daniel told Ruth and me to take a little walk in the garden; in that twilit garden we kissed for the first time, and in the morning we went to St Thomas's Church where Francis Underhill was now the curate and where Ruth worked among the poor she loved so much.

Every day during my visit Mrs Daniel, Rachel, Ruth and myself were planning the decoration of their new house, the perfectly proportioned rooms of which deserved more attractive wallpaper than that which the late Provost had given them. There was one moment of acute embarrassment for all of us after we had been in the drawing-room where Mrs Daniel had decided she was going to have light-crimson damask curtains, with which decision both her daughters were disagreeing while I, no doubt anxious to stand well with Mrs Daniel, was applauding her choice.

"Well, don't let's argue any more about the curtains," she said. "We must decide about the papers in the bedrooms." So up the wide curved staircase we went to the first landing.

"Oh dear, oh dear, the poor dear Inges," Mrs Daniel exclaimed as she contemplated the paper that covered the passages and even some of the bedrooms as well, the pattern of which seemed to consist of nothing but small blackbeetles wandering about on a grey background. I do not recall seeing such a gloomy wallpaper anywhere, and have wondered whether that gloomy wallpaper may not have influenced the youth of Dean Inge and led to the epithet always attached to him by the popular Press.

As Mrs Daniel gave that exclamation about the poor dear Inges the door of one of the bedrooms opened and out came Mrs Inge, Miss Inge and Canon Inge as he was at this date. They had been visiting the room where the Provost had died. All were in complete black: all had the red noses supposed to indicate chronic dyspepsia; Mrs Inge and Miss Inge were wiping the tears from their eyes.

"Oh dear," Mrs Daniel bubbled. "Oh, I am so sorry we were

making such a noise. We didn't know you were in the house."

"It is we who are the intruders," said Canon Inge in that dry voice of his. "It is we who should apologize," and with a bow he led his mother and sister downstairs and out into the quad.

"What a dreadful thing to have happened," Mrs Daniel declared. "I never felt so embarrassed in my life. Do you think they heard what I said?"

"They heard what you said because they came out of the room just as you said it," Rachel told her.

"Oh, but they may have thought Mother was sympathizing with them," said Ruth, always eager to console or reassure. "The poor dear Inges weren't to know it was their wallpaper which made you call them that."

Presently we all forgot about the poor dear Inges in choosing the paper for that garden-room under the terrace from which a flight of stone steps swept down on either side to the big lawn in front; for that garden-room where Ruth and I would sit so often and talk about the future we chose a pattern of brightly coloured birds whose colours for me have never faded.

Our next tour of *Twelfth Night* must have started early in August. Bertie Forsyth was back with us for Malvolio but this time Orsino was played by Charles Maude. Alban Hood was an absentee and I had the best Sir Andrew I had yet had in Arthur Eckersley, an old O.U.D.S. member who had gone down in 1901. He was then engaged in minor journalism, and nine years' hence would write in *Punch* the review of *Carnival* that set the ball of success rolling for a young man's second novel. Beryl Faber was not with us; her place was taken by an actress whose name I have forgotten. She always knew better than everybody else how a line should be said or an exit made, and we grew tired of hearing her say 'when I was with Mr Benson we always did this,' or 'I think I'll try that speech another way to-night.' How maliciously amused we were when instead of making Viola say 'I would *I* had a beard but I would not have it grow on *my* chin' she said with a terrific sigh 'I would I had a beard but I would not have it grow on my *chin*.'

We played first in the Charterhouse gardens for some local good cause, and stayed in Godalming with various residents, but all I remember of Charterhouse is meeting Malcolm Hogg and his sister Ethel Woods in deep mourning for their father Quintin Hogg, the founder of the Polytechnic, who had recently died. We went to one or two other places which I have forgotten. Then we went to Tamworth where Raymond Wavell and I stayed some ten miles away in a mediaeval house beside a lake. I wish I could remember the name of that house or the name of our host, for the house and its setting had a serene beauty which I should like to behold again.

But the most vivid memory of that time is staying at Hams Hall in Staffordshire with the first Lord Norton. Hams Hall is now the headquarters of Birmingham electricity. Lord Norton, born 150 years ago as I write these words, was a wonderful relic of an earlier age. He had been an Under-Secretary of the Colonies and a President of the Board of Trade; Adderley Street in Cape Town is named after him. In his Gladstone collar and heavy cravat Lord Norton was a formidable figure at the head of his own dining-table. With difficulty he had been persuaded to surrender to having dinner at what he considered the preposterously late hour of half-past six, and when it was over the ladies, who included grand-daughters and great-granddaughters, were banished to the drawing-room and the men were invited to draw up their chairs and take port with his lordship. I shall not affirm positively that he drank three bottles, but he certainly did put away a great deal of port during the two hours or more we sat round the table. If one of us strolling players looked the worse for wear a couple of footmen would come along and help him up to bed.

The echo of Lord Norton's voice, slightly cracked with age, comes back from that August evening as he talks of Queen Victoria: "Yes, I remember when I was at Oxford we all thought her a pretty little gal. Very fond of dancing she was till she settled down. That's what I complain of about the young folks to-day, they don't settle down."

On the subject of smoking Lord Norton was adamant. I was warned by Ruth Adderley, one of his granddaughters, to be careful about this. "One of our friends who was staying at Hams last summer lit a cigarette as he was going out into the garden and grandfather saw him, and when he came in his bags were packed and the trap was waiting to drive him to the station."

"But can't we smoke when we're in the garden?" I asked.

"Oh, of course when you're out in the garden it's all right but this friend lit his cigarette while he was still in the hall."

We gave two riotous performancces in that great garden. I suggested to Sir Andrew Aguecheek that at one moment in the duel scene he should climb up a tree to avoid Viola's rapier. Arthur Eckersley did so but in coming down again he tore his trunks and in his confusion made an exit right into the audience. Another ludicrous incident recurs from that last tour we made with the *Twelfth Night* pastoral.

In those days many undergraduates made a sacred business of colouring a meerschaum pipe. They had to be wiped carefully at intervals when they were sweating because moisture was fatal to the process. Charles Maude had a meerschaum pipe which he was colouring with devotion; one evening instead of leaving it in his dressing-room he walked along to stand by for his entrance, still smoking it. The cue came sooner than he had expected, and on he went along the woodland path.

"Charles," I called after him. "Your pipe!"

He snatched it from his mouth and then paused for an agonized second or two. Alas, he had no pocket in his Elizabethan trunks and hose. He was compelled to take the sacred meerschaum from his mouth and throw it into a clump of very wet nettles.

Harry Pirie-Gordon and I went up to Oxford a week early in order to get our rooms as we wanted them. 43 High was one of two gabled houses between which was a passage, dividing two shops, that led to their respective doors. 43 High was run by Miss Prince and Miss Allen. Miss Prince, known as the Prugger, was a large grim woman of over sixty whom I never saw smile. Miss Allen was about half the age of Miss Prince and very plump. The two of them slept in a double-bed in a room on the left of the only door in to Number 43, opposite which a narrow staircase led up to our sitting-room with its wide projecting window looking out on the High. My bedroom was above Miss Prince and Miss Allen, Harry's bedroom above mine. There was a small w.c. and cupboard on the other side of the passage to our sitting-room. I can see now Miss Prince's face of offended amazement when we told her that we wanted the gas cut off in our part of the house.

"The gas cut off?" she gasped. "You'll do no such thing. Miss Allen and me aren't going to be bothered with messy lamps."

"We aren't going to have lamps. We're going to have candles."

And candles we did have. Big wax altar candles on the chimney shelf, candles in brass sconces, and by our chairs reading candles which we took up to bed with us every night. The staircase and the passage were lighted by sanctuary lamps with floating wicks. The dining-room table was also candlelit.

"And all the pictures in every room must be taken down," we said.

"Not Nebuchadnezzar's Feast," Miss Prince exclaimed, gazing with pride at a large steel engraving of that calamitous event hanging above the fireplace. We had no mercy on Nebuchadnezzar's Feast. We covered the hideous wallpaper with a green tapestry on which were golden fleurs-de-lys and griffins' heads. Our pictures were Arundel prints; they would have been Medici prints if the society had then existed. The triptych screen that framed Memling's Crucifixion is still in one of my rooms to-day. I can best recapture the pleasure those digs of ours in 43 High gave me when I was twenty by some extracts from an article I wrote that autumn in *The Oxford Point of View*: it was called 'The Undergraduate's Garden,' inspired by Xavier de Maistre's journey round his room and the prose of Walter Pater:

"Xavier de Maistre took forty-two days and four times as many pages to complete the circuit of a room which combined the stimulating surroundings of the library with the discretion and quieter atmosphere of the bedroom. To me there is always something slightly indelicate in the idea of a combined apartment, something suggestive of eked-out fortnights at Margate. . . . A bedroom should be the body's hermitage. . . . The masculine bedroom should contain properly no more than a bed, a bath, and a window open to receive the invigorating currents of fresh air; yet I am prepared to concede to the luxurious an unvarnished washstand, even a dressing-table, on the definite understanding that it should never be used as a beach to gather and to garner the flotsam and jetsam of the day's idleness and the day's work. I hold it unseemly that the frail face of the morning should smile its welcome upon the appendages of a dead yesterday—'ces regards flétris par la veille' in the words of M. Coppée. Let a monastic ideal of decoration accord with the monastic scheme of architecture under which for so many years all Oxford bedrooms were built; have no querulous pattern weeping on your walls, nor let your lids flutter into sleep to the tune of a dancing design; just as the careful diner will not disturb the mechanical alternations of his fork between plate and mouth in a vain attempt to track the fugitive steps of a *leit-motif*. . . . If you must have photographs of your friends and of your friends' friends in groups whose composition would offend a Doré, let them never trespass without the threshold of the dining-room. Should it happen that fickle chance beggar you of eating companions, the solitude of your meal will be made less noticeable if you sit surrounded by the conventional figures of your friends. . . . You may reflect how purposeless is this photography which presents you with starched marionettes for living souls, and whose only contribution to beauty lies in the elimination of a too predominant mole. . . . And this hearth, round which in post-prandial security you coin apparelled paradox and postulate unchallenged aphorism, take care that it be in itself deserving of these sacrosanct confidences. See to it that this illuminated shrine which we may not unfairly salute as the ὄμφαλος of the room, has its presiding genius, its Delphic priestess. Few would wish to refuse La Gioconda the place of honour; she 'upon whose head all the ends of the world are come', may appropriately sit enthroned on the chimney shelf with her elusive smile, her arms folded so suggestively as she watches the fruitless efforts of man to see in the flame his own fiery soul. Flank her not with college shields, as did the hero of a lately published ephemeral novel, but with two austere pieces of blue or green china of antique shape and wrought by hand. Sometimes, when you are tired of the realities of life you may light two tall wax candles, and as the shadows flicker across her subtle countenance, freshen your mind with cool dreams of dead ambitions and old beliefs. . . .

"And what background will you choose for your goddess? That must depend on your interpretation of the picture. If with Pater, whom it would be mere impertinence in me to praise, you regard her as summing up in her expression all the periods of the world's history, then let her rest against a tapestry of eyeless blue infinite and invariable. But if (and this is my personal belief) you hold her to be the consummation of what men call mediaevalism, and her smile to be the cynical expression of faith which knowing all knows the folly of what men call knowledge, then let her rest against a dim green arras figured with fantastic beasts and golden flowers; such arras as might have hung in long forgotten castles whose topmost turret peered anxiously above the changeless glooms years upon years ago. Mona Lisa has been called 'the painter's picture', and it is a commonplace of criticism to style Spenser 'the poet's poet'. Would not the criticism gain in accuracy what it lost in triteness if we were to reverse the application?

"After the hearth . . . there are many claimants for pride of place in your room. There are the bookshelves, the desk, but before these, I think, we should rank the window and its surroundings. If the gods have been very good to you, your window will be a bay window from which you will be able to gaze along that majestic sweep of buildings not unlike one of the grander reaches of the Thames and called happily enough the High. One may pursue the analogy and say that Queen's Lane has all the quiet charm and inconclusive meandering of one of the Thames backwaters. . . .

"Opposite my desk hangs *Primavera*. Every time I look at it an exquisite emotion thrills me—more intangible than the generality of emotions. I know nothing comparable to it except the feeling I have whenever I read the first few stanzas of St Agnes' Eve. It possesses an almost intoxicating beauty—the oranges in the dark wooded background, the opalescent forms of the Graces, the ground dappled with light flowers, the loose blue robe of the West Wind, and above all the fairy flowery vestment of Spring herself. For the rest, I can see, as I sit writing these words, the calm golden-green sky of Giorgione's Madonna and Child, the angels of Benozzo Gozzoli, the stormy low blue line of sky in Memling's Crucifixion, the kindly austerity of the four saints whose kindliness is typified by the warm red vestment of St Jerome. Further along the wall are the sea-green armour of St

George and the sea-green robe of the Princess in Pisanello's fresco; while at my elbow is the marvellous multitudinous-hued carpet on which in reverend adoration kneel the Meyer family. And all this pleasure you too may have if you will pocket your pride and content your soul with a careful choice of Arundel prints. . . .

"A few more admonitions and I have done. Beware of electric light: it is the symbol of Modernity. Beware, too, of gas; it is a bastard symbol of Modernity, and moreover has a pestilential odour as from some cauldron brewed in a witch's kitchen. Most of all avoid the sonorously named Incandescent variety, which is the symbol of an Anaemic Civilization. Put your faith in good wax candles which smell only when hastily extinguished. . . . And now on this wet weary October night, in this room where the flickering candles make monstrous shadows on the walls, more than ever does the world seem peopled with phantoms; and as I gaze at the lonely street and watch the dark entry which leads towards the front door, I remember it was in just such an entry that François Villon robbed the dead woman on that white fifteenth-century night. I remember too how Gérard de Nerval hanged himself outside the low tavern in the Rue de la Vieille-Lanterne; yet I would have gladly welcomed either in this room. I see no weather-worn homeless poet, and so to bed."

In the August number of *The Oxford Point of View* I had written:

"I cannot understand this sudden attack on motor-cars. If people objected to them because they were ugly and unreliable and noisy or because they did not possess a pleasant smell, I should be in the vanguard of the protestants. Such is not the case, however. They are disliked for their rapidity. They are reviled for their only virtue, their one reason for existence. If twelve men choose to risk their necks I really fail to see what it has to do with Peckham. Chariot races are no longer the mode and therefore all honour to the men who try to revive, if not their outward glory of display, at any rate the spirit that urged men to such risks in the past."

This paragraph was provoked by a silly season correspondence in the Press and meetings all over the place to demand that a speed-limit of 20 miles an hour should be imposed on road motor-races. Coming up that term, I had seen as the hansom reached Carfax a prominent sign MORRIS'S OXFORD GARAGE for which a part of the old Oxford covered market had been used. Some days later I took my bicycle to have a puncture mended into Morris's bicycle shop at 48 High, which was managed by Lord Nuffield's father. "Could you let me have my bike back in an hour? I've got a lecture in Queen's at eleven and I'll call in for it when I get out."

"We're very busy this morning," said Manager Morris, "but leave your machine and I'll see what we can do."

"What's this tremendous place you've just opened, Morris's Oxford Garage? When do you think you're going to fill that with cars?' I asked. And suddenly from the other side of the shop a youngish man with intense dark eyes, the future Lord Nuffield himself, said with a fierce conviction that swept away any possibility of argument: "That garage won't hold the cars that will want it in ten years' time."

I was so deeply impressed by this prophecy that I wrote a paragraph in *The Varsity* which, alas, has not survived among my papers, to say the University must realize that the motor-car would be the transport of the future and that it was the duty of the University and the Mayor and Corporation of Oxford to make an enclave of the University by building a road round the city which would start before Worcester College, cross the Woodstock road and the Banbury road and run on through Cowley Meadows to meet another circular road starting below the Castle and running on through Christ Church meadows to join the main road beyond Magdalen Bridge.

Cowley Meadows to-day have been covered by Morris's works and they are still arguing, as I write these words, about that road through Christ Church meadows. If they do not settle this argument for another sixty years Magdalen Bridge and Magdalen Tower will have fallen down like London Bridge in the nursery rhyme.

The London County Council has been guilty of more acts of vandalism than either the Luftwaffe or the R.A.F. I recall that this very autumn Clifford's Inn with its lovely hall was sold to speculative builders for £100,000; the passive, sluggish vandalism of the University of Oxford in allowing the noblest street in Europe to suffer the equivalent of an actual destruction is not less culpable and if at last Oxford should turn into a red-brick University to match the spiritual and intellectual transformation it is already undergoing only Nemesis will smile.

Soon after that Michaelmas term opened I went into the bookshop of William George's Sons in the High, which was being run during their minority by the brothers Chaundy. "Well," I asked, "how did you enjoy your visit to France with Gynes last vac?"

"Enjoy it?" Leslie Chaundy exploded. "It's the last time my brother and I will ever go abroad with Gynes. We couldn't understand the way everyone was bowing and scraping to Gynes until we found out he'd been calling himself Viscount Gynes and telling everybody we were his valets."

Gynes was the College messenger at Magdalen, whose job it was to bicycle round delivering to addresses in Oxford the various letters from undergraduates he found waiting for him in the lodge. The sender put his initials on the bottom left-hand corner of the envelope and was charged a penny for each one. Gynes had been messenger for over ten years and his golden age was the early 'nineties when Lord Alfred Douglas was bringing out the *Spirit Lamp* from Magdalen and Oscar Wilde was a frequent visitor to his old college. Gynes became a devotee of the 'decadence' and used to enjoy showing me in his room along Cowley Road the volumes he had of Ernest Dowson, Lionel Johnson, Arthur Symons and many other poets of the period, some of them autographed. I can hear his vibrant voice reading with a slight Oxfordshire accent the sonnets of Lord Alfred Douglas which he particularly admired, and presently asking me to excuse him if he took off his boots because his feet were tired after bicycling all over Oxford. The book-collecting side of Gynes and his reminiscences of the 'nineties which interested me so much were not what made him an important figure in the life of the College. For most of the undergraduates it was his prowess at golf. He had the freedom of the links at Hincksey and was in constant demand as a coach. When after the First World War Gunstone retired from the stewardship of the J.C.R. Gynes seemed the only member of the college staff who could succeed so rich a personality as Gunner.

"Well, what do you think of my room now?" the old man asked me when I visited Oxford after the First War and went to call on him at the house of his son, who had the chemist shop underneath our old digs at 43 High. "It's a bit too much like the outside of a chocolate box to my notion."

"I certainly don't see you against that colour scheme, Gunner, but then it isn't you any longer."

"Ah, that horrible war brought many changes. The men aren't the same as the men in my time. Do you know, they don't sing the Magdalen song any more? Well, they don't have any more 'afters' to-day."

How many of those who once joined in the chorus of that song which for us was Auld Lang Syne would sing no more ever again any song!

Let the spirit of the past
Like a mantle round us cast
Be our heritage and glory set before us,
And we'll raise and raise again
The victorious refrain
Of 'Magdalena floreat' in chorus.

I used to have a copy of that old song, and if I can find it before I write Octave Five and am sitting with Bob Boothby in Raymond Wavell's old room in Swither's, underneath my own of twenty years earlier, I shall reprint it for what I am sure will be the incredulous eyes of Magdalen men to-day with no time for the past.

The political question in 1903 was whether Joseph Chamberlain's Tariff Reform would be successful in restoring life to a Unionist party that seemed to be slowly fading away in a lethargic senescence. Maurice Woods, the elder son of the late President of Trinity (who was now Master of the Temple) and Margaret L. Woods, whose novels good though they were never seemed as remarkable as herself, was galvanizing the Canning Club, having resigned from the Russell. With all the fervour of converts to Protection he and other young Tory conspirators were going about muttering fiercely that Balfour must go, just as a quarter of a century hence equally fierce young Tory conspirators would be going about fiercely muttering that Baldwin must go. And as I write these words I have no doubt that fierce young Tory conspirators are going about muttering that Macmillan must go: plotting against their leaders seems to be endemic with Tories. I was firmly for Free Trade, and as Secretary of the Strafford Club never tired of telling Maurice Woods, Henry Lygon and the rest that none of them began to know what a genuine Tory was. I was a Jacobite Tory in the middle of the eighteenth century, who hated a Whig as much as Dr Johnson. Now that the Liberal party looked like emerging from Whiggery I thought I should probably follow Winston Churchill's example and, as it were, cross the floor of the House.

The young member for Oldham came to Oxford sometime that term, and I went to hear him speak at the Corn Exchange. I see him now striding up and down that platform, with reddish curly hair prematurely thinning and a pink cherubic face, in a frock-coat which had evidently been made for him before he went to South Africa and was now definitely on the tight side. At this date he had an impediment in his speech and speaking as he did with the rapidity of a machine-gun his words were often impossible to follow. It did not matter. The force with which he spoke and the vigour of his gestures roused enthusiastic applause whether the audience was able to know just exactly what he was saying or not; certainly I came out of the Corn Exchange that day completely sure that if Great Britain abandoned Free Trade no amount of writing about flannelled fools at the wicket and muddied oafs in the goal by Rudyard Kipling could save the British Empire from ultimate collapse.

Edward Compton as Garrick. From the painting by Herkomer

It had been decided that Ruth and I could not become formally engaged until we were both twenty-one, but that as it must soon be obvious there was what was called an 'understanding' between us we might go for a walk together twice a week. Not long before she died Lady Peck, an elder sister of my dearly loved Ronald Knox, told me that her most romantic memory of that Oxford of long ago was seeing Ruth and me on some of those walks. Neither of us realized at the time that we were playing Ferdinand and Miranda to an interested audience; we were as unconscious of them as if we had indeed both been walking on Prospero's enchanted island. All I can recall is a faint irritation when one of the young women of North Oxford would say, 'I saw you and Ruth yesterday afternoon.'

One of those walks was to Headington to have tea with Miss Rhoda Broughton in her little house only the width of the pavement away from the main road through the village. She was then about sixty with a neat head of iron-grey hair, a clear complexion and bright observant eyes. She had a sharp tongue but she was kind to Ruth and me. Perhaps we reminded her of two of those young people of whose loves she used to write in those earlier novels of hers which had shocked an earlier generation. I recall her saying that afternoon: "I began as Zola and I am ending as Charlotte Yonge."

An absurd trifle which lingers in my memory from that tea-party with Rhoda Broughton is seeing her blow out the spirit-lamp with a sort of pea-shooter. And as we walked homeward down Headington Hill Ruth said she was sure that Rhoda Broughton must have had an unhappy love affair long ago.

Much as I had enjoyed the planning for the house in which the Daniels were going to live I sadly missed that daisied room in Worcester House. I hesitate to say that I had a presentiment of unhappiness, because it is too easy to talk of presentiment in the past. I remember the sharp moment of disappointment in the new sitting-room that was to be Rachel's and Ruth's. Yet, it was a delightful room looking out across the garden to the oldest part of the college.

Every Sunday Mrs Daniel invited various of the Worcester undergraduates to tea, which Rachel and Ruth were inclined to find a bit of an ordeal when the party consisted of freshers. So my help to deal with the problem of putting them at ease was always enlisted. There was one freshman who needed nobody to put him at ease, and this was Oliver Gogarty, who was proposing to add an Oxford degree in medicine to his Trinity College, Dublin degree. He was at least a couple of years older than myself and whatever wit I had been granted paled beside what can fairly be called the dazzling wit of Gogarty. He was Buck Milligan of James Joyce's *Ulysses* and I do not propose to attempt an evocation of Oliver Gogarty when he was in his twenties; his portrait has been painted by a master. I shall have more to say about him in my sixth Octave, when he and I were in our forties. I introduced him in 1903 to Christopher Stone, who was captivated by his ebullient ribaldry and metrical skill.

Christopher was still fluent in verse. He had published while still at Eton a volume of extraordinary accomplishment for a seventeen-year old called *Lusus Pueriles*, and was set on making a name in literature. Even as the threat to my future had been the Civil Service, so the threat to him was schoolmastering. His father, the Revd. E. D. Stone, had been an Eton housemaster and afterwards had had the famous prep. school of Stone House near Broadstairs; his eldest brother, the Rev. Frank Stone, was now a master at Radley; his elder brother E. W. Stone was now a housemaster at Eton; another elder brother, Will Stone, had been master of the Sixth at Marlborough before his early death. Christopher used to confide in me how desperately he was determined not to be a schoolmaster and naturally I supported with fervour such a resolve. We would go to London when we had taken our degrees and, although he would have to get a permanent job if possible on one of the weeklies, and I should have to get through my law exams and be called to the Bar, we would both of us make a name, he by writing novels and I by writing plays. Christopher was deeply in love with a sister of his great friend Robin Buxton, but of course he had no hope of being considered an eligible match for a rich banking family unless he could make a name for himself, and not merely a name but also money. I should not have to compete with money; the Daniels were unworldly and if I could earn enough to keep Ruth in simplicity I ought to be able to count on marrying her within three years.

Meanwhile Christopher and I had to get our degrees. I said that for my fourth year I was proposing to give up the High and retire to the Old Parsonage in Banbury Road, as far as I could get from Magdalen and the temptation of continuous sociability. I should be nearer to Sligger, and in Balliol people understood better the demands of work than they did in Magdalen. I felt confident of a First in History and should have as good a chance as anybody of a Fellowship at All Souls. That would mean £200 a year for seven years, and if my father would allow me £150 a year which was half of what he was forking out now, and if the Provost would allow Ruth £100 a year that would mean

Ruth and I could be married in just over two years' time. Would it not be a good idea if Christopher made up his mind to share digs with me at the Old Parsonage, that mediaeval house which stood in such surprising contrast to the rest of Banbury Road? Would it not be a good idea if Christopher decided to quit Meadows and come to the Old Parsonage for his fourth year? He would be almost as far from the House as I should be from Magdalen. Christopher agreed with me. His Third in Honour Mods had been rather a shock, and somehow he must get at least a Second in Greats.

"You'll never get even a Second," I told him, "if you don't stop bicycling all over Oxford, calling on different people for ten minutes." So we went along to the Old Parsonage and booked our rooms there for October the following year. I was so pleased with the prospect that I called in at Balliol to tell Sligger what I had done.

"This will save me sending you a note," he told me. "I want you to come along on " whatever day it was "and meet an American called Pearsall Smith. Don't be late, because he always goes to bed at nine. He told me he wanted to meet a few young men, but don't mind if he gives you the idea that the last person in the world was yourself." I did not feel I particularly wanted to meet this odd American but I promised to come.

On the way to give my news about the Old Parsonage to the Daniels I saw Horatio Symonds coming out of his house in Beaumont Street. 'Pego' Symonds, as he was known to undergraduates, was the physician to the University and a third cousin of mine, the third of a line of Oxford doctors. I told him about the Old Parsonage and he congratulated me on displaying more common sense than he had thought I possessed. I quoted in my first Octave the extract from John Addington Symonds' fragment of autobiography in which he told how he had destroyed a mass of correspondence from his Puritan ancestors because it depressed him so much. The portraits of some of those Puritan ancestors of his and mine were hanging in Horatio Symonds' dining-room, and a grim funereal lot they were. There was nothing of the Puritan about Horatio; yet I suppose when he made that remark about my common sense it was a tribute to that eighth of me which throughout my life would owe something to its Puritan ancestry.

I cannot remember where it was in Balliol that Sligger's party was held that evening; it was certainly not in his rooms and I think it must have been in the Senior Common Room. I was excited to see Hilaire Belloc there but when I asked Sligger to introduce me I was told that he had gone. "Poor Belloc, he has never forgiven us," said Sligger; he was alluding to Belloc's mortification when Balliol failed to make him a Fellow. "But come along and I'll introduce you to Pearsall Smith."

I saw a tall thin man with a sharp nose and seeming by the way he kept peering about him with fidgetty gestures to be short-sighted. A minute later I was fascinated by his talk. He was in Oxford to gather more material for his book about Sir Henry Wotton, and would be working every day in the Bodleian. So absorbed was I by Pearsall Smith's conversation that I did not hear the first strokes of Tom chiming from Christ Church those 101 slow strokes that signified the hour of nine, after the last of which if an undergraduate was in his own college he could not go out. For Logan Pearsall Smith it was a curfew.

"I must go now," he said, no trace of Philadelphia in that voice of his. "If I talk after nine o'clock I cannot sleep. I suffer from insomnia and when I go away I always bring dark curtains with which to shut out the light in my bedroom and I have to bring with me a special pillow shaped like a small bolster and rather hard." I hesitated a moment and then plunged.

"I suppose you wouldn't have time to come to lunch with me at 43 High?" I asked. To my surprise and gratification Pearsall Smith said he would be glad to come, and that was the beginning of a friendship which had a profound influence over my literary future.

Two or three days later he came and I showed him that article of mine called 'The Undergraduate's Garden.' I see him now peering over the pages and hear him from time to time murmuring aloud to himself the fragment of a sentence.

"Yes, yes, you have it in you. The authentic note of English prose sounds from time to time. Of course, there are all kinds of faults, but faults can be corrected. What matters is the cadence, and I hear the authentic cadence. Concealed alliteration. Variety of broad vowel sounds. For prose or verse both are indispensable, and for prose the cadence, the cadence. Sir Thomas Browne. 'The iniquity of oblivion blindly scattereth her poppy.' And above all to avoid every unnecessary sibilant. Sibilants are the curse of the English language. And that dreadful tintinnabulation of gerunds and present participles. Ing, ing, ing, for ever ings."

Logan Pearsall Smith was the first person to instil in me the austere doctrine of art for art's sake, regarded from the standpoint of a Quaker not as a kind of brilliant paradox in the way it was preached by Oscar Wilde. I owe him an immense debt and, although the moment would come when I should feel bound to disappoint him by attempting larger themes than he believed were any longer worth trying to achieve in hopeless competition with the past of literature, his advice at this stage of my development was of crucial value. To Logan Pearsall Smith I owe primarily my determination sixty years later always to make whatever I write as good as I am capable of making it.

And now it is time to move on to what was for me the fateful year of 1904.

TWENTY-ONE YEARS OLD: 1904

I SPENT my twenty-first birthday at 1 Nevern Square but remember nothing about it except getting £10 from my father which I spent on books to which James Parker added one from himself.

Instead of giving the conventional Twenty-Firster at one of the Oxford hotels or clubs, Harry Pirie-Gordon and I gave a dinner at 43 High to six majors and a minor of which I have the menu. Harry had just taken on the editorship of the *Isis*.

The guests were Harold Hartley, Claude Kirby, Alban Hood, Christopher Stone, Hugh Francis, and Raymond Wavell.

That Saturday night dinner was the first Harry Pirie-Gordon and I gave of many during that Hilary term and Trinity term. We never asked more than six guests and strove to surprise them every time with some remarkable dish. On one occasion we had a roast swan, which was voted uneatable, and on another a roast peahen which was a success. But what we considered our triumph was the boar's head. Dr Sewell, Warden of New College since 1860, had died in the previous autumn and had been succeeded by the famous Spooner, which of course meant that new and obviously mythical spoonerisms were being attributed to him all the time. I feel sure that he never did say at the All Souls' dinner, when the boar's head was carried in with due solemnity, 'There is nothing I like better than a hot and steaming whore's bed', but we liked to think he had when we sat down to our boar's head that night. Nor do I believe that he really ever did embarrass his young lady partner at croquet when, meaning to call out reproachfully 'You've missed the post', he turned that into a spoonerism.

On the other side of the High from us was the shop of Cooper and Son, Italian Warehousemen. Frank Cooper, the son, a good-looking, immensely obliging and very competent young man, presided over that superlative shop. There was no trouble he would not take to discover all sorts of rareties in the way of food. Cooper and Co's Oxford marmalade is still famous and is still better than any other commercial marmalade, but I am glad I knew what it was when it was Cooper and Son's Oxford marmalade.

For those dinners of ours on Saturday nights Harry Pirie-Gordon and I made a point of varying the company as much as the dishes. We would ask a don, a couple of 'aesthetes', a couple of 'hearties', and somebody from our own intimate circle of friends. One of our guests was F. W. Bussell, the Vice-Principal of Brasenose, who stood out as a personality even among the many outstanding eccentrics of that day. He was not only a great classical scholar and the leading authority on mediaeval Latin, he was also a theologian with first class honours, a doctor of divinity and on top of that a doctor of music. His hobby as a parson was the collection of extinct livings swallowed up by the North Sea round the coast of East Anglia. His costume was unusual for an Anglican clergyman. It consisted of a black frogged riding-coat buttoned by the top button over a black silk waistcoat, above which was a white bow-tie and a bowler hat. He had a small waxed moustache. On one of the evenings he dined with us he arrived in galoshes, which he called his *bottines*. It was that evening that he borrowed from me the fifth volume of the *Yellow Book*, which he forgot to return. Many many years later I wrote an article for the quarterly called *Oxford* about the University characters of my time and gave a brief portrait of Bussell. He had retired from academic life to marry and live at Worthing, whence he wrote to say that he had never worn a bowler but that he was horrified to find that fifth volume of the *Yellow Book* in his library and was sending it back immediately. I wrote to apologize for ascribing to him a bowler. A few days later Bussell sent me a snapshot of himself and an undergraduate seated outside some village inn, in which he was wearing a bowler. On the back of it he had written '*Peccavi. F.W.B.*' He used to keep B.N.C. continually amused by the notices he pinned on the board in the lodge. I remember only one of them.

> 'The Vice-Principal learns with horror and bitter remorse that the following gentlemen failed last week to keep the minimum number of chapels, attendance at which is the little all that the College expects.'

Jack Gilliat was the President of the O.U.D.S. this year with Malcolm Hogg as Secretary, Horatio Symonds as Treasurer, and myself with the new office of Business Manager. Malcolm Hogg was responsible for the social side of the club and I was responsible for the play in that February. The allotment of Eights Week to the annual production the previous year had not been as financially successful as we had hoped, and it was decided to revert to the usual date of an O.U.D.S. production in mid-February. The play chosen was *As You Like It*, in which I was to play Touchstone. When this was announced the President of Magdalen asked me to come and see him.

"Don't you think it would be a mistake for you to act in the O.U.D.S. play in view of your Schools?" he asked.

"But I'm not taking Schools till June year, Mr President."

"Well, in view of what I hear about this June, you might want to take your Schools this year," he said, showing those rather large teeth of his in a wide smile. I realized he was referring to my engagement to Ruth, of which Mrs Daniel must have told him.

"But, Mr President, I've taken rooms in the Old Parsonage in Banbury Road for my fourth year and am meaning to work really hard."

"I'm glad to hear it, but it seems to me that it would be wise if you started to work really hard before next autumn. Don't you think you are doing too much outside your work—editing your paper, acting with the O.U.D.S., speaking at debates in various colleges, entertaining people at smoking concerts, and Mr Fletcher tells me not attending his lectures as often as you should be?"

I did not think for a moment that there was any serious intention to deprive me of a fourth year but I decided it would be politic to pay heed to that warning and said that if the President thought it was a mistake for me to act in *As You Like It* I would not do so. He showed his teeth in that smile of his which always seemed a little mechanical.

I was disappointed at having to give up Touchstone, which had been the part older playgoers always associated with my grandfather, but I was soon as much absorbed in my job as Business Manager. On February 4th I appeared as the week's 'Who's Who in the *Varsity*:'

"Mr Mackenzie was born some years before his arrival in Oxford.

"When not playing Rugby football for his college, or lacrosse for ulterior motives, he threw himself heartily into the task of educating the youth of Oxford through the medium of journalism. *The Oxford Point of View* is now well known; and this unique venture in University literature owed its origin and development to the efforts of our hero.

"But what he has already done is nothing to what is to come. Anyone who has heard his dreams for the future may tremble for the fate of an astonished world.

"His character is marked by an extraordinary versatility, which enables him to talk best on those subjects in which he has the least knowledge. His political views are typical of the Strafford Club, of which he was some time secretary.

"The recent disturbances in Morocco are probably due to his meteoric progress through that ill-fated district. The Sultan is still in terror of the return of our modern Crusader.

"If you wish to understand him thoroughly study his clothing."

The allusion to lacrosse above refers to the start of lacrosse at the

University in the previous year. As a former player of lacrosse when St Paul's still played that splendid game in the Lent term I was roped in and in fact played for the University in two or three matches. Then I got a jab in the groin and decided it was not a game to play with beginners. A half-blue was unimaginable in those days, even more unimaginable than the half-blue just awarded for lawn tennis. That 'pat-ball' players should be given a half-blue seemed about as absurd as to grant a half-blue for ping-pong; for all I know ping-pong may have been granted a half-blue by now. That the game of tennis as noble and ancient as the game of golf should provide ping-pong with the name 'table tennis' and that lawn tennis should arrogate to itself 'tennis' without a prefix might make the Kings of Scotland and of England turn in their graves.

The performance of *As You Like It* was a great success and we took over £500. Even that was not enough and it was decided that next year we should have to do a Greek play to get the Club out of debt. I wrote a notice of *As You Like It* for the *Isis* from which I take a few quotes:

"*Charles* (Mr Pirie-Gordon) is better as a wrestler than as an actor. Mr Cadogan is a very charming *First Lord* but a rather uncertain shot. We learn that besides three stags, at least one scene-shifter was severely frightened, and that the backcloth is perforated. Mr Stone is a delightful Amiens and sings his songs exquisitely.

"Miss Rachel Daniel as *Celia* seemed to have stepped out of a Fête Champêtre and brought with her all the grace of the olden times. She acts as well as she looks."

The Mr Cadogan who played the First Lord was Alec Cadogan,[1] who although only in his first year at Balliol was already equipped to be an ambassador anywhere. The O.U.D.S. recognized his diplomatic quality and elected him President in the following year. Christopher Stone's success as Amiens was a surprise to most people in the University, because they knew him as an immensely popular turn at smoking concerts when he used always to sing falsetto, his star performance being *If no one ever marries me*.

In that week Mr E. Montague Compton Mackenzie of Magdalen was the 259th Isis Idol following immediately after Mr William Temple of Balliol, the future Archibshop of Canterbury.

"There is so much to be said about Mr Mackenzie as he flaunts in our midst to-day, that his earlier effervescences may well be left to the

[1] Rt. Hon. Sir Alexander Cadogan, O.M., G.C.M.G., K.C.B.

imaginative reader. In his third term he started *The Oxford Point of View*, of which he is still Editor; and although all Oxford may not endorse our Idol's personal point of view, that is Oxford's fault.

"His appearances in the O.U.D.S. programmes and at numerous smokers have always been received with enthusiasm. Of his personal appearance little need be said. His precipitous hair, keen and vivid features, yellow tie, green shirt and conspicuous attire are well known to most of us; and no small circle of friends is familiar with his courteously barbaric manners, his mediaeval room at 43 High, and his admirable library. But those who know him best wonder most at the fact that though he has so large a mind yet he knows it thoroughly; and, with an imagination which staggers reason and a sense of humour which gravels it, he never fails to brace and to exhaust the pedestrian intelligence.

"The fecundity of his ideas is better understood in the reflection that so many of them pass away and vanish. His crowded interests and occupations are almost unhealthy in their exuberance; and when he can find time to devote more than five minutes to a new conception, the results of his industry will become palpable. His literary work is sometimes thrashed out after four or five discarded beginnings. but more often feverishly committed to paper in crepuscular handwriting as the ideas bristle, and it is no unusual occurrence for him to write an article for *The Oxford Point of View* after a late breakfast, go to a lecture, reorganize the O.U.D.S., and buy a new edition of Rabelais —all in one morning.

"From all of which it may be gathered that our Idol is self-confident, so unaffectedly self-confident that he carries conviction. Unlike many of his friends, he does things, not because other people do not do them, but because he thinks they are best done in his particular way, He has of course his peculiarities of thought, attire, and action, and would be the last to wish for their mitigation. His lightning discrimination has stood him in good stead in his exploration into the purlieus of mediaevalism, literature, art, drama, and whatever else attracts his interest or fancy.

"To penetrate even deeper into the recesses of Mr Mackenzie's character, it may be said that he is at once strikingly old and startingly young. Hardly a thought passes through his brain but comprehends some grand prospect: he is a born organizer of theory, aware of infinity no less than of detail, an inspiring and inspired optimist. Nothing seems impossible as pictured by him, for eloquence vivifies his imagination. In debate his oratory is overwhelming, and in the bombardment of personalities his humour is most richly displayed. But when all is said and done there remains the fact that he is very young; and when such words as 'cocksure' and 'boyish enthusiasm are whispered, the wiseacre smiles sedately."

I must admit after reading that Idol I am not surprised that about this time my mother said she wondered if Monty would ever do anything except go round the world amusing people. Anyway, it is reassuring to read in the *Isis* of 57 years later that "the grand old man of *Sinister Street* is the most delightful author alive" because it encourages me to suppose that I can still amuse the undergraduate of to-day as presumably I was able to amuse them when I was twenty.

Years and years after this, just before the last war, I was in Oxford and went to see Miss Allen who must have been nearly 70 by then.

"Oh, you was cunning," she said. "Do you remember that night you come back from some dinner and found your bed heaped up with books? You come right downstairs and into the room where me and Miss Prince slept. And you said 'Miss Allen' you said, 'are those books on my bed mine or Mr Pirie-Gordon's?' And I said 'they're Mr Pirie-Gordon's,' and you went right upstairs and threw them all out of your bedroom window. Oh, you was cunning! And Miss Prince was that annoyed. 'Miss Allen,' she said because she always called me Miss Allen even when we was in bed together, 'of all the lodgers we've ever had there's none of them given me such trouble as that Mr Mackenzie.' But I liked it, though I didn't dare tell Miss Prince so at the time. I reckon it's never been the same at 43 since you and Mr Pirie-Gordon left."

Harry and I were always thinking out 'good jokes'; one of them was expensive. I dropped a brogue from our dining-room window on the head of a policeman who was standing below. He picked it up and went off with it to the House where J. L. Myres[1] was now the Junior Proctor. A messenger left a note at 43 to say Mr Myres would like to see Mr E. M. C. Mackenzie of Magdalen at nine o'clock to-morrow morning.

When I got to Myres's rooms in Christ Church he was sitting there with my brogue under his Assyrian beard.

"Is this your shoe, Mr Mackenzie?"

"Yes, sir."

"Two guineas."

"What for?"

[1] The late Sir John Myres.

"Assaulting the city police with this shoe."

"It was an accident. Surely one can't be fined two guineas because one's brogue slips when one is pulling it off and falls out of a window."

"Two guineas," Myres repeated.

I paid up.

"And here is your shoe," he said, impassive as one of his own excavated figures when archeologizing in Asia Minor.

We shall meet Myres again in 1916.

By now Pearsall Smith had persuaded me that if I wished to be the writer of poems and plays I aspired to be it was essential I should withdraw from the world and test my vocation for literature as sternly as if I were testing a vocation for the monastic life. Christopher Stone, who had also come under the influence of Pearsall Smith, agreed to share with me a cottage in a remote countryside. I think it must have been Orlo Williams who told us of a cottage to let in Burford which had been rented for a while some years previously while the house his father had bought in Taynton, two miles away on the road to Stow-on-the-Wold, had been got ready for their occupation. Christopher and I bicycled the 18 miles from Oxford to Burford, and as we turned off from the road to Cheltenham another 18 miles west and rode down that wide ancient main street of the little town I thought, whatever the cottage is like, here must I live.

Nobody who visits Burford to-day, that tranquil street defiled by rows of parked cars, its outskirts suburbanized by small houses, can hope to feel the spell that Burford could cast. At the bottom of the High Street, just before the fifteenth-century bridge over the Windrush, was a line of almshouses called Wysdom after the Symon Wysdom who had endowed them in the sixteenth century. We crossed that ancient bridge with its angular nooks on either side, the refuge to-day for pedestrians when motor cars hoot angrily at having to slow down for such a ridiculously narrow bridge. Beyond this were two houses with a wooden gateway between them, through which one passed into a garden filled with ancient espalier apple-trees, mostly Ribston pippins, at the end of which was a small Elizabethan house lengthened at either side by wings added later. The house had been divided, two thirds of it forming the cottage which Christopher and I contemplated renting, the other third lived in by the owner. Over the door of the original house was the original carved stone hood: over the door immediately next to it was a modern hood of the same size but uncarved. The owner was a grumpy old gentleman called Sylvester, the last of a long line of Sylvesters, one of whom had built the Lady Chapel in Burford's magnificent church. Hence the name Ladyham—Our Lady's field by the water. Those fields by the water begin at Petersham just beyond Richmond, and westward of that every suffix 'ham' implies the vicinity of water. Eastward, beginning with Hampstead, every suffix of 'ham' is the equivalent of 'home'.

Ladyham was indeed a field by the water. From the millpool on the right of the bridge looking up the High Street a wide millstream flowed along between the churchyard and the orchard behind Ladyham, from which the narrow Windrush flowed round the back of the house; a privy of fine design at the back of our cottage was served by the Windrush, which was crossed by a small bridge at the Sylvesters' back door opposite which was a barn.

In our cottage there was a dining-room on the left of the narrow entrance hall, with a kitchen next to it. Upstairs was a large sitting-room with a wide bay-window overlooking the orchard on one side and another window looking westward up the valley of the Windrush. Beyond this were two bedrooms, and a small curved staircase ascended to a little bedroom with a dormer-window in the roof, which Christopher immediately decided should be his. Two ancient espalier pear trees covered our side of the house and another covered the sister cottage. There was a well beside a sycamore tree in front, from which we would draw our water, and a small semicircle of garden surrounded by a low railing. Moreover, besides this we should have the little walled bee-garden on the other side of the ten-acre water-meadow on the southern slope of the rising ground. There were plums and that best of all gages, Jefferson's Drop, growing against the three walls, but no longer any bee-hives.

We asked old Sylvester what rent he required, and were told £14. 10s a year to which would be added £2 for the rates. We at once agreed to take the cottage on a three-year lease.

In the seventh week of the Hilary term there was an examination for those taking Honour Schools, at the end of which the various dons, all sitting round the High Table in hall with the President at the head of it, made remarks complimentary or otherwise about the result.

"It's useless for him to stay up for a fourth year," said Fletcher when my turn came to hear the result of what were called the Easter collections, or 'colleckers' as we called them.

"Well, I did warn Mr Mackenzie earlier in the term, Mr Fletcher, that he seemed to be interested in too many things that would interfere with his work for his Schools," said the President.

"He doesn't seem to have paid much attention to your warning, President," said Fletcher.

"I gave up acting in the O.U.D.S. play," I protested angrily. "And I told you, Mr President, that I had taken rooms in the Old Parsonage in order to be able to work really hard for a First next year."

"He has no chance of a First. He'll be lucky if he gets a Third in his Finals in June," Fletcher snapped.

"Did Mr Urquhart make that prophecy?" I asked.

"Mr Urquhart in Balliol has no say in what we decide in Magdalen."

I felt my heart beginning to beat and the blood draining from my cheeks with anger.

"I'll make a prophecy to you, Mr Fletcher. I obviously can't get a First for you with hardly more than two months to get it, but I shall try to get you a Second because it's the only Second you *will* get this year, and if you had let me stay on for my fourth year I should have got you the only First you will get next year."

The President, smiling his toothy smile, intervened before Fletcher could reply.

"Well, I think I can promise you that if you do get a Second the College will be glad to let you stay up another year and read for the new Honours School of English Literature."

"Oh no, Mr President, if I go down in June I shall go down for good. I cannot afford to waste my time working for the College to get a First in English Literature to make up for its not getting a single First in History."

I think the President may have felt some qualms, because the next time he went to see the Daniels Ruth told him how unjust he had been. Then Warren told her he had not intervened with Fletcher on my behalf because he had thought it would be better for me, in view of my forthcoming engagement to her, if I started at once to think seriously of my career.

"And I told him," said Ruth, "that your career had nothing to do with anybody except you and me."

Soon after that the President told me he had had a letter from St Loe Strachey to say that John Buchan was leaving the staff of the *Spectator*, where he was acting as number two to C. L. Graves, in order to edit the *Johannesburg Star*, and that he was looking out for a young man to take his place. "And if you get a Second in your Schools," he said with that wide smile, "I shall write and suggest your name to Mr Strachey."

"I do not agree with the *Spectator*'s attitude, Mr President, and if I did go in for journalism it is the last paper with which I should want to be associated."

Two or three parties had been made up to visit the proposed retreat of Christopher and myself; it had received the blessing of Logan Pearsall Smith, who had presented us with a diamond pencil so that, instead of inscribing their names in a book, visitors' could scratch them on one of the big panes of the bay-window in what old Mr Sylvester called the drawing-room. George Montagu came to stay in Oxford some time early in March bringing with him Robert Whitworth Jones. 'Bobbie' Whitworth Jones was on the London stage and had been playing the young lover in Pinero's play *Iris*, in which Oscar Asche was the brutal husband. He was a tall extremely emotional and lovable character who had been at Radley, to which he was passionately devoted; he had been a pupil of Christopher's elder brother, Frank Stone. He and George Montagu accompanied us on one of those Burford expeditions, when Whitworth Jones discovered that one of the houses on either side of the gate into Ladyham was to let, and he and George Montagu decided to take it. George was still an M.P. and felt that he needed an occasional complete rest from political life and the wear and tear of London 'Society'.

Then in May the blow fell. Old Mr Sylvester had a stroke, tumbled into the river behind the house and was drowned. We were notified that both leases would be cancelled and that the Ladyham estate, consisting of the two houses at the entrance to Ladyham itself and the twelve acres of land, would be put up for auction in July provided no previous offer had been made and accepted.

"You must buy it," Bobbie Whitworth Jones declared.

"Buy it?" I exclaimed. "How do you think Polly and I can do that?"

"Never mind about Polly Stone; you must buy it. I have asked the solicitor what offer he thought would be acceptable and he told me that £1500 would probably be accepted. You can offer £1400 and I'm pretty sure that would secure the place. Then I will buy a half-share from you."

"And where on earth do you think I'm going to find £1400?" I asked.

"You will insure your life for £2000 and borrow the money giving your policy as security to the London and Counties Bank."

The blow to all my plans that leaving Ladyham would mean made me what must be called reckless. I approached some insurance company, I forget which, with a view to taking out a life policy for £2000. Another blow fell. The insurance company did not consider my life had enough promise of lasting long enough to risk insuring. Their doctor obviously thought I was a likely victim for tuberculosis. In 1903 tuberculosis was still a major threat, and I believe that the success with which the doctors have almost mastered tuberculosis is one reason for the increase of lung cancer. Those who would otherwise have died of tuberculosis when young now live on to the time when cancer attacks age and it is their weak spot which cancer attacks.

Bobbie Whitworth Jones was not in the least discouraged when he heard of the refusal of a policy to me.

"You must insure Pirie-Gordon's life and he will make over the policy to you as a security."

So Harry Pirie-Gordon's life was insured, and to cut a long story short I was able to buy Ladyham for £1400, of which Bobbie Whitworth Jones found half. I never can remember the details of financial arrangements, and anyway that is enough about Ladyham for the moment.

In that Easter vac Ruth came to stay with us at Beech, where my mother loved her as much as I hoped she would. So too did my two youngest sisters, Katie and Fay, and indeed all my family. My mother thought it would be wise to write to my father to tell him about my engagement to Ruth in June, and also about my proposal to live in Burford. She would be with him then on tour, and she would explain to him all I had told her about Burford. One of her reasons for joining the C.C.C. was that she and my father were bringing out a new edition of the Compton Birthday Book with two quotations from each play produced by the Compton Comedy Company and the date of the first performance of every one. A souvenir of that new edition remains in a letter from Henry James:

Reform Club
Pall Mall S.W.
Feb. 10th 1904

Dear Mrs Compton,

I was born horribly long ago—long before you and Compton were even dreamed of: on April 15*th* 1843. *But don't let the Birthday Book give me away too much! Be vague about the year!*

May the poor dear "American" shine indeed in some modest corner of it, antidiluvian as he now seems! I look back upon him as on a strange parenthesis of my existence and yet not unkindly—and quite romantically. And I should still

Ladyham

43 High Street

like nothing better than to write another play if I could afford it! With kind remembrances to Newman. [My father's part in The American]

Yours most truly

Henry James

The letter I wrote to my father has also survived in the same packet, but like most of my letters in youth undated. So were many of Henry James's letters when he was younger. The careful dating of letters may be a sign of age; to-day mine are always given day, month and year.

I expect you have already guessed that I was much in love with Ruth Daniel. I am going to be engaged to her in June. Of course that does not mean immediate marriage or anything you would consider foolish but I cannot be grateful enough for the splendid influence she has had over me, an influence which has shown itself very strongly in all my work since last June—an influence which I think you would notice at once were you to see me now. . . . I should have told you before but knew you were worried with productions etc and so hesitated to give you any more to think about.

This year I intend (with your approval) to live at Burford. . . . The cottage is quite ideal and the rent including a walled garden some 100 yards from the house is £16 in all. This will be much cheaper and healthier than living in London. I propose to take it on a three-years' lease and go straight there in June. I am going to live with a man called Stone, who is taking up literature as a profession. We are going to borrow a good deal of furniture at first. I shall come up to town to eat dinners and to theatres four times a year, enough to keep me in touch with things but not enough to be distracted by the world. It will be two years before I have finished my dinners but I shall take my bar exams soon and be ready to be called when the time comes. I intend to specialize in Ecclesiastical Law and Canon Law and shall write on law to earn a name. I have in my head two plays, a book of essays, and a novel out of which I hope to make a name. I have had an offer for a mediaeval play which if good enough a man is willing to back, and I should very much like to write you a mediaeval play with a part for yourself.

Now as to money. I want you to give me the £300 you would have given if I had stayed up for a fourth year, for that year beginning in June. That will pay my debts at Oxford, keep me for a year and leave enough to pay for some furniture. After that I want you to allow me £150 which will include everything and is not as much as would be necessary in London. . . . I am working so hard for my Schools that I hardly know how to endure it. I hope to scrape a second but of course a year suddenly taken off throws things out of gear.

I do not know what those two plays were going to be about, but I do vaguely recall walking along the Broad with James Elroy Flecker (who had been introduced to me by John Mavrogordato) and telling him about a trilogy I was momentarily inspired to write under the influence of Merejkowski's *Death of the Gods*. I seem to see Flecker's bullet head nodding in slow approbation of my theme, but that theme has vanished from my memory. Yes, that letter shows how just the writer of that Isis Idol was when he called me very young. I recall round about now hearing somebody say what a fantastic success it had been for young Hubert Henry Davies to have two plays running in the West End at his age. This referred to *Cousin Kate* and *Mrs Gorringe's Necklace*.

"Young?" I exclaimed. "Young? You surely don't call twenty-four young?" I was already feeling very old at twenty-one.

We were all much shaken when a day or two after we went back to Oxford for that summer term we found every hatter in the place had filled his window with the 'new motoring-caps', which were much like any cap you see to-day. I myself had been considering whether I would not venture to invest in a Trilby hat to celebrate abolishing the brief fashion of parting one's hair in the middle and following a fashion started by Gilbert Wills,[1] now in his fourth year at Magdalen, of brushing one's hair back without a parting. There was only one man in Magdalen who wore a Trilby hat. This was Charles Prescott,[2] but he was now in his fourth year and had come up two years older than any body else after having had to give up the 10th Hussars for his health. I did not feel I could compete with Charles Prescott, always immensely amiable as he was to his juniors. I was less taken with the 'new motoring-caps'; indeed, we all declared them to be unfit for civilized wear. The first Magdalen man that bought one was Henry Lygon.

"My god!" exclaimed somebody looking out of our window at 43. "Look at Henry Lygon in one of those bloody awful new motoring-caps!"

And sure enough there was Henry in a motoring-cap of a light Lovat tweed walking along on the other side of the High on his Lygon toes. I need hardly add that we were soon all wearing those 'bloody awful motoring-caps'.

It was on Friday April 29th that Henry came into 43 High one morning wearing one of the new collars of the same pattern as the shirt. Whatever I may have done to shock Oxford by wearing a green shirt with a yellow tie I always wore a white collar. We ragged Henry about his non-white collar and Harry Pirie-Gordon tickled him while we took it off.

[1] The late Lord Dulverton. [2] The late Sir Charles Prescott, Bt.

This was the time when the popular Press was full of the Guards 'ragging' scandal, when some poor subaltern was supposed to have been mercilessly treated by his fellow officers. "I'm going to write to the *Daily Mail* about your collar, Henry," I told him and forthwith wrote the following letter:

Sir,

May I call the attention of your valuable paper to a gross case of ragging at Oxford in which the brother of a well-known Liberal peer was held down and severely bitten in the legs, stomach and ribs by three gentlemen (sic) merely for wearing a white collar with blue lines round it.

Yours faithfully,
M. C. Mackenzie

43 *High Street,* *April* 29
Oxford.

"You don't suppose, Monty, do you, that they'll print that tosh?" Henry Lygon scoffed.

"We'll see," I told him.

The next day was Saturday and, as it happened, Harry Pirie-Gordon and I were not giving our usual Saturday night dinner. I had probably made up my mind to have an industrious evening with the First or Third Crusade. Just before seven I went into 43 High to get my gown for dining in hall. I was greeted by Miss Allen.

"Oh, there's been a gentleman here from the *Daily Mail*, Mr Mackenzie. He says it's very important for him to see you and he give me his card. He's coming back at half-past seven." I looked at the card and read '*Mr Frank Dilnot. Daily Mail.*'

"When he comes back, Miss Allen, show him up to our room and give him some Grand Marnier." Grand Marnier was the fashionable sweet liqueur in Oxford at this date. "I'll come back the moment hall is over."

In hall I quickly improvized a scene for the *Daily Mail*, with suitable parts for people to play in it and know they were to play them. Then Harry and two or three others hurried back with me to 43 High, where we found Mr Frank Dilnot deep in the basket-chair into which Miss Allen had shown him. Mona Lisa with her enigmatic smile was eyeing him from between the two big wax candles. The sanctuary lamps on either side of the fireplace were burning in their little crimson glass bowls. On the tapestried walls the golden fleur de lys and griffins glowed dimly in the shadows. I lighted the candles in the brass sconces to give more light, for I could see that Mr Dilnot was ill at ease in such an unfamiliar setting.

"And you say that ragging in Oxford is even more serious than the stories we have been hearing about the Guards?"

"It's much more widely spread," I assured him. "Well, there are so many things one can be ragged for in Oxford." Mr Dilnot by now had taken out his note-book.

"For instance if an undergraduate wears a top-hat with a gown he may be ragged. If he wears patent-leather boots in his first term he may be ragged. They're very down on anybody who breaks the strict rules of dress. That was what upset them when Lord Beauchamp's brother wore that white collar with blue lines round it. I wrote to the *Daily Mail* about his being bitten."

"I know. That is why the Editor sent me down to Oxford to investigate."

"Up," I said.

"Up?"

"Yes, we always talk of going up to Oxford. If anybody said down to Oxford, he would certainly be ragged."

I went on to invent more and more imaginary rags for more and more ridiculous reasons while as fast as he could Mr Dilnot made notes. The others occasionally made faces at me to warn me against becoming too tall with my stories and making the reporter suspicious. I paid no attention. Then I said in a grave voice: "But what is really bad for the University is that any undergraduate who tries to work is almost inevitably ragged. Only last week a man had his room completely wrecked merely because he refused to make up a four at bridge and said he had to work."

"Do they ever indulge in—er—corporal punishment?"

I realized he was hopeful of titillating readers with a paragraph about corporal punishment, which had been a feature of the famous Guards' ragging scandal; I decided to disappoint him.

"No, I've not heard of any corporal punishment being inflicted. Debagging of course is frequent."

"Debagging?"

"Taking off a chap's trousers."

"Which would involve exposure of course?"

"Oh, not if he was wearing a shirt of the usual length. No, no, if a chap has been debagged he'll be allowed to pick up his trousers and go off to his room to put them on again. No, I don't consider debagging a threat to morals. But what is really serious is the growing feeling against the Rhodes scholars. And the *Daily Mail* is partly to blame for that."

"The *Daily Mail*?" Mr Dilnot exclaimed. "But surely the *Daily Mail* has always supported Mr Cecil Rhodes' wonderful bequest."

"That's the trouble. A lot of people have resented your saying that the advent of the Rhodes scholars would transform a provincial University into an Imperial one. We do not consider ourselves a provincial University."

"I'll call the Editor's attention to that," Mr Dilnot promised.

"Yes, I hope you will. There was a nasty riot last week in the Cowley Road and frankly I'm afraid we're going to see more rioting soon. It may become very serious. We don't want to upset Mr Rudyard Kipling again. He's only just beginning to get over the shocks he had in the Boer War. After all, we are patriotic in Oxford. You may remember that when Mr Lloyd George came to address a meeting here during the war he had to escape from the hall, disguised as a policeman."

My tales were interrupted by the entrance of an Etonian demy called Leach, who came staggering into the room with a pile of about a dozen books. I had cast Leach for this part because of the normal pallor of his complexion.

"They won't let me work. They won't let me work. Oh, do let me work here in peace."

Harry Pirie-Gordon rose to his full height. looking exactly like himself as Charles the Wrestler in *As You Like It*.

"Don't be afraid, Leach. You can work in peace here and nobody is going to rag you in *this* room. But you'll be quieter upstairs in the dining-room where you can spread out your books on our dinner-table."

"Oh, thanks awfully, Pirie-Gordon. I'll go up and start working at once." And Leach went out of the room with his pile of books.

No sooner had he left than Hugh Francis came in, wearing his Leander blazer and pink Leander tie, which as cox of one of the Trial Eights he had earned the right to wear.

"Look here, you chaps, you've got to help me. They're after me! I want to work and they say I've got to go out and cox the Eight. I can't go out tonight with the Eight. I must read about Spinoza's Categorical Imperative, or am I muddling up Spinoza with Kant? I was coxing the Eight all this morning and all this afternoon, and I'm getting in such a muddle over my work. I must be allowed to work to-night."

Harry Pirie-Gordon as Charles the Wrestler reassured him: "You're not going out with the Eight. *We'll* see to that, Francis."

At this moment we heard angry shouts above the tramp of feet along the entry below, and presently there burst into the room half a dozen of the rowing 'push', C. A. Willis in the van. 'Chunky' Willis, who was the bow of the University Eight and would one day be Governor of the Nile Provinces in the Sudan Civil Service, demanded in ferocious tones: "Where is that little cur Francis?" Then he thrust out his chest and beat upon it like a gorilla with clenched fists. "Ah, there you are, you little squirt! Come out and cox the Eight, you little worm. If you don't come out at once we're going to rag you." The other members of the rowing 'push' growled in menacing approval of Chunky's threat.

"Stay where you are, Francis," said Harry Pirie-Gordon. "Nobody will dare to rag you here." And with this Harry began to roll up his sleeves and became more like Charles the Wrestler than ever.

"And this is Mr Frank Dilnot who is investigating ragging at Oxford for the *Daily Mail*," he said. The rowing 'push', muttering to one another, retired.

"It was certainly lucky for Mr Francis that *you* were here, Mr Pirie-Gordon," said Mr Dilnot. "Yes, thank you, I will have one more Grand Marnier, and then I must hurry to get the last train back to London." He had barely swallowed the liqueur and put his notebook in his pocket than we heard again the tramp of feet and angry shouts in the entry followed by loud knocks on the door of 43 High.

I ran out and called "Bolt the door, Miss Allen. Don't let anybody in." Then I came back into the room and said, "I'm awfully sorry, Mr Dilnot, but I'm afraid they are determined to rag you."

"What am I do to?" Mr Dilnot gasped.

"There's only one thing you can do," I told him. "You must escape before they break down the door."

"Escape? But how?"

"We'll let you down out of the window by a sheet. Harry, go and get a sheet as quick as you can before the door gives way."

A few moments later we let Mr Dilnot down into the High out of our window, and the last view we had of him was running past Queen's College toward the station in the moonlight.

The general verdict of those who had been present was that as usual I had overdone it, and that inevitably on his way back to London the reporter would realize that the whole evening must have been a hoax. I maintained that Mr Frank Dilnot would not have allowed himself to be let down into the High by a sheet if he had suspected a hoax. And I was right.

On Monday May the 2nd there was a column and a half in the *Daily Mail* about ragging at Oxford, in which many of the stories I had told Mr Dilnot were reproduced, though nothing was said about Mr Dilnot's own escape. In no time at all copies of the *Daily Mail* were at a premium and were being sold for sixpence a piece. Here is some of what was published:

DAILY MAIL Monday, May 2 1904

"RAGGING" AT OXFORD

Some Experiences of Undergraduates

Causes of the Craze

A few days ago a letter reached the 'Daily Mail' office from an Oxford undergraduate who described the punishment inflicted on a fellow undergraduate and who went on to state that "ragging" at the University was general. A representative of the 'Daily Mail' was thereupon sent to Oxford to investigate, and he found the case to be understated rather than overstated.

A handsome young giant, sixteen stone in weight, who had been at the University three years, and whom no one would ever think of "ragging", lay back in a comfortable arm-chair in his rooms after dinner in Hall, and explained, while a college friend put in occasional remarks.

"This week there was a very bad case," he said. "The young brother of a well-known peer was held down by three undergraduates, and he was then bitten severely in the legs and ribs. The offence for which this punishment was inflicted was the wearing of a collar with blue lines upon it; Oxford etiquette requires a white collar."

Here is a list of some of the "offences" which lead to "ragging":—

Wearing patent leather boots during first year at Oxford.

Carrying a walking-stick when in cap and gown.

Wearing silk hat.

Wearing cap and gown except when unavoidable.

Lack of hospitality.

Lack of money.

Showing signs of hard study.

Provincial accent.

While the two undergraduates were explaining matters a third walked into the room. He was a man who had actually been "ragged". "It's no laughing matter," he said. My sin is that I am studying hard for an examination. Their latest exploit was to try and smoke me out. I awoke at half-past two the other morning feeling half stifled, and found the room full of smoke. They had lighted a smouldering fire outside under my window."

DRAMATIC INTERRUPTIONS

The speaker's story was interrupted by the boisterous entry of two noisy undergraduates, typical "raggers". They gave a cheery greeting to the owner of the rooms, and walking up to the man who had just been speaking, sneeringly swore at him. He smoked on philosophically, They made sarcastic inquiries as to how his work was progressing, and then twisted his chair round violently. As they were only two to one, and as there would have been the young giant who occupied the rooms to reckon with, they did nothing more for the time, and left as abruptly as they came.

Five minutes later there was another dramatic interruption. Continual shouts and a sound of running came from the court below. Then somebody dashed in at the door of the undergraduate's rooms and rushed up the stairs, followed by what appeared to be a howling mob. Panting and excited the fugitive knocked entreatingly at the door ."Open quick," he cried. His pursuers were on his heels.

The young giant flew to the door, opened it, and allowed a fair-haired young fellow in cap and gown to enter, and then shut it in the face of the mob which had now reached the landing. The stranger staggered in exhausted.

A fusillade of blows rattled against the door, and there were loud and angry shouts of "Let us in," and "Where is he?" "Let's get at him." "We'll wait for him."

The fair-haired young man uttered an earnest benediction. He had escaped a "ragging" by a hair's breadth.

"To what do you attribute your immunity from 'ragging'?" asked the interviewer of the undergraduate who occupied the rooms.

The young giant shrugged his huge shoulders carelessly.

"I get on very well with them all," he said. "Besides, I used to take an interest in heavy-weight boxing."

The *Daily Mail* started to print fantastic letters from correspondents about ragging, and then two days later the correspondence stopped abruptly.

The reason for this was that the *Daily Express* found out about the hoax and devoted a column to shedding crocodile's tears over such unkindness to a great paper. Here is an extract:

"There is much indignation in 'Varsity circles at Oxford at the action of certain ingenious but misguided undergraduates who have seen fit to inveigle a great metropolitan newspaper—the 'Daily Mail' —into printing a story about 'ragging' at one of the colleges.

"The sympathy with the 'Daily Mail' is the more widespread because of the fact that the very means which made the hoax possible was the earnest endeavour of our contemporary to probe the matter and find out the truth.

There is no possible reason for hilarity in a matter of such grave import touching upon the prerogatives of the Press in the gathering of news."

Commiseration with the *Daily Mail* was hardly apparent that evening when the *Star* reported what had happened under the headlines

SHANGHAIED
Daily Mail Frogmarched
by Oxford Undergraduates

In those days the *Daily Express* was a struggling halfpenny paper with a small circulation and no influence at all. The *Daily Mail* tried to pay them out for those crocodile's tears by hoaxing the *Daily Express* with a story about a baby's being carried off by an eagle in the wilds of Sutherland, and then condoling with the *Daily Express*. It fell flat, however, because so few people read the *Daily Express* in 1904.

If I had had a head that was easily turned it might have been spinning round like a top by now, so often was I called upon to tell the story of the *Daily Mail* rag. I recall a dinner with the Daniels when Dr Merry, the Rector of Lincoln, was one of the guests. No man could have had a more appropriate surname, for with his jovial bearded face he was merriment incarnate and the leading exponent of Aristophanes. He laughed and laughed when I was made to tell the story after dinner and declared that it was as good as a scene from Aristophanes himself. Another guest that night was C. L. Shadwell, the translator of Dante who had been Walter Pater's intimate friend. He was not yet Provost of Oriel but still Censor of the Lodging Houses. Shadwell had a large smooth face along which never a ripple of humour played. He had a habit of holding up his hand as a signal for the other guests at a dinner-table to keep silent while he spoke. Having made this gesture, he leaned over the table to ask me why undergraduates persisted in walking along the gutter in the High to the great inconvenience of people like himself who always preferred the edge of the pavement and were therefore continually being jostled.

"Well, I suppose some of us walk along the edge of the road for the same reason that you walk along the edge of the pavement, because we like it," I replied.

And later that evening Dr Merry told me how pleased he had been when I stood up to Shadwell. "That reply of yours silenced him and gave me a good laugh."

Frank Dilnot later became editor of the *Daily Herald*, and in a volume of reminiscences he told about his experience that evening at Oxford with much good-nature, claiming that any other reporter would have been hoaxed like himself.

The *Daily Mail* itself was as generous as its reporter. Nine years later it would be the first paper to acclaim *Sinister Street*, as prior to that it had been the first paper to acclaim *Zuleika Dobson*—in his own copy of which Max Beerbohm had stuck a tiny extract from the review of it in the *Daily Express*: "Mr Max Beerbohm may be able to draw but he certainly cannot write," which shows that the *Daily Express* was still hoping to put the *Daily Mail* in the wrong.

Mention of Max Beerbohm reminds me that he came to breakfast with us at 43 High in that summer term. It was Reggie Turner who wrote to tell me Max was paying a visit to Merton, and that he had told Max I should be asking him to breakfast.

We were in something like a flutter at 43 High when that venerable literary figure of just over thirty accepted our invitation, and I spent a good hour deciding upon the guests who should be granted the honour of meeting him. Finally I chose Claude Kirby, Christopher Stone, Tom Spring Rice, John Mavrogordato and Lance Andrewes. That breakfast cannot be recorded as a success. We sat back waiting for Max to talk like his *Works*, the little red duodecimo volume of which I had and which one day, alas, I should have to sell when tiding over some financial crisis. Max failed to respond. He sat there with his fingers only just appearing out of a tight pair of cuffs and hardly said more than 'no' or 'yes' to the remarks we strove to make in the hope of a witty commentary. We felt he was unutterably bored by us all and no doubt our remarks became more and more fatuous. Even I, not noticeably deficient in chatter, became silent, hoping that Max would be able to keep his cuffs out of the jar of Oxford marmalade when he was helping himself to it. Ten years later when I was staying with Max at Rapallo I asked him if he remembered that breakfast.

"I was petrified," he declared. "Nothing makes me so nervous as talking to undergraduates."

"We thought you were bored by us."

"No, no," he said. "I was simply frightened to death."

About this time Harry Pirie-Gordon became preoccupied with 'jokes'. The success of the *Daily Mail* rag may have fired us to improve even upon that. Harry's 'joke' was a good one. He bought the whole of the front row of stalls for a performance of *The Walls of Jericho* at the Garrick Theatre. Then he sent round the tickets to various people with instructions that a ticket was to be sent to any really bald man they knew. So when the evening came the whole front row of the stalls was filled with almost completely bald men. The audience began to titter before the curtain went up and when the bald men all looked round to see what was making the audience titter it began to laugh.

I was unable to get away to see the effect of the joke but according to Harry the bald men remained completely mystified through every interval.

My own 'joke' was less successful. At that date there was a quarrel between the General Post Office and the Great Western Railway over the mails. So the G.P.O. refused to send the mails from Oxford by train, and every night the scarlet coach of the Royal Mail left Oxford for London with four changes of horses on the way. There was an armed guard beside the driver and I thought it would be fun to hold up the Royal Mail. We worked on an elaborate ambush, but it was pouring in buckets on the night we had chosen for the deed, and we decided to put it off. Then we discovered you could get 14 years' penal servitude for holding up the Royal Mail; we decided to abandon our 'joke'.

Somebody had presented the College with a pair of black swans, and to make up for the fiasco of the Royal Mail I got hold of an Easter egg rather larger than an ostrich's egg and put it on top of one of those twiggy growths that affect willows, with a notice requesting visitors not to disturb the swan's egg. We derived much pleasure from listening to the fatuous comments of visitors in Addison's Walk, none of whom seemed to suspect that even a black swan could hardly lay an egg larger than that of an ostrich.

With so many preoccupations frivolous or otherwise I look back to that last summer term of mine with astonishment that I even succeeded in getting a pass 'in the gulf', let alone a class in the Honours School of Modern History.

Ruth and I took the two walks a week we were allowed, the favourite of which was to Godstow where once upon a time Fair Rosamund used to welcome Henry II; we seemed in Godstow meadows to be as far away from present Oxford as those lovers who lived between the First and Third Crusades. There was a party in the garden of the Provost's Lodgings at which I met Laurence Hope, the author of the Indian Love Lyrics, one of which at least was unavoidable at any ballad concert. I thought her affected and self-consciously trying to live up to the glamorous Orient of which she was the emotional exponent. Here too I met again Ellen Terry, whom I had not seen since that visit to her dressing-room at the Lyceum in 1898. Ellen Terry was as charming as she always was, but I found her daughter Edith Craig tiresome: I always think of her as Ailsa Craig, for she was rocky and superior.

The guest by whom I was most impressed was Cunningham

Grahame. If somebody had told me in June 1904 that one day I should be a great friend of that inspiring hidalgo I should have been incredulous. He was far from easy for an undergraduate to talk to in those days, but he appeared suddenly to be aware of my existence when I told him I had been to Morocco and I lost my shyness. Another guest was an old Worcester man called Macmeikan, a delightful fellow who was tutor to young Lord Tavistock, the Duke of Bedford's heir, a fifteen-year boy who for some mysterious reason was then supposed to be slightly wanting. I found him extremely intelligent and Macmeikan was devoted to him. I never met him after he succeeded to the dukedom, but corresponded with him once or twice over questions to which we had the same answers.

I had made up my mind that if I succeeded in acquiring Ladyham I would somehow turn the two cottages back into one house. Almost next door to Cooper and Son's shop was the renowned second-hand furniture shop of Walford and Spokes, presided over by Mr Spokes. I asked Mr Spokes if he would come over to Burford with me and give an estimate of what it would cost to make the transformation I planned. The estimate was £400. I knew it would be hopeless to ask my father for the money; the only chance was to fire my mother's interest. My instinct was right. Just as she had transformed Canadian Cottage into the roomy bungalow it became, her creative impulse was again irresistible. As soon as she saw Ladyham she was captivated by the transformation I planned to make. Throughout her married life she had raided her marriage settlement. My father must have known she was doing this, but like so many men he shut his eyes to his wife's generous extravagance. She would come to the end of that marriage settlement in 1909, but fortunately for her when she did so *The Arcadians* was enjoying its immense success, and my father who had a third interest in it with Milton Bode, his partner, and Robert Courtneidge, was well in the money. That is only a momentary anticipation of events in my fourth Octave. In 1904 she was to let me have the money for the transformation of Lady Ham: I had decided to make two words of Ladyham at the same time as I made one house of it again.

We knocked down the Sylvester staircase and closed up the Sylvester front door. We abolished the Sylvester kitchen and now had a large hall with an open grate, beyond which there was a room for Christopher's study. We abolished the ancient privy whose two seats and a small child's seat were served by the Windrush and turned it into an outside larder. We put the second stone hood over the old

Sylvester back door and installed a w.c. Harry Pirie-Gordon presented us with a heavily-nailed thick oak door to stand beneath the old carved hood, for which he paid £20. When we were knocking down the partition between the two staircases we found a parchment deed which gave us the date of the original house. It was 1585. Why it should have been walled up was difficult to say. It may have been in dread of the Levellers (whose mutiny was crushed by Cromwell and Fairfax) when they were taken prisoner and shut up in the tower of Burford church; three of them were shot against the west door, the bullet-marks being still visible.

Worcester House was being pulled down; the Provost managed to save that wooden Jacobean hood plastered inside and this he gave to me for what had been the back door of the larger cottage, and for that door he gave me the brass dolphin of the Worcester House front-door. We built a wide low wall at each end of Lady Ham on which we could sit beside a lawn on either side of the entrance path. We built a circular wall round the well. 'Lean down, lean down to the water, Mélisande.' The little dining-room was papered in apple-green. My library upstairs with rectangular book-shelves on either side of the fireplace was covered with a green canvas paper which I remember cost what seemed the extravagant sum of half-a-crown a square yard. The bedrooms were all distempered in ivory, but Christopher's study was papered in brown. Brown wallpaper was much in the mode about now. Christopher insisted on sticking to his little attic bedroom. Mine was next the library, and we had two spare rooms.

Meanwhile, Walford and Spokes were putting leaded casements in Bobbie Whitworth Jones's house where George Montagu would instal his Aeoline organ to which I owe the first glimmerings of musical appreciation.

As if there were not already too many distractions for the all too rapid approach of Schools the Reverend Harold Davidson arrived at 43 High to beg a lodging for two nights because he was preaching somewhere in Oxford. We told him there wasn't a vacant bed. "Oh, I don't want a bed. I'll curl up anywhere like a bug in a rug," he declared in that relentless voice of his. "I'm raising money for fallen girls and I must not miss the opportunity of a collection. Why, here's the very place to sleep," he exclaimed, going over to the window-seat.

We told him he could not possibly sleep on a narrow window-seat, and in the end he elected to sleep under the dining-room table with a couple of blankets and a pillow that Miss Allen found for him in spite of a protest from Miss Prince. Then he started to write his sermon, from which he would keep reading excerpts until Harry and I told him that if he wanted to write a sermon he must go and write it in the lavatory where we locked him in. Half an hour later he appeared in the sitting-room.

"I've finished my sermon," he announced.

"But how on earth did you get out of the lavatory?" we asked in amazement.

"Oh-ho," he chuckled. "Stone walls do not a prison make for Davidson. I got out through the window. A bit of a squeeze but I managed it and slid down the drain-pipe."

"My goodness," Miss Allen declared later. "When Miss Prince saw him come slithering down that pipe out of that tiny little window she couldn't believe her own eyes. He's a proper little monkey, that's what he is. And Miss Prince, she said it didn't matter if he was a monkey or a reverend he wasn't never going to sleep again at 43."

When the vigil of those fateful five days of Schools came I decided the only way I could possibly get that Second to which I had rashly committed myself was to sit up every night and cram. The physical side of the cramming was to be provided by quails in aspic which Frank Cooper had produced from his great repertory of recherché comestibles; the only liquid was to be very strong black coffee. It was quite an effort of determination and endurance, and after the strain of the nightly mental cramming my own fatigue was not allayed by the sight of the women candidates, not yet undergraduettes as they would be called at first when they became members of the University, bent feverishly over their answers and scribbling away in a frenzy of concentration, all of it in order to get the honorary equivalent of an Oxford degree, but not the degree itself. I seem to hear now the frantic scratching of the quill pens which almost everybody used in those days. Indeed, I should use a quill myself for a long time; a packet of 25 from Vincent's used to cost half a crown.

I did well enough on the first four days to rouse a faint hope of a First after all. I knew I must have got a couple of alphas for the Three Crusades, and later I would hear that I had got an alpha plus for the political economy paper! Considering that I had never opened Mills's *Political Economy* this would have been a genuine miracle but for a practical explanation. Somebody had lent me a little exercise-book with full and clearly arranged notes of A. L. Smith's lectures on Mills.

These, after one of those all night sittings, I knew by heart next morning. Disaster fell on the fifth day, which was occupied by the two papers on my General Period—919-1273. This with Sligger's usually benign encouragement I had read with some application during the two years after Pass Mods. Moreover, when I came out of Schools that afternoon and walked across to 43 High in order to get out of the sombre attire, toss my cap and gown in a corner and divest myself of that idiotic white bow tie, I felt that I had done two quite good papers.

When I went up for my viva in July the only question I was asked was where Rome was.

"In Italy," I answered, surprised by what seemed such a fatuously superfluous question.

"But whereabouts in Italy?" the examiner asked.

"Roughly in the middle of it."

"One would not think so from the map you drew of Italy in the thirteenth century in which Rome has moved down towards the toe of Italy."

When I went out Fletcher followed me, beaming with an unusual warmth of good will.

"Well, you've got a capital safe Second," he told me. "You just might have viva'd yourself into a First with betas on your English history papers, two alpha plus pluses in your special subject, and alpha pluses in Political Economy and Political Science. But what on earth happened to you in your General Period? You had a delta in one paper and a delta minus in the other, which of course completely knocked out a First."

I realized that the fifth night of sitting up eating quails in aspic and drinking black coffee had been too much, and that what I had supposed was my lucid account of the rise of the Franciscan friars and my subtle analysis of the relations between Pope Sylvester II and the young Emperor Otto I must have been on a level with my putting Rome near the toe of Italy on that map. How true it was that when one thought one had done well in a paper it was a sign one's brain had not been severely tried, and that when one thought one had done badly it was a sign one really had made one's brain work and so, feeling fatigued, one was pessimistic. I should be taught that lesson in the future when I was writing *Carnival* and, reading over in the morning what I had thought so good the night before, should cancel those pages.

Back to June 1904. I have mentioned already that it was the custom for users of the History library on going down to present books, and in accord with that custom I had presented the library with Lingard's History of England in the hope that it might correct some of Froude's brilliant falsification of Tudor history. Then Fletcher asked us if we should not like to subscribe two guineas each toward the expense of acquiring the *Dictionary of National Biography*, the 63 guineas for which had placed a heavy strain on the finances of the History library. I felt that Fletcher's request after his attitude at the Easter collections was adding insult to injury and, although I grudgingly parted with those two guineas, resentment endured. At the last bonner of the term I stole away from the noisy mob dancing round it and urged by the verity of wine, went up to the History library, carried down those 63 large volumes, climbed laboriously over the fence into the deer park and built them up into a pile over enough paper to set them burning. I had lighted this private bonfire and was contemplating my handiwork when luckily both for the *Dictionary of National Biography* and myself two or three of my friends who had missed me from the bonner and had gone to look for me arrived in the nick of time and the volumes were hastily rescued. If those volumes of the D.N.B. still grace the shelves of the History library in Magdalen the curious enquirer may still see in the corners of two of the volumes the faint brown mark of a burn. I found two little brown spots still visible when I last looked at them, twenty years after they were made.

I recall no feeling of sentimental regret at going down. It has been a lifelong habit of mine never to regret what I could not have, and to dwell instead on the disadvantage of whatever it was I had wanted if I had obtained it. I now felt what a mistake it would have been if I had stayed up another year. True, I might have got a First but an All Souls fellowship would have been too uncertain a possibility to make that fourth year worth while. What value would a First be to my ambition? The possession of Lady Ham was worth infinitely more than rooms in the Old Parsonage for three terms. Being tied to the grind of reading for my finals would interfere with poetry and plays and essays and everything else I was expecting to write. Harry was keeping on our rooms at 43 for his fourth year. He had given up the *Isis* editorship and would carry on as editor of *The Oxford Point of View*. I could earn a bit of money by coaching girls from Maggie Hall or Somerville in history, and use 43 High for a weekly visit to Oxford to do such coaching. I would go in for the Newdigate: Garibaldi was an attractive subject. Anyway, what mattered Oxford except for Ruth, to whom my engagement would be announced at the beginning of Commem.; and at the three balls to which we were going, one of them in Worcester itself, she would be wearing her engagement ring. It was an emerald, the birthstone of May, set in minute diamonds. I had bought it at Rowell's and the fifteen guineas it had cost had been paid by letting one more bill for books have its payment postponed for a while. Bills were certainly a problem. I owed over £300, mostly for books, but by going to live in Burford I should be so well in reach of Oxford that the booksellers would not be worried about the credit they would be giving.

I think the first ball to which Ruth and I went was at Christ Church, but I recall more vividly the Masonic ball given by the Apollo Lodge. I see now Harold Hartley and Harry Pirie-Gordon as Templars in their crimson cloaks taking part in a special quadrille with a lot of courtly sword play. Harry was absorbed in Masonry and mounting from degree to degree with ever more expensive and elaborate aprons. He usually kept his Masonic books locked up, but once I found the lid of the small coffer in which he kept them open and I looked through them in the hope of discovering a few secrets. I was much amused by the large mysterious eyes appearing on the pages of what were apparently manuals of services and ritual for various degrees, but I remained unimpressed by the services and the ritual. I told Harry I had read his abracadabra; he did not seem in the least disconcerted, contenting himself with a hieratic gesture of solemn disapproval. So I bought a book called *Y a-t-il des Femmes dans la Franc-Maçonnerie Française?* by Octave Mirbeau, in which was page after page of female masons wearing very little more than a masonic apron, and gave it to Harry, telling him it was a great deal more interesting than his masonic literature.

The last ball was the Worcester ball in the College Hall, when Ruth was told by her mother and sister that she must keep at least twelve dances for Worcester undergraduates. I was consoled for not dancing every dance with Ruth by being told by various North Oxford friends of hers how lovely and happy Ruth looked since our engagement was announced.

At the last Royal Academy banquet, two months ago to a day from my writing these words in France, one of the guests opposite me at table asked me to settle an argument he was having with his next door neighbour.

"You were at Magdalen, weren't you, not Worcester?"

On my "Yes" the neighbour said,

"Well, I remember seeing you at a ball in Worcester years ago with a very pretty girl with light-brown hair."

"That was 59 years ago," I told him. "And the girl with light-brown hair was the daughter of the Provost, to whom I was engaged."

It was close on eight o'clock in the morning when we sat outside for photographs to be taken of the dancers by Hills and Saunders or Gilman; no photograph could evoke the memory of that last ball at which I should dance with Ruth like that casual remark made in Burlington House. And as I write of it now I hear the silent echo in my mind of those waltzes of long ago—*Choristers*, *Valse Amoureuse*, *Frères Joyeux*, *Gold and Silver*, and most poignantly of all the *Eton Boating Song*. I hear again a steward say to a young man, "I'm sorry, sir, but if I see you reversing again I shall have to ask you to leave the floor of the ball-room." This will sound extremely comic to the elaborate waltzers of to-day, but when one was waltzing round in the intoxication of that rhythm all depended on that rhythm's being sustained; if one couple started to reverse it could easily happen that three couples would crash to the floor as they came in contact with an unexpected obstacle, with an ankle or two sprained or even a leg broken.

When I got back to 43 High and went to bed that morning I had a strange experience. I was just dozing off when I felt as if I had been hit a tremendous blow on the heart, and as I was hit I found myself on the floor having turned a complete somersault when I was projected out of bed. I thought it would be wise to consult Dr Collier about that somersault. He told me it must have been what he called a pseudo-angina; when I asked him if it was serious he reassured me: "All the same, you'd be wise not to spend quite such another hectic fortnight as you seem to have been spending." Whatever it was, I have never had a repetition of that extraordinary somersault out of bed.

As I go down from Oxford I ask myself if I have been able to present my life there as convincingly as I was able to present the life of Michael Fane in *Sinister Street*. The latter was an easier task because I could manipulate my characters like marionettes, and only two or three of them were partial portraits of real people. In autobiography one has to stick to the facts and I have not made much effort to analyze my mental processes; to do so would convey a wrong impression of myself because I was and still am incapable of much introversion. Although there was in me a complete conviction that one day I should make a name, my course toward that name was by no means clear beyond my conviction that it would be in some form of writing. In embarking upon the Burford experiment I was influenced by Pearsall Smith's belief in a vocational approach to literature and in the absolute necessity of cutting oneself off from the wider world during one's novitiate. At this date he and I had a plan to found a sort of mother-house in Oxford, to which those less fortunate than myself who in spite of their devotion to literature were hampered by another profession, could retire from time to time to commune together without involving themselves in the academic life of the University. We went so far as to look over a house in Merton Street which would be suitable for such a little centre, and for a time Pearsall Smith played with the idea of taking the house himself and endowing it for such a purpose.

I suppose I must have seemed to the academic eye as wilfully neglectful of making the most of my abilities as I had seemed to my schoolmasters, and I see plainly how much I must have exasperated many people; being almost completely indifferent to the opinion of other people, I laid upon myself the entire burden of success or failure and I should have reproached nobody except myself if I had failed. I was a puzzle to my father, but fortunately I had in my mother somebody who could, as it were, gamble upon me, though, let it be added, she would from time to time advocate for my future far more preposterous steps than any I advocated for myself.

The Daniels had a houseboat at Lechlade where they had spent much time in summers gone by. Now, with Worcester House pulled down, Mrs Daniel seemed to feel suddenly that with it had gone the Oxford of her young married life; it was decided to bring the houseboat from Lechlade to Oxford and get it sold. They were to spend a last week on it after Commem. and then it would be towed to Oxford. I stayed with Mrs Daniel, Rachel and Ruth on the houseboat for that last week, and one day Ruth and I walked to Kelmscott Manor to call on Mrs William Morris. She sat in a yew parlour in the middle of the lawn, and kept pressing upon me tankards of ale. I felt I must try to maintain the pre-Raphaelite tradition and I drank much more than I wanted to. Mrs Morris sat in that yew parlour, looking as if she were still sitting for Rossetti. Her daughter May was there; it was she who kept being sent for another tankard of ale. She also showed Ruth and me round the inside of the Manor and when we walked back across the water-meadows to the houseboat we felt as if we had been for a while in a house under a spell.

I cannot bring myself to tell in cold factual prose of that journey down the Upper Thames from Lechlade to Oxford; I have told it in *Guy and Pauline*.

My memories of those first weeks at Lady Ham are almost inextricably confused. Christopher Stone went off to tutor the second Lord Leverhulme, who was now at Eton and bound for Trinity College, Cambridge. William Lever had recently built himself a much larger house and I recall Christopher's speaking with much affection of Mrs Lever and telling me how she used to wonder why her husband wanted to build such a large house when they had been so comfortable in their eight-roomed house which she had found it so much easier to manage.

Dear Gunner came over from Oxford to see Lady Ham. I recall from that visit his pleasure that Alan Don[1] had been elected President of the J.C.R. He had for him admiration and affection and thought he would have a good influence on next year's freshmen.

W. H. Hutton[2], still a don at St John's College, lived in the Great House, an impressive Caroline survival that matched Hutton himself. When I dined with him I felt I was living in the reign of Charles I and that Laud was still Archbishop of Canterbury, and basked in his approval of my design for living.

Across the river from Lady Ham was the house of Dr Cheatle, who would hand on an unique personality to his eldest son, now a medical student. Dr Cheatle had a gruff exterior that concealed the warm heart of a devoted physician always ready to drive miles in his gig to tend a patient, and yet managed to make the patients in his consulting room feel they were committing a crime by having anything the matter with them. There were two younger sons, Roland and Walter, and two daughters, Mary and Gladys. Mrs Cheatle undertook to find us a housekeeper for Lady Ham, and Miss Harris an elderly spinster was engaged.

Then one day William Search came along to ask if I would take him on as gardener and handyman at a pound a week. I found Search a man after my own heart and in spite of being warned against him as a Radical of the deepest dye, with an independence of behaviour and outlook that made him an impossible servant, I engaged him. To-day Search would be a Communist; if he had lived in the days of Chartism he would have been a Chartist. There was a former Chartist settlement near Burford, where in Charterville the world was to see a practical example of equality in action. Every little house was to have

[1] The Very Reverend A. C. Don, K.C.V.O., Dean of Westminster.
[2] The late Dean of Winchester.

its little bit of land and the results of industry were to be shared. The experiment lasted only about two years and was a complete failure, but I believe the cluster of houses still remains as what at any rate in my time at Burford was a blot on the landscape, but a much less offensive blot on the landscape than the suburbanisation of Burford which came after. Search was a tremendous reader but, with the little education he had until he was taken away from school at twelve to work for an impoverished family, his reading was wild and he was almost incapable of distinguishing fact from fiction. He loved long words as much as Mrs Malaprop and dealt with them as ruthlessly. Hydrangeas became 'hydragangers' and the fuzzy growths on willow-trees were 'cantankerous' growths.

Search was profoundly suspicious of the establishment of the Other House, as he called the house of Bobby Whitworth Jones and George Montagu. The fact that the latter was a Tory M.P. and going to be an earl one day he felt as a reflection upon his integrity whenever he touched his cap to him.

"Why is he a member of Parliament?" he would ask indignantly. "Because the people of Huntingdon vote for him because his uncle is a big shot in Huntingdon and they wouldn't think it respectful not to vote for him. Still, even though he is going to be a lord one day I'd trust Mr Montagu more than what I would Mr Jones. The trouble with him is he doesn't know the difference between a shilling and a pound. Extravaganza? He's a walking extravaganza. Look at this wall he's on at you to build. Seventy pounds! And for what? For the Other House to have their own garden."

"But it gives us a walled garden too, Search. In fact, Mr Whitworth Jones is paying much more than his share. We shall have much more than half of that wall."

This dry wall six feet high ran from the road across the big water-meadow as far as Lady Ham. To-day its venerable appearance fills me with pride when I look at it and reflect that such a wall would cost at least £500 to build not half as well to-day. Yet my share of that wall was only £35.

Search's doubts about Bobby Whitworth Jones's financial wisdom were caused by the leaded casements he had had made for the Other House: "What was wrong with the windows as they were?" he would ask indignantly.

It would have been halfway through July that I went down to Somerset to stay with the Daniels. All the way in the train I was humming to myself 'O Mistress Mine' and when the compartment emptied a station or two before we reached Frome I was able to sing aloud that loveliest of all Shakespeare's lyrics:

O mistress mine, where are you roaming?
O stay and hear; your true love's coming,
That can sing both high and low:
'Trip no farther, pretty sweeting;
Journeys end in lovers meeting,
Every wise man's son doth know.
What is love? 'tis not hereafter;
Present mirth hath present laughter;
What's to come is still unsure:
In delay there lies no plenty;
Then come kiss me, sweet and twenty,
Youth's a stuff will not endure.

And there was Ruth on the platform. In my joy at seeing her I left in the empty compartment a green kangaroo-skin pouch with four ounces of John Cotton's Medium Mixture in it.

As I remember, it was a brother of the Provost who was the leading solicitor in Frome with a country house at Nunny. This was full of cousins when Ruth was there and I was put up in the charming little village, joining the house party after breakfast and going back to the village at bedtime. Ruth and I spent much of our time in a garden room off a terrace looking down into the combe. There were long drives through the lovely countryside of Somerset, with which in all England only Dorset can compete in variety of scenery. Were I indeed as 'romantic' as all my life I have been called I might be tempted to claim that ancestral voices called to me in Somerset because my paternal grandmother was a Somerset Montague and George Montagu had told me that they were the oldest Montagues of all. For myself I was more impressed by being able to say to my Juliet that I was Romeo and a Montague.

In the garden of the Daniels' town-house in Frome was a wide terrace at either end of which was a gazebo, and from one gazebo to the other the softest whisper was carried along the high wall at the back of the terrace. Sitting each of us in one of those dome-shaped gazebos, from which one looked down over the roofs of Frome, Ruth and I would whisper our vows.

And then one afternoon Rachel, passing by that garden room, saw Ruth sitting upon my knee, for which she reproached her younger sister for behaving like a housemaid. From that moment the passionate emotion of young love was tormented by a questioning self-consciousness. A day or two after this we drove to Glastonbury, where Ruth and I climbed to the summit of that Tor on which foul Henry had hanged the abbot of that great monastery. It was here, sitting on the short turf, the green vale of Avalon outspread below, that Ruth told me what a strain upon her our year of love was becoming and let me know how disappointed she had been when I refused the President's offer to recommend me as John Buchan's successor on the staff of the *Spectator*. If I had accepted that offer marriage would have been so much nearer, but when would marriage come if I spent all the precious time that would have brought it nearer in writing poetry at Lady Ham? Whatever defence of my attitude I may have given it would have seemed to her inspired by nothing except an utter selfishness, as I must now admit. At eighty the selfishness of youth is so much more easily recognized than it is at twenty-one.

Ruth came to see me off by the train and for some reason there was over an hour to wait, and we went for a walk along a straight dusty road which returns to my memory like a scene in one of Hardy's novels as the background of what was coming to seem a hopeless emotional situation. As I sat in the compartment the mood in which I had sung to myself 'O Mistress Mine,' seemed as far away as that first kiss in the July twilight a year ago. The compartment was again empty of other passengers. In a birdcage on the seat opposite was a Manx kitten given to me by the owner of the cottage in Nunny where I had slept: it was Ruth who had called him Twinkle.

I was back in Burford by August Bank Holiday. This I know because on the west window of my old library I scratched with my diamond pencil:

On August 1st 1904
A Camberwell Beauty flew out of
this window

I had gone up to fetch something from the library before making my way up to a cricket-match on the Burford ground. When I entered the room I saw a butterfly I had never seen in England. It was a Camberwell Beauty on the top of my green roll-topped desk beside the open west window. I doubt if Moses looking down from Sinai on the promised land flowing with milk and honey got a bigger thrill than I got from that creamy rivulet of colour flowing round those dark outspread wings. Unfortunately my panama was on my head and like an ass I tried to clap it over the butterfly, only to see it fly out of the window which, of course, I should have shut immediately. I went out of the window after the noble butterfly and slithered down the pear-tree to the ground, but by the time I reached the gate it was out of sight. I went sadly back to the library, scratched the record of this entomological event upon the pane, and walked up to the cricket-match where, my mind still full of that Camberwell Beauty, I was bowled first ball.

At Lady Ham I kept turning from one literary project to another. I translated a one-act play of François Coppée into blank verse. I made a one-act play out of a Guy de Maupassant short story. I started to write a blank-verse drama about Joan of Arc. A fragment of Joan of Arc's speech after her condemnation has survived typed by myself on my Hammond typewriter from some almost illegible scrawl written with a copying-ink pencil with which I would compose until the fag of rewriting out *Carnival* in ink in the year 1911 would cure me of a stupid habit.

From that typewritten fragment of Joan of Arc's last speech I quote some lines, wondering if anybody who read them to-day as the work of a twenty-one-year-old would consider that any future lay before him:

"*My lords of England, give me leave I pray*
To speak my little utterance to the world.
The sentence you have deemed it fit to pass
I will not challenge by a word, nor yet
With fretful protestations of my wrong
Kindle the short-lived flame of quick remorse,
Nor with regrets as vain as ill-told beads
Vex the inspiréd reason of your doom.
But for this land of France, this fair green land,
Fain would I speak with such a clarion voice
As shall put fire into the hearts of men
Whose oldest ancestors are yet unborn,
So that their children's children may salute
My name with tideless acclamations,
Ah! Even now I hear their noisy praise—
Here lies the woman whose thin cry whistled
Across disaster's grey and angry flood,
And woke to victory the arms of France—
My lords, this piping treble heard afar
Was a faint echo of the voice of God."

I turned from Joan of Arc to Garibaldi, who was the subject for that year's Newdigate, of which I wrote the opening lines:

From high Rome Garibaldi fled,
From Rome on that disastrous day,

When Frenchmen stumbled through her dead,
Huddled like leaves along the way.
A ragged unkempt band of men,
Whose footsteps faltered wearily,
Marched through the rank Campagna fen,
Beggared of all save liberty.
The faded crimson of their coats
Was stained to brightness by their blood;
Thin rang the broken trumpet-notes,
The mouthpiece caked with fulsome mud;
And rent was every sodden drum
Since the sad echoes of its beat
Had rolled from the Janiculum
Along the Trastevere Street.

It went on for another twenty lines, which I read to Sligger, who pointed out that their shirts were crimson not their coats. I might have tackled that with fresh rhymes, but what completely discouraged me was to be told that it was "Trastévere" not "Trastevére" and the loss of that resounding quadrisyllable made me abandon any further effort to grapple with the Newdigate; it is obvious I must have been in a fever to accomplish something that would justify my withdrawal to Burford. What was the use of being convinced that I was right to do what I was doing for my literary future unless I could prove to myself that I was right and that I was not indulging myself in an illusion of my vocation like some stage-struck young woman? That I think must be the explanation of what, when I look back at it, seems an exasperating inability to make up my mind what I really did want to write, being sustained inwardly by the conviction of my own ultimate success but fretted by a continuous uncertainty about the way to achieve it.

All through that autumn in her daily letters to me Ruth always seemed her old self, but I suppose my daily letters to her must have seemed to show her more and more certainly all the time that I was more wrapped up in my future as a writer than in bringing our marriage nearer. Every time I went into Oxford that autumn she seemed to be more and more under a nervous strain. That sitting-room of hers and Rachel's in the Provost's Lodging became associated in my mind always with those doubts that used to torment her, doubts that used to culminate more and more often in what was a mutual exasperation which letters each to the other taking all the blame for it did nothing really to allay. It began to seem as if our love had fled to that daisied room which had cherished it, that daisied room in Worcester House which was gone for ever. Ruth always came down with me when those afternoons ended and before letting me out of the front-door we would kiss in the hall and vow to one another that next time I came we would not spoil the time we spent together.

On a wet November afternoon Ruth had been more agitated than ever before; no doubt if I had been older and wiser I should have recognized that she was on the verge of a nervous breakdown. All I was aware of, as she let me out of the front-door in the corner of that Worcester quad, was somehow that her last kiss had been meaningless. I turned to see her standing there for a moment with the door ajar and was on the point of going back when the door closed; walking out of the Worcester lodge in the dripping darkness of that November evening on my way to the station, I felt for the first, and indeed I believe I can say for the only time in my life, the emotion of despair. All the way through Yarnton and Ascot-under-Wychwood to Shipton-under-Wychwood, the station for Burford, I sat in a gloom and when I got into the bus that made the slow journey of five miles I had no desire for the two horses walking up the long hill over the wold ever to reach the top of it and trot again. I felt I could not bear the evening before me, when after excusing myself for toying with the supper Miss Harris would put before me I would go up to the library and sit deep in my basket chair, listening to the splash of the swollen Windrush beneath the bay-window, looking at Smut the bull-dog lying before the fire and Twinkle lying asleep in the grandfather chair beside it, and trying to read whatever book it was which I felt I ought to be reading.

Two days later Mrs Daniel wrote to say Ruth had seemed so overwrought lately that it had been decided it would be a good thing if she went to Paris for a change of scene, where she would stay for a month or perhaps even longer with Kathleen Bruce. Kathleen Bruce[1] was the daughter of Canon Bruce, a great friend of the Daniels, who would soon marry Captain Robert Scott and become the mother of Peter Scott. She was a great friend of the painter Shannon and was now studying art in Paris.

I heard the news with a sort of relief at the thought that those afternoons of mutual misunderstanding were at an end for a time, but also with a sharp remorse because I blamed myself for being unable to give up what I believed was the right plan to secure my future as a writer, instead of getting down more practically to the task of earning enough money on which to marry. I could write to Arthur Bourchier and ask

[1] The late Lady Kennet.

him if the offer he had made me last year was still open, but if I surrendered to the stage that would seem surrender to an art which would destroy my dream of literary eminence. True, Shakespeare had managed to be an actor and his own immortal self, but profoundly as I believed in my own ultimate success I felt that emulation of Shakespeare would be an exaggerated optimism.

A young Russian officer came for a week-end that autumn to stay at the Other House, his last days in England, having been ordered East for the war with Japan. He was most encouraging about an Impromptu in verse I had written to the Pathetic Symphony performed by George Montagu on his Aeoline. I was exasperated at this time by the absurdly pro-Japanese attitude of the British Press. In the illustrated weeklies the Russian soldiers were always depicted rather like untidy mangy bears and the Japanese as spruce as clockwork soldiers. That young Russian officer was killed very soon after he reached the Far East.

The self-questioning and depression about the rightness of my decision to hang on at Lady Ham were relieved by an invitation to stay with Pearsall Smith in Sussex where Lord Turnour, as he then was, was fighting a bye-election. This he won, to become at twenty-one the baby of the House of Commons, from which 47 years later, as Lord Winterton, still the member for Horsham, he would retire as father of the House. We had regarded him at Oxford as a model for caricaturists when anxious to satirize the brainless young aristocrat; we should have derided the notion that a Turnour could ever ripen to the impressive maturity of a Winterton. As the holder of an Irish peerage he would continue as member for Horsham when he succeeded to the earldom, and when he was given a peerage of the U.K. he remained a respected figure in the House of Lords for another ten years.

The first thing that happened when I reached Fernhurst was to be told we were going to a political meeting held by Turnour's Liberal opponent, whose name I forget, though I remember thinking Pearsall Smith was never cut out to be a political speaker.

My stay with Logan Pearsall Smith in a house called High Buildings brings back to me the sight of Logan sitting on one side of a great log-fire, myself on the other, and I hear from all those years ago the echo of Logan's jerky voice as he looks up at the chimney piece and mutters: "Nine o'clock. No more talking. I cannot sleep if I talk after nine o'clock." And silence descends until we go up to bed at ten, with a quick little good-night from Logan as if he were afraid that even one word added to it might give him a sleepless night.

I told him about Ruth's going to Paris, but although he applauded my resolve to continue as I was doing at Lady Ham I was not perfectly reassured about my behaviour. Then Robert Trevelyan came to stay in some house near High Buildings, and Logan showed him some of my poems.

"Bobby Trevelyan sees very great promise in your poems, and he is a hard critic," I was told.

Then Trevelyan himself gave me words of encouragement when we met at Horsham station, he going one way I the other. I must have said something to him about that abortive Newdigate of mine because I remember his telling me that his brother George was contemplating a book about Garibaldi. Had George Macaulay Trevelyan's *Garibaldi and the Defence of the Roman Republic* been written and read with the pleasure it gave me a couple of years later I might have been inspired to finish that Newdigate poem.

As well as longer poems I had been writing sonnets during the last two months, finding the discipline they imposed of great value to my control of words. Pearsall Smith, who was now writing his first *Trivia*, some of which were published in the November number of *The Oxford Point of View*, decided to see what he could do with the sonnet.

Before I went back to Burford my host gave me some furniture for Lady Ham, among which were six high Venetian chairs with carved backs. When I demurred at accepting such a gift Logan said I need not think he was being too generous; they were not genuinely old and he was tired of being disillusioned about the taste of friends who claimed to be connoisseurs when they admired them as examples of Venetian art in the seventeenth century. Another piece of furniture Logan gave me was a wide low divan with a spring which for many years would be a solace when I was racked by neuritis.

Early in January Pearsall Smith moved from Fernhurst to a little house in Grove Street, Oxford, off the High, where he intended to live until he had finished his book on Henry Wotton. From there he came over for a night or two to Burford where we compared our sonnets. One evening he handed me a sonnet he had written on a sheet of Bromo. On that flimsy toilet paper in faint handwriting it has somehow survived:

To M. C. M.

Oh poet, by forgotten Burford town
You live beneath the ancient song of bells
Amid strange twilights, strange autumnal spells
Where rivers whisper to the waning Moon;

Hither from Oxford when old daylight shone
Came youths who riding by the holy wells
Saw knights all woe-begone and damozels
And banners gleaming on the rainy down,
The voices that their poet heard you hear,
You too have passed the moss-encrusted door,
Into the gothic glimmering world, and so,
Young wizard of the ancient past and dear,
The strange magician's mantle that he wore
Dipped in rich dyes has fallen now on you.

Christopher was at home in Abingdon for Christmas, and after a round of dinners I was only too glad to spend a quiet evening in my library. Miss Harris, my housekeeper, was visiting friends; Search had insisted on sitting in the kitchen until she came back in case I wanted anything. It was an absolutely still night of hard frost without a cloud in the sky to obscure moon or stars. I had just gone back to my chair after looking out to see if our otter was wandering about in the orchard; having caught sight of him on one of those mysterious visits of his, the object of which I never could guess, I heard somewhere in the room a noise like the whispering of wind in reeds. I could see nothing to account for the sound but that I was not imagining it was evident from the fact that Smut was pricking her ears and that Twinkle lying in his grandfather-chair looked up to listen, The sound moved with a kind of ghostly whistle about the room; presently I rang the bell for Search and asked him what he heard. He was standing in the open door; as he said it must be a moth, the sound went past him out into the passage.

"I saw no moth go past you," I told him.

"No more didn't I. I can still hear it. It's out in the passage. It's going up to Mr Stone's room."

Search took the paraffin lamp from its bracket by the library door and we followed the sound up the staircase to Christopher's attic; as we reached it the sound went on into the great garret that ran the length of the house. The sound kept just ahead of us as we followed it with the lamp until we reached the wall at the far end when the sound stopped.

This remains the only completely inexplicable occurrence I have ever encountered. The night was as breathless as only a night of hard frost can be; no sound made by wind was an explanation, much as the sound resembled the whisper of wind in reeds. No moth large enough to make that sound could possibly have been unseen, and that could be said of any bat. I gave it up at the time and I give it up sixty years later. As we followed that sound I did not for a moment imagine it to be a ghostly manifestation. Virgil's words about the unhappy ghosts who, unable to cross Lethe, make a sound like wind in the reeds along its banks did not spring to mind. I was merely as much flummoxed then for an explanation as I am to-day.

If I were as 'romantic' as my friends still accuse me of being, I might believe that sound was an omen of a letter I should receive not many days after it had sighed so inexplicably through the house.

Earlier in December I had been asked by Alec Cadogan, now President of the O.U.D.S., if I could come to Oxford in February to play in *The Clouds* of Aristophanes. Cyril Bailey and J. L. Myres were going to produce it; Sir Hubert Parry was doing the music. Just about then W. H. Hutton had been made Archdeacon of Peterborough and would be leaving St John's; he had kindly suggested to Sligger that I would be a good person to take on the coaching of some of the students who came to him from one of the women's colleges. This Sligger had arranged and Harry Pirie-Gordon gladly made our old room available.

I felt I could take part in the Greek play without seeming to be once more turning aside from the work in hand to another preoccupation. I promised to play Phidippides in *The Clouds* next term and wrote to tell Ruth. She did not answer herself, but her mother wrote to say that Ruth had decided it would be better for herself and better for me if she broke off our engagement; she felt that she was standing in the way of my happiness in the way I was planning my future and she could not bear to feel she was a hindrance now and no longer a help. That was affecting her health, and she kept worrying about my troubles. She hoped that I would take back the engagement ring to the shop where I bought it if I still owed any money there. By the same post came a tiny cardboard box inside which was her engagement ring. For a moment I thought of writing to Ruth to say I should not act in the Greek play if she felt it would make people think I was not taking our engagement seriously. Then it seemed that an age of misunderstanding stretched before us and that the thing for us to do was to forget.

On a grey January morning I carried Ruth's letters into the orchard to burn. There were over 400 of them and when the last piece of paper inscribed with her hand was black I felt as though I had been burning letters for an eon. That night I took the emerald engagement ring and dropped it in the mill pool. That anybody but Ruth herself should wear it was unimaginable.

It has been an almost intolerable effort of will to tell the factual story of that love of long ago; if it seems coldly told it has not been coldly felt.

TWENTY-TWO YEARS OLD: 1905

THE breaking off of my engagement left me with a sense of failure and when my twenty-second birthday came I woke feeling mine had been a wasted life. I was now twenty-two, and I had not yet made the faintest mark upon the world. I was slightly cheered by reading Milton's sonnet on his twenty-second birthday. After all, my great predecessor at St Paul's had gone up to Cambridge when he was only sixteen, whereas owing to the absurdly protracted adolescence of our modern notions of education I had been compelled to wait until I was eighteen before I went up to Oxford.

How soon hath time the subtle thief of youth,
Stolen on his wing my three and twentieth year!
My hasting days fly on with full career,
But my late spring no bud or blossom shew'th.

Perhaps I ought not to worry too much until my twenty-fifth year.

During that visit to Lady Ham earlier in January Pearsall Smith had read through all the poems I had been writing; I had also told him about the breaking off of my engagement and my doubts whether it was right for me to cling any longer to this novitiate of literature to which I had vowed myself. Was it in very fact a surrender to self-indulgence? Four days after my birthday I received the following letter from him, and that this should have been the only letter to me which has survived from this period of my life is evidence of the value it was to me at a moment of anxious self-questioning:

2 Grove Street,
Oxford
Jan. 20. 1905

My dear Monty,

Yes. I was immensely impressed by your work. You have found your road and already taken a great jump forward in it. I am sure it will lead you far—very far indeed. Live on as you are doing now in the atmosphere of the great things, and make your work like them, definite and objective. The artist should not give us feelings, but put a thing before us that makes us feel. I often remember Goethe's saying 'the ancients wrote the horrible, the moderns write horribly; they wrote the agreeable, we agreeably.'

As to Burford stick to it—nothing can really move you if you decide to stay. The world owes you a living and if you sit tight it will give it to you, although it may bluster a bit. The great and obvious unbelieved secret of life is this. One can do anything one wants.

All this is shocking advice to give youth! Come to lunch on Tuesday if you aren't otherwise engaged. I have some extra furniture you might possibly like for Burford. . . . I am most anxious for you to see this little house.

Yours ever

Logan Pearsall Smith

And indeed that little house in Grove Street was the perfect expression of Logan himself at this time. For me it was a reassuring retreat from the way I felt Oxford might be gossiping about the broken engagement. I hear now Logan's voice across the breakfast table saying: "You must isolate yourself from this nagging question of what are people saying. You must pay no attention to criticism unless you are able to feel that the critic has as good a mind as yourself. Poor Philip Morrell had a very difficult time when after his engagement was broken he became engaged to Lady Ottoline Cavendish-Bentinck. Naturally Oxford gossiped and chattered; they felt he had broken his engagement because he could not resist marrying the daughter of a duke.

"I'm not getting engaged to anybody else."

"No, but you must be careful just now not to appear in the least interested by any girl."

I stayed sometimes with Logan and sometimes with Hugh Sidgwick and Tom Spring Rice at 20 Holywell when I came to Oxford for rehearsals of *The Clouds* and the coaching of the two girls from Somerville or Maggie Hall. I cannot remember the appearance of the two girls as they sat scribbling notes of my observations, but I can see now their chaperon in a purple velvet blouse knitting away in the window-seat of what was now Harry Pirie-Gordon's room at 43 High. The virtue of young women students was anxiously protected in those days; indeed, I believe if gas masks could have allowed them to take down their notes fast enough they might have been compelled to wear them when they were being coached by anybody under fifty.

The Greek Play Committee presented an impressive array of Oxford scholarship that included six Heads of Houses, the Regius Professor of Greek, I. Bywater, the Corpus Professor of Latin, Robinson Ellis, and the Corpus Reader in Greek, A. Sidgwick. It was appropriate that the Provost of Oriel, D. B. Munro of the *Homeric*

Grammar should be a member, and even more appropriate that Dr Merry, the Vice-Chancellor and leading authority on Aristophanes, should preside. His first job was to give permission for the Chorus of Clouds to be clothed in feminine attire and thereby be an exception to the sacrosanct rule that women must always play women's parts in Oxford. Sir Hubert Parry of Exeter, Professor of Music, was composing the music and Dr Hugh Allen of New College was going to train the Chorus. J. L. Myres was to be responsible for the archaeological correctness of the scenery; Cyril Bailey, A. D. Godley, and Christopher Cookson were going to direct the stage arrangements, and the first two were to make a metrical version of the Acting Edition of the play which would be on sale for eighteenpence.

At the end of that impressive Committee of scholarship were the names of the Hon. A. M. M. Cadogan of Balliol, the President of the O.U.D.S., J. L. Philipps of Queen's, the Business Manager of the O.U.D.S. who had given such an admirable performance of Adam in *As You Like It*, and E. M. C. Mackenzie of Magdalen.

I feel that this great play of the poet I love best in all literature has a lesson for to-day even more vital than it had for Athens two and a half millenniums ago, and I cannot resist reprinting from the programme the argument of the play:

"Aristophanes' Comedy *The Clouds* was first produced in Athens in 434 B.C. at the great Dionysia where it obtained only the third prize. Its intention is to point out the effects of educational novelties on minds incapable of understanding them. Socrates, who, when the play was first acted, was in the prime of life, is caricatured as the representative of the Sophists."

Let me interrupt for a moment to observe that E. L. Scott, an undergraduate of Univ., was in appearance a remarkable prefiguration of Sir Charles Snow, who on March 1st 1905, the date of the first performance, would have to wait another seven months and a half before he would be born.

"Strepsiades, an old-fashioned Athenian farmer, had got into debt through the extravagance of his son Phidippides. He tries to induce the young man to give up the turf and become a student in Socrates' school (the Phrontisterion) so that he may learn the Unjust Argument and so baffle his father's creditors. When his son refuses the old man resolves to go himself and be initiated by Socrates as a pupil. He is granted an interview with the Chorus of Clouds—patron deities of a cloudy philosophy—and forswearing his old beliefs, he is committed to Socrates' care.

"At the opening of Act II Strepsiades is studying under difficulties, in the Phrontisterion or Thinking Shop from which Socrates expels him for stupidity. The Chorus advise him to send his son instead, and this time Strepsiades succeeds in persuading Phidippides to become a pupil. The Just and Unjust Arguments—personifying respectively old and new educational methods—are here introduced and state their rival claims to be Phidippides' tutor. New ideas carry the day."

That was a difficult scene for Phidippides who in the orange tunic and lemon-yellow cloak designed by Miss Lorimer of Somerville had to stand for twenty minutes in an Attic attitude of graceful attention without saying a word. However, I felt richly rewarded when one of the dramatic critics wrote that I looked like a Greek vase of the best period.

"In Act III Strepsiades reappears at the door of the Phrontisterion, where he finds his son transformed from a butterfly of fashion into a master of dialectic. Father and son dine together to celebrate the occasion but presently Strepsiades returns in great dismay. Age and youth have quarrelled at dinner, Phidippides has not only given his parent a beating, but is prepared to justify it by arguments, and to beat his mother into the bargain. This so horrifies Strepsiades that he repents at once of having cast off old ideas of religion and honesty, and he revenges himself on the Socratic philosophy by setting fire to the Phrontisterion."

Strepsiades was played by a freshman from Univ. called C. W. Mercer, who had the great success he deserved for a fine performance. One day he would have a much greater success with another performance by becoming Dornford Yates.

Parry's music was masterly. I can still hear from the "Sinfonia Academica" that motor-horn challenging the solo violin. "To symbolize the relation between modern progress and the Classics, the latest infant prodigy, the motor-horn, practises the Beethoven Violin Concerto, though its compass limits its efforts to the first bar; a struggle between the motor-horn and the solo violin ends in the triumph of the former." Parry with his glorious sense of humour could express equally well the poetry of Aristophanes. And I can still hear the opening line of one of the Choruses ἀένιαι νέφελαι, Ye heavenly Clouds. That Chorus of tenors and basses in feminine attire and long hair were marvellously trained by Hugh Allen[1] who was himself an Aristophanic figure of ruthless authority. Max

[1] The late Sir Hugh Allen.

Graham, the Balliol stroke and Blue, was one of the tenors; Tom Spring Rice, Timmy Jekyll, Bing Compton[1] and Archie Gordon, who only a year or two later would be killed in a motor-bicycle accident, all Balliol, were among the basses, and T. G. Gibson of New College was a superlative Coryphaeus. I can hear him now asking me how on earth he was going to prevent Hugh Allen from tearing his hair out.

The great occasion for us all was the matinée on Thursday, March 4th, when the hosts of Cambridge descended upon us, all of them we felt highly critical of our efforts and determined to compare *The Clouds* unfavourably with *The Wasps* which had been given in Cambridge the previous year with music by Vaughan Williams. The overture to *The Wasps* is still a popular gramophone record, but alas, there are no records of Hubert Parry's magnificent choruses in *The Clouds*.

In the scene when Phidippides, as a young racing blood who has been transformed into an Athenian beatnik by the Unjust Argument, receives the visit from his father I used to wait in the wings for my cue wearing nothing but a very short pair of shorts and the orange tunic. The weather was bitterly cold and wet, and while I was waiting I used to wrap a heavy greatcoat round me and stand in carpet-slippers. My cue came. I threw off the coat but forgot to step out of the carpet-slippers, and there I was standing in the middle of the stage in a pair of red and blue carpet-slippers. I felt that the hosts of Cambridge would descend upon this hideous anachronism with glee. I felt that the honour of my own University was at stake. I stepped out of the slippers and called with an imperious gesture to Eddie Keeling[2] standing in the wings,

"ὦ δοῦλε!" "(O slave!)"

Then I pointed to the carpet-slippers on the stage and with a respectful acknowledgement of the command the slave picked up the slippers and carried them into the wings. Ten years later Eddie Keeling and I would carry off with equal aplomb two or three breaches of military etiquette at Gallipoli. I am entitled to boast of our aplomb because not one of the hosts of Cambridge noticed that gloss upon the text of Aristophanes.

I had to carry off a much more painful incident on the last night, when at the end of the play Phidippides declares Zeus does not exist and that the Whirligig now reigns. To suit the action to the word I had to whirl around a whip and on that last night caught my cheek

[1] The Marquess of Northampton.

[2] Edward Wallis Keeling who was H.B.M.'s Minister in Venezuela and Consul-General in Tangier.

with the thong. I had a weal on my cheek that did not disappear for nearly a fortnight.

To our great disappointment Alec Cadogan fell ill with a bad go of influenza in the middle of the week and had to call on me to take the chair at the usual O.U.D.S. supper. He had done a splendid job, but even the satisfaction of taking more than £950 and thereby completely restoring the finances of the O.U.D.S. was not able to lower his temperature. We had a great supper at the Clarendon with speeches galore, and after the sober guests had departed some of the less sober guests painted the classical busts round the Sheldonian bright red; others climbed into Pembroke and pulled some of the Pemmy[1] boxing champions out of bed. How they managed to make that extremely difficult climb and get out again before they were knocked out by the Pemmy boxers only champagne could tell.

It has always been a mystery to me how anybody can remember what he thought was happening in delirium as having actually happened, or how anybody can remember his extravagant behaviour and mental attitude when under the influence of alcohol. No doubt much may be forgotten, but why does any of it remain in the mind? I had experience of both during this Octave, an example of the latter occurring this very February.

Round about St Valentine's day Raymond Wavell came of age, and, although a younger son, inherited a great deal of money, much of it as I remember in Welsh slate quarries. The only condition of the inheritance was that he would have to add Paxton to his name and become R. G. Wavell-Paxton. He celebrated the occasion by giving a dinner to eleven of his friends at the Café Royal. I was in London on the morning of his birthday and walked round from Nevern Square to Rosary Gardens to wish him many happy returns. "Come and look at the suite I've bought," he said, and he showed me proudly a Chesterfield and two armchairs covered in red morocco leather. The purchase of that luxurious furniture had been Raymond's first step to assuring himself that he was now rich.

The dinner was entirely Magdalen as I remember, and refreshed by a sorbet in the middle when we smoked cigarettes to show what men of the world we were. It was a noble repast and there was unlimited champagne. After dinner we repaired to three boxes at the Empire, where Genée was dancing in the ballet *Sylvia*. With that invincible certitude of penetrating to the heart of things which wine

[1] It may be worth recording in a footnote that between 1901 and 1905 Worcester was known as Wuggins, Queen's as Quagga's and Jesus as Jaggers.

induces, I decided that the great prima ballerina instead of dancing herself was letting the theatre dance round her and standing motionless in the middle of the stage. I felt this was a slight to the audience and taking off my tailcoat I threw it down into the stalls where it landed over the head of an elderly gentleman who was gazing at the ballet through his opera glasses. Presently one of the commissionaires came up into the box with my coat and said: "Now, gentlemen, you're having a lovely evening. Don't go and spoil it and have to get yourselves turned out."

The next thing I remember is walking up and down the promenade with Kenneth Carlisle, the captain of the Oxford Cricket Eleven. The expensive tarts in long trailing skirts covered with sequins were walking backwards and forwards, the skirts pulled tightly round their behinds to show them off to the best advantage. On one of these skirts Kenneth Carlisle put his foot as if he were getting back quickly into safety in a close escape from being stumped by the wicket-keeper. The indignant owner of the skirt turned round and said to Kenneth in accents of withering scorn: "And I suppose you call yourself an effing gentleman!"

The next thing I remember is walking along Coventry Street with Kenneth and solving a problem with the gravity of an Einstein.

"You know, Kenneth, when you're rather tight the houses on each side of the road always keep turning round and round you. Now if we go round and round the houses will keep perfectly still like Genée just now."

"Yes, that sounds rather a good idea," Kenneth agreed and we proceeded to walk on along Coventry Street, revolving slowly. This made us feel giddy and we decided it would be more comfortable to let the houses continue to go round and round instead of ourselves.

The next thing I remember is putting my foot on one of the spokes of the wheel of a hansom-cab as it was being walked along by the edge of the pavement to catch a fare. As the wheel went round, up I came until I could pat the cabby on the back and jump before the spoke began to go down and in doing so break my ankle. I did that to another couple of cabs and I remain astonished I did not break an ankle.

Our rendez-vous with the rest of the Twenty-firsters was for supper at the Continental in Lower Regent Street; later on it would become the headquarters of Ciro's famous club. It was getting on for midnight when we arrived, and for some lunatic reason I got it into my head that the right thing to order was a turbot. The large fish arrived almost at the same moment as the waiters were saying 'Time, please, ladies and gentlemen.' I seized the turbot by the tail with the intention of throwing it at the maître d'hôtel, but the tail broke, and the next thing I remember is finding myself in a hansom with a black woman. I felt pretty sure that she *was* black but I felt it would be only fair to make perfectly sure I was right. I saw a policeman standing by the corner near Piccadilly and pushing up the lid of the communicating trap I asked the cabby to pull up for me to get out a moment.

"Excuse me, officer," I said, "will you be kind enough to tell me whether the lady I was sitting next to in that cab is black or white?"

"She's black, sir," he said with a grin.

"Thanks very much, officer," and slipping him half a crown I hurried off.

The next thing I remember is finding myself at Oxford Circus and hearing a rather pretty girl say "Good evening, darling."

"Good evening," I replied with a smile.

"Where are you going now, darling?"

"I don't think I was going anywhere in particular."

"Wouldn't you like to come back with me? My boy has just sent me a case of bubbly from Maidenhead and I must have somebody to drink it with me."

"Where do you live?"

"In Shaftesbury Avenue."

I hailed a hansom, and she gave the address of some flats in Shaftesbury Avenue. Her flat must have been about five floors up and, when we got there, sure enough there was a case of half a dozen bottles of Moët-Chandon.

"Here's to life," she said as we started on the first bottle, which when we had finished it I threw out of the window. By the time we had drunk two more bottles, both of which I threw out of the window, neither of us was in a state to do anything but lie down on the bed and go to sleep. When morning came, a grey wet February dawn, I looked out of the window. Down below in Shaftesbury Avenue the street-cleaners were sweeping up the broken glass of those bottles I had flung out during the night. I looked at my hostess; she was still fast asleep. Luckily I had a fiver on me which I left upon the dressing-table, and going down the many stairs of those flats I reached Shaftesbury Avenue where I soon found a cab to drive me to Nevern Square. I now had an *idée fixe*. I must somehow catch the 9.50 a.m. train to Oxford in order to be back at 43 High by eleven to coach my two pupils in whatever part of the Middle Ages we had reached. The others would all come back later in the day with tales about my behaviour; I would be there before them and tell the story myself. I undressed and lay down for half an hour, but could not surrender to sleep. Then I got up, had a cold bath to pull myself together, put on a tweed suit, went downstairs to whistle for a hansom, and caught the 9.50 to Oxford which in those days, before British Railways made railway-travel an expensive farce, reached Oxford at 10.50. At eleven o'clock I was coaching my pupils chaperoned by that elderly spinster with her knitting and purple velvet blouse.

"Nobody back yet?" I asked in the Magdalen lodge when I got there soon after noon. "Well, we had quite a night, and you really should have seen Kenneth Carlisle in the Empire promenade." I was first with the stories.

On February 17th for the first and only time in my life I kept a diary which lasted, ever dwindling, day by day until May. It reveals the state of my mind at the time better than I should be able to recapture it in retrospect and I think it worth while to print some extracts from it before I burn most of it.

February 17. Oxford.

With the delight of possessing a note-book self-designed, and better with paper made by hand, I start my diary. I remember years ago starting one in a Christmas present. New Year's day proved fatal; the entry for Jan. 2 was 'had a stomach-ache' and there my premature attempt at autobiography stopped dead. This year has already been weighty enough and no one quite knows what I have suffered in the matter of my broken engagement. Polly [Christopher Stone] *was wonderful, especially when I consider his preconceived notions about such things. He is learning humanity. As yet he hardly knows the meaning of frailty. I have heard nothing of Ruth since. She is in Somerset, and when I think of that summer landscape bare in the pale February sun I think of it in dismay. I have to realise somehow that it was all a mistake—the wind can never wed the rain. I must make a vow not to sentimentalize the past. Outwardly I smile. Within I have that dull ache of disappointment as when one waits for a long expected eagerly desired guest, and the bell rings, bringing with it a note to apologize. . . .*

Logan came in much put about because he found a tiresome assonance in his Eton sonnet. I suggested 'towers' instead of 'trees'. . . . Polly's sonnet on Eton was disappointing, but I doubt if anyone can do justice to the thing he loves best. It leads almost inevitably to a relapse into the self-consciousness of extreme youth: the feeling of getting into an omnibus full of people. . . . After breakfast I polished my primrose sonnet and tried to get a word to express the live gold of daffodils—failed—then I worried about money which I do about once a month. . . .

That 'primrose sonnet' was printed in the *Oxford Magazine* a fortnight later:

To the first primrose in my garden :

I found thee in a sheltered garden nook,
Amid the aconites, and snowdrops wan:
The parsimonious February sun
Must sure have lent thee that half-careworn look
Of childish wonderment, swift overtook
By fancied loves and fears, and life begun:
What April-call aroused thee, quiet nun,
That thy dark cloister is too soon forsook?
The western sky still holds a thought of rain.
The thrush is singing in the sycamore
To mellow the fast-lengthening eventide;
But fickle is the windy weather-vane,
And daffodils keep close their golden store
Which will light up the glades when thou hast died.

Robert Bridges to lunch. Bridges condemned Bradley's Inaugural Lecture, (as Professor of Poetry). I don't believe he had read it. He cracked up Woolridge as a writer. . . . Went for a delightful walk in Iffley with Logan. We built up embryo Balzacian romances about the houses. I vow that a red-brick villa is as romantic as a stone castle. . . . As we walked through the village, I was thinking poignantly of the time in June when I last walked through it with Ruth . . . heard the shouting of the rowing Bacchanals. Walked home by towing-path. Stayed on the barge to watch the last division of the Toggers 'Well rowed, Magdalen!' though they were far behind and there seemed no peculiar call for congraulations. Taught my absurd pupils. . . . Dinner: tried to define poetry, 'the rhythmic and melodious expression of the meaning of life.' Rehearsal of The Clouds. Read my sonnets to Tom Spring Rice and drank a glass of stout. Went back to 20 Holywell with T.S.R. and Alec Cadogan. Discussed where right faded into wrong in amorous play with women. Tom only allowed kissing. Johnny Hely-Hutchinson was more daring.

I have not mentioned Hely-Hutchinson yet. He was at Trinity, the son of Sir Walter Hely-Hutchinson who had been Governor of Cape Colony and was supposed to be the original of *His Excellency* in Robert Marshal's amusing Haymarket farce. His younger brother Maurice would one day make a valuable contribution to the music of the B.B.C.

February 20. A long rehearsal at which I felt really ill and my chest was hurting like hell. . . . If ever this diary is read for the sake of elucidating my character I fear some Matthew Arnold of the future will find me a good target for the arrows of his austerity. But already in imagination I revile him for a fool and tell him that his life of self-restraint springs from the jealousy of a eunuch who cannot compass his pleasures. His remarks about Keats's love-letters are really damnable.

February 21. *Polly came in and insisted on my seeing a doctor. Was told to go to bed and keep quiet.*

February 22. *Felt better. Bridges came in about* 12.30 *and made a proposal about an Oxford letter to the new* Academy. *He seems to like me. He said one annoying thing. Apropos of Anderson Graham's previous editorship of* Country Life, *he thought the* Academy *might succeed because* Country Life *had been so difficult. Then said he, 'You know,* Country Life *is read by a so much better class than the* Athenaeum. *The worst of literature nowadays is that it's all in the hands of literary people.' I said I thought there was also the danger of the modern artist being so eager to prove himself a gentleman that he forgot to show himself an artist. It is strange how a solitary man and a really great poet like Bridges idealizes the absurd English country gentleman who is all too often a compound of cruelty, snobbishness, pretentiousness, pride and brainlessness, whose like is not to be found anywhere outside a German university or regiment.*

February 23. *To a debate on the British empire. I deplored the win or lose spirit of the age. War is the result of that. In old days it was for the settlement of a dispute. Now it is for the exploitation of a political theory or the test of financial security. I was appalled by the crassness of most of the speakers. Young men really are very stupid.*

The diary stopped for three weeks; when it began again in mid-March it was entirely taken up with my agitation over the illness and death of that beloved bulldog Smut, of whom as a memorial upon my shelves still stands the copy of Malory's *Morte d'Arthur* with the marks of her teeth as a puppy. I was recalling the evening when I had made Smut lie in the grandfather-chair which was Twinkle's own chair and how Twinkle had come in, when Miss Harris brought up the coffee after dinner, and looked coldly at Smut. She had wagged a propitiatory stump of a tail and explained to Twinkle that it was my fault not hers that she was lying in Twinkle's chair. Twinkle had retired for two hours under that divan which Pearsall Smith had given me and when he came out he had jumped on the divan for his evening snooze before asking me to let him out at midnight for his amorous adventures. At four o'clock in the morning after the day when Smut died Twinkle had climbed up the pear-tree that grew below and round the window of my bedroom and from the gutter had jumped through the window open at the top to my bed. From then on every morning when I woke he was asleep at the foot of my bed.

Some time in that early spring Philip Lloyd-Graeme gave us an Irish staghound puppy with a pedigree going back to the reign of Queen Anne. I called him Sir Charles Grandison because he was such a perfect specimen of the aristocratic fool. Brainless though he was he was also so good-tempered that the most aggressive dogs found it impossible to pick a quarrel with him. Only once did he really disgrace himself; that was when Henry Lygon, who was staying with us at the time, left a gold hunter watch lying on the lawn to find when he came back for it that Charles had chewed it. Henry was naturally furious, but, as we told him, he should not leave gold watches lying about on lawns.

About the same time as 'Charles' reached us Colonel Longmore, my commanding officer in the volunteers, wrote to ask if I would care to have a bulldog who had made himself unpopular in Hertford by killing other dogs. In fresh surroundings he might be less quarrelsome. So 'Billy' arrived, and from the moment of his arrival Search became his devoted slave. Billy's habit on a walk was to find the largest stone he could and carry it back with growls to Lady Ham, the muscles of his thick neck taut with the weight in his mouth. These rocks, for they were more like rocks than stones, were then buried by Billy in the garden. Billy's other ambition, apart from carrying in his mouth heavier stones than any bulldog had ever carried, was to get into the bus arriving from Shipton station. This alarmed the other passengers when they were getting out. One evening the driver caught Billy a crack with his whip, whereupon Billy climbed up to the box and bit the driver's leg. Naturally there was a fuss and I decided that Billy would have to be shot.

"Shoot my boon companion?" Search protested. "Nobody's going to shoot my boon companion. It's as clear as gin it weren't his fault. If the bloody driver hadn't hit him with his bloody whip Billy wouldn't have climbed up and bit him. That Conservatory big mouth deserved what he got."

So Search took his boon companion back to his own cottage, where for the next two or three years he lived, being exercised only at night by Search but even then contriving to carry back from those walks heavy stones to bury in the tiny garden. Then Billy died and upon his grave Search laid some of his big stones.

When my engagement was broken off I went through a period of passionate atheism similar to that of my Aunt Ellen of which I wrote in 1900. In the diary I find:

March 14. *The other night I saw the young moon keeling over in the western sky; above her was Venus and then Jupiter. What a necklace the heavens wore that night. And fools who dabble in religious sentiment must needs talk of the Star of Bethlehem, that jack o'lantern which has misled a universe.*

I am tempted to omit an entry in my diary on the following day because it is so ridiculously 'youthful', but I think the opinion, however raw the expression of it, foreshadows what to-day is accepted. I am recording a conversation with a girl I knew.

March 15. *The discussion turned on the pre-matrimonial morality of the average man. Like all well-brought up English girls she was horrified at the idea of cynical love for a night. I pointed out that men at* 16 *or* 17 *have all the impulses of a man without the stability and that it is not fair to condemn a man for the first exercise of puberty. She conceded my point but continued to think it was horrible. Some would say, I suppose, that I had no right to initiate a series of ideas of which without me she would have remained ignorant. I don't think so. It seems to me monstrous that women are still expected to adopt the mental attitude of the seraglio without any of the compensations of that sedentary existence. I do reprehend this sickly cult for ignorance miscalled innocence. The only claim such innocence can possess is the potentiality for knowledge. Girls as soon as they reach puberty should be instructed in all sexual questions. Half the unhappy marriages are due to the shock of finding what physical intimacy is involved in marriage. Of girls who marry for money, I said that they prostituted their bodies as absolutely as the poorest street-walker who sells her body for sixpence to a dissolute labourer.*

March 16

Received £7. 2*s from pupils which was welcome enough as I had not a penny in the bank. Interviewed Wall, Burford's leading liberal: I offered to serve on the committee. . . . The pink-edged ash-keys looked exquisite to-day, and it is wonderful to coast downhill before the wind with nothing but the moaning of the telegraph wires and the song of innumerable larks. The earth looked rich and brown, and there were hares in the furrows, but the floods are rising and the nights are gusty. George is undergoing a rest-cure. So like him to cure love-sickness with the help of a doctor.*

George Montagu had just told me that a fortune-teller had prophesied he would be married in July. "But I can't think who it can be, my dear," he said, that drooping eyelid of his almost shutting out the eye. "There was an American girl I met last year and I did think of proposing to her, but whenever I led up to the subject of marriage she always seemed to shy away from it. She's coming over from

America again this season. Do you think I'm going to marry Alberta Sturgess?"

"Dear George, the only person to give you the answer to that will be Miss Sturgess herself."

"Yes, I suppose you're right. But it is an extraordinary thing, because I had no idea of getting married this July. The only person I can imagine myself being married to is Alberta, and if she refuses me I don't see how I can be married in July. It's really worrying. I think I'll take a rest-cure."

George's rest-cure lasted hardly a week. When he came back to Burford he brought with him his mother, Lady Agneta, who was a combination of Queen Victoria and Oscar Wilde's Lady Bracknell. She arrived in beautiful April weather. "What divine weather you've brought with you, Lady Agneta," said Bobbie Whitworth Jones.

"Hardly divine, Mr Whitworth Jones," she observed, raising her lorgnette to reprove him with her eyes.

Johnny Hely-Hutchinson came to stay for a bit in that Easter vac, bringing us a present of a fur rug his father had brought back from South Africa for Lord Salisbury, who died while he was on the voyage home. Johnny Hely-Hutchinson found it unpresented and gave it to Lady Ham. He and I and Christopher were asked along to the Other House after dinner that Sunday night. Johnny went in a pair of carpet-slippers, and I can see now Lady Agneta's look of frozen superiority as she gazed at those slippers through her lorgnette. When we had gone she said to Bobbie: "I thought you told me that young man was a cousin of Lord Donoughmore, Mr Whitworth Jones."

"Yes, he's a first cousin."

"Extremely unusual behaviour for a well-connected young man to come to coffee after dinner in carpet-slippers," Lady Agneta observed severely.

It was about now that Roger Fry came to Burford with his wife. At this date he was in the middle of painting in the old English water-colour manner, and came to call on us at Lady Ham. On the window that was our visitors' book he scratched with the diamond pencil *The fresh green lap of fair King Richard's land.* Mrs Fry stayed behind in Burford when her husband left, and painted a picture of Burford High Street in the Chinese manner. She was a strange remote woman with whom I found it difficult to converse.

March 30. *A great upset. Mrs Church whom George engaged as housekeeper for the Other House for the Anglican propensities of her name has eloped with the linen. There had been talk for some time of Mrs Church's intrigue with a lazy young man some years younger than herself who used to smoke Bobbie's Russian cigarettes and he has apparently gone with the linen. Search said it was plainly a case of immortality between them. . . . I found the first cowslip of the year and saw in our orchard the first wryneck. The cuckoo must follow soon. As thrilling a sight to me as any I know is the sight of a thrush sitting. The black eyes, half-frightened half-defiant, the tenderness and grace provide a sensation to which nothing could do justice except Pan himself. I wonder if nature never did betray the heart that loved her. If I were in a mystic mood I should agree. But the question of the supernatural I cannot pretend to answer. In many ways I am absolutely materialistic, but unforgettable moments arise when the soul of earth seems to glisten in the twilight, but this may be only a desire to attribute rather than ascertain causation. I suppose this is the old pathetic fallacy again.*

During that early spring of 1905 I was mostly alone at Lady Ham. George Montagu and Whitworth Jones came for week-ends; Christopher did not come until the Easter vac began. I used often to play George's Aeoline to myself. He had a fine collection of rolls—all the Beethoven symphonies, Tchaikovsky's Fifth and Sixth, the Second Brahms, the Jupiter of Mozart, but what really started me off on the Aeolian was the Marche Slav of Tchaikovsky. That Aeolian of George Montagu's would one day in a March seventeen years hence play a vital part in the direction of my life.

I have mentioned the otter that used to visit the orchard every evening. I cannot claim that we became friends, and yet in a way we did because it would continue to nuzzle about in the grass, in search of what I could never discover, even when I was walking about in the orchard. At first it used to hurry back into the river but it seemed to gain more and more confidence and at last paid no attention to my arrival, evidently having decided that I meant it no harm.

I do not remember just when it was that the otter hunt had a meet in Burford. I feel angry to-day when I remember that infernal hunt. A lot of idiotic young men and women with poles arrived in the orchard and I went out to turn them off our Lady Ham land. The Master had the impudence to express his surprise at my lack of sportsmanship. Then one of the young men started poking his pole into the mill stream whereupon Search pushed him into it.

"Do you realize that is an assault?" the pompous Master asked.

"Yes, and I realize there will be quite a few more assaults," I said, "unless you realize you are all trespassers on my land. So get off it with your blasted hounds before I shoot one of them." And the otter hunt retired to pursue their foul sport further down the Windrush.

April 2. *Read all the morning* Graziella *by Lamartine which bored me. The book was sent to me in curious circumstances. A young woman staying here with George Montagu happened to break a window in my library. She with a turn of fancy ascribed it to the enlivening influence of Raphael, a sun spirit, and sent me this book bound in an odd chamois leather cover with inserts of different coloured silk—the symbolism of which was to be explained when next we met. She is one of your intensely egotistical moderns with a mania for mutual self-analysis. Some men and women practise it with almost sensual persistennce. However, she does play Chopin divinely and is oddly psychical. It is she who told George he was going to be married in July. We shall see if she is really as psychical as George believes. . . . After lunch I read* Emerald Uthwart *and* The Child in the House *of Pater. Maurice Woods says reading Pater is like drinking buttermilk. I must admit there's a kind of drooling sweetness about him which is like a bad imitation of Keats. I doubt if he has any real knowledge of humanity. Nevertheless I cannot disown the man who wrote that page about Mona Lisa and I believe he has an influence which is valuable at the right moment. I should always prescribe him as a corrective for Carlyle.*

Soon after three there was a terrific knock at the door and I saw Hubert Parry in motoring costume. He is a most *delightful man. His conversation is discharged like a child firing off a toy-pistol, revelling in the noise. He was charmed with the house and the well. 'Pelléas and Mélisande, what, ah, devilish good, what?—grand—splendid.' Then I read a bit of a parody I had started of* Princess Maleine *which I called* Princess Migraine *who was rescued by Prince Aspirin. Parry sat down at the piano and began to improvize a parody of Debussy. I don't know enough about Debussy to know how good it was but I chanted my* Princess Migraine *to his Debussy accompaniment. Then suddenly he jumped up and was very amusing about Torrey and Alexander and their glory song. "They're converting 'em in baker's dozens and the conversion doesn't last a month. This revivalism is all my eye and Betty Martin, and now they're printing conversions among the births, deaths and marriages in provincial newspapers. Well, good-bye, my dear boy. I must get along now to Gloucester." I walked with him to his big car. When he got in and tooted his horn in farewell the village kids fled in affright. I think they thought he was going to chase them.*

I went to London for a week or two in May and recorded my impressions of the plays I saw.

May 20.

In the afternoon to the Adelphi and H. B. Irving as Hamlet. A fine performance and a notable advance on Forbes Robertson in the part. I hear complaints of his lack of emotion, but the reverse seems to me the case. . . . nothing so bad as Oscar Asche's Claudius is conceivable. In the great penitent speech he was like a butcher who had been converted by Torrey and Alexander.

May 23.

Went to see Martin Harvey as Hamlet. What a ludicrous performance! He looked like a grasshopper, shock-headed Peter, a French decadent poet, an acrobat—anything but Hamlet. And then this funny little figure of fun went bellowing about the stage. Glenny as Claudius looked like a greasy King of Clubs but spoke his lines well. Miss de Silva a poor Ophelia. She had a confidante in purple for the mad scene. Why imitate Tilburina? Stephen Philips as the Ghost looked majestic, and once or twice spoke a line quite well.

May 24.

Went to Candida *with my mother. What an excellent play. It amused me the way the audience consistently misunderstood everything. What they laughed at most was Marchbank. Granville Barker was to blame for this because he persistently misinterpreted the part. Eugene should be attractive,* ingénu, *yes, but not a ploughboy with feet too large for him. C. V. France as the Parson was excellent. Sydney Fairbrother admirable. Kate Rorke was wrong. When Eugene is horrified at the idea of her peeling onions, one felt it was the only métier she would adopt with success. However, I thoroughly enjoyed the performance and am amused to see how popular G.B.S. is becoming. And he deserves to be. He is not a charlatan, as so many think; indeed, he is the only dramatist with a mind that we have.*

May 27.

To Everybody's Secret. *Tiresome, sugary, sentimental piece with nothing to recommend it except the clever acting of a little girl called Iris Hawkins who was quite splendid. Cyril Maude as always was agreeable and attractive.*

By this May I had managed to fall in love with two girls at once. Almost the last entry in that short-lived diary of mine lets me know that on May 25th I took Phyllis to *Tristan and Isolde* at Covent Garden with Richter conducting. We sat in the top tier of boxes; I commend the experience to any enterprising young lover of to-day. After the opera we went to a ball at the Empress Rooms in Kensington High Street and danced until 3 a.m., after which '*we drove about London for an hour in the green dawn and by God, London can be a wonderful place.*'

Ten days later I had an equally thrilling experience with Amaryllis. She was a student at the Royal Free Hospital, living at the hostel in Hunter Street which, I believe, was built by Mrs Bernard Shaw. Amaryllis shared rooms with a girl who had gone to Eton for the Fourth of June and invited me to supper with her that Sunday night. I am not sure what time it was that visitors were supposed to leave the hostel. At any rate when the time came Amaryllis let me stay on. It was just after sunrise of a golden June morning when I left her. It was quite an apprehensive descent down three flights of stone stairs to reach the great gothic front door of the hostel. However, luck was with me and as I tiptoed my way along corridors and down stairs I met nobody. Then I had to unbolt the big front door. Mercifully the bolts were well oiled, but my heart was beating as I closed it behind me and walked down the steps into Hunter Street; I had reached Mecklenburg Square before I was able to join with love and laugh at locksmiths.

Amaryllis was a precursor of the girls of to-day who regard life so much more sensibly than most of the girls of my generation. The lessons she taught me are a commonplace at eighty; at twenty-two they were a revelation.

In my diary for May 22nd I wrote:

I went to see Robbie Ross in Hornton Street. More Adey and Reggie Turner were there. Robbie read some of the letters he had been getting from people about De Profundis. *George Alexander had written to say that after reading it "he was bound to confess that he shed tears". Robbie said he hoped he would shed more than tears and pay royalties to Wilde's estate if he revives the plays whose acting rights he bought for almost nothing when Wilde went bankrupt. At this moment Bosie Douglas came in and stood on the fender fidgeting and scratching himself as usual and kept sliding off it. Then Robbie read a letter from G. B. Shaw to point out that* De Profundis *was Wilde's final score off the British public, and that it was a gigantic* blague, *the final pose even in prison. Douglas said Shaw was probably right and Robbie got angry. Douglas criticized Wilde's life in Paris and Robbie said the one most to blame for that was Douglas himself. Douglas lost his temper, kicked the fender and marched out of the room. He came back for a moment and told Robbie he did not know what he was talking about. Then he slammed the door, and presently downstairs we heard the front door slam. More Adey was walking about looking more vague than ever and Reggie Turner said Bosie was so impossible that he should have to put him in his next novel when all the reviewers would say that Mr Turner's characters were far from true to life. . . . Robbie read a letter from a man called Dorretly who lived at Birkenhead in which he said that Wilde was the English Christ and asked if Robbie knew where he could obtain a cabinet photograph of Oscar Wilde because he wanted to place it beside one he already possessed of Hall Caine. "With two authors like that," Reggie said, "he ought to get a cabinet photograph of my publisher to represent Barabbas."*

In my book *On Moral Courage* I wrote an account of that evening from memory, and the discovery of this diary has warned me once more what tricks memory can play. I thought the month was March instead of May and gave Alfred Douglas a coat with an astrakhan collar which obviously he could not have been wearing in May. I also wrote of him standing with his back to the fire, and there would hardly have been a fire burning late in May even in London. I had often seen in earlier days Bosie Douglas in a greatcoat with an astrakhan collar and it remained as a kind of permanent property in my picture of him conjured by memory.

War may have been finally declared by Robbie Ross and Bosie Douglas on that May evening in Hornton Street. In *On Moral Courage* I wrote: "In 1912 Martin Secker published a book about Oscar Wilde by Arthur Ransome, and Alfred Douglas sued for libel. Ross provided the defence with the suppressed portion of *De Profundis*. Douglas lost his case. Thence onwards Douglas carried on a vendetta in print against Ross of such viciousness that he was driven into bringing a libel action against his enemy. On that occasion the jury disagreed but the malevolent hounding of him by Alfred Douglas severely affected his health and probably shortened his life. His devotion to Wilde was not only courageous but also practical, and nobody deserved less than he the sneers at him in Mr St John Ervine's book, *A Present Time Appraisal of Oscar Wilde*.

That book was published in 1951; now in 1963 Rupert Croft-Cooke has written *Bosie*, which presents Douglas as the offspring of Sir Galahad and Boadicea. I have no objection to hero-worship provided it does not entail a silly caricature of those whom the hero did not worship. To anybody who knew Robbie Ross, Rupert Croft-Cooke's presentation of him is just that. I respect more than Rupert Croft-Cooke's hero his brother the Marquess, who when living in Edith Villas, West Kensington, applied to the magistrate at the West London police court for permission to shoot at motorists exceeding the speed-limit.

Back in Burford that June I heard that Fisher Dilke and Ethel Clifford were to spend part of their honeymoon at the Other House. All my friends at Oxford were in the throes of Schools and I was alone in Lady Ham when they arrived. Ethel, whose poetry I much admired came round to borrow a book, and having just read *La Cousine Bette* for the second time with renewed enthusiasm I lent it to her. Next morning Ethel came round and rated me for lending a girl such a book on her honeymoon. I appeased her with a sonnet:

Lady of dreams, whose antique minstrelsy,
Echoes along the yellow shores of sleep,
And passes with its singing up the steep
Pierian slope where the nine Muses lie;

The Earl of Sandwich

Robert Whitworth Jones

Apollo sent thee wreaths of rosemary,
That thou might'st so remember still to keep
Thy tears for all who have forgot to weep,
A consolation and a litany.

I too have travelled under the slow moon,
And watched princesses, in dim sea-green gowns,
Combing their locks at casements diamonded.
Sure am I now it was thy far-heard tune
Which held them charmed among the roses red,
So that the moonlight silvered all their crowns.

Fisher Dilke was as handsome a man as I ever saw, but not at that date a great conversationalist. We used to go for long walks together, Fisher always wearing Trinity Hall slacks, that is white flannel trousers with a black stripe, in the course of which even a chatterbox like myself was reduced to silence by Fisher's resolute taciturnity. Toward the end of the time Ethel's younger sister Turkey came to stay with the Dilkes. I have forgotten her Christian name, if indeed I ever knew it. I used to take her for long voyages up and down the Windrush in my canoe. Once we went as far as Minster Lovell to see that ruined mediaeval manor house where legend said was discovered the chest in which a daughter of the house had hidden herself in a game, and in which her skeleton was found years later because she had been unable to get out. The story is told in Bayly's poem *The Mistletoe Bough.*

Then Mrs W. K. Clifford came to stay and, perhaps not considering me an 'eligible young man', took her daughter with her when she went away in case those voyages in a canoe should lead to emotional developments. There was no question in fact of such developments, but Mrs Clifford was right to be cautious, for indeed a young poet with an allowance of £150 a year from his father *was* most ineligible.

It would have been just after the Dilkes left that George Montagu came to Burford with the news that he and Alberta Sturgess were to be married at the end of July. "You must admit now, my dear Monty, that—— really is psychical," he said to me, that eyelid of his drooping triumphantly. The dash represents that odd girl who broke one of the panes in my library and gave me *Graziella.*

It must have been earlier in that July that I went to Cambridge to act in a one-act play by Thomas Heywood called *Worke for Cutlers.* This had been discovered in the library of Trinity Hall by A. Forbes Sieveking. Sieveking was the leading authority on old gardens, about which he had written books of more interest to the architect than the florist. He was also a devotee of fencing and a friend of Captain Hutton, the leading authority on swordsmanship and a distinguished figure in his dark and light blue Bath Club tie, who was to superintend the proper performance of *Worke for Cutlers*, which was an argument between Sword, Rapier and Dagger. Sieveking was to play Sword, I was to play Rapier and Alec Ross was to be Dagger. Alec Ross was an elder brother of Robbie Ross and in spite of having lost an eye was a fencing devotee. The piece was to be given as a pastoral on a cloudless July afternoon in the gardens of Trinity Hall, the centre of the audience being the moon-faced genial E. A. Beck, the Master of the Hall. To complete the Elizabethan atmosphere there was to be music given by the Dolmetsch family, all dressed in Elizabethan costume. I wore heavy black and gold trunks and black silk hose, with a very stiff and very large ruff, and tried to manage as gracefully as I could a genuine Elizabethan rapier well over six-feet long.

Alec Ross and I stayed with Sir Clifford Allbutt, the Regius Professor of Physics. Allbutt was a delightful man with only one fault: he was anti-tobacco; smoking in his house was absolutely forbidden. Alec and I had adjoining bedrooms and we used to lean out of our windows and smoke much needed cigarettes as we talked to one another. Down below the delicious scent of the tobacco plant in the border made the night fragrant, their white blooms glimmering in the moonlight. "I'm glad the Professor's anti-nicotianism doesn't forbid the plant," I said to Alec Ross.

They were a delightful three days in the sunny peace of the Cambridge Long Vacation in which, as I remember, so much more sensibly than at Oxford, undergraduates anxious to work could keep a term.

Christopher Stone was still away when I returned to Burford, coaching Esmé Chinnery at Cobham in Surrey for the arduous task of passing Little Go. He had been offered this job by Mrs Chinnery, the widow of a rich stockbroker; writing to his sister Faith about it, he had said he did not think he could take it because I should be alone at Lady Ham. From her he had received an indignant letter, asking if this 'Monty' about whom he made such a fuss was to interfere with his life. She was growing tired of always hearing about 'Monty'. In fact Faith Stone had met me for the first time in the previous year at her brother's rooms in Meadows. She recorded this meeting in the first volume of her reminiscences called *As Much As I Dare*:

"On May 25th, 1904 I sat in Christopher's shaded room in Christ

Church, having tea with some half-dozen undergraduates, suffering violent toothache, and waiting with some apprehension for the arrival of the Magdalen poet, who was very late.

"Then the door opened, and he was in the room. My first impression was of a bright-green emerald tie, and an enormous pair of eyes which seemed luminous in the darkened room. As he came into the light of the bay window, I saw the rose-leaf complexion, the small pretty Cupid's bow mouth, the sloping poet's brow, and then the wan crooked smile which so surprisingly tautened the Cupid's bow of a mouth. I saw that the eyes were deep violet blue.

"This then was Monty Mackenzie. I was overwhelmed by the manner in which his personality took charge of the room and everything it contained. Everything else, including myself became insignificant. I was not at all pleased.

" 'Toothache?' he was saying. 'Give your sister a glass of port, Polly. Port. The best thing for toothache.'

"I was given a glass, and sipped it unwillingly. I felt small and helpless, acutely conscious that no power on earth could shake the immanence of this too vivid personality. He was there, secure as a planet in our firmament. I watched him as he talked, enchanting his audience (for indeed it seemed to be instantly that); I noted as he held the floor, his graceful telling gestures, so rare in England, and the beauty of the great head, and the wideness of the cheek-bones, the fine sharpness of the shapely nose."

After reading that I am not surprised Faith had grown tired of always hearing about 'Monty'. And if I ever prescribed port for toothache I certainly deserved to lose all my own teeth twenty years later.

At this point I could kick myself for having stopped keeping that diary at the end of May, because the correct sequence of events is impossible to guarantee. Sometime toward the end of this July I was staying with Logan Pearsall Smith in Sussex. I recollect going with him to call on the Clutton Brocks and being tremendously impressed by Clutton Brock, and from that visit I recall being captivated by a huge bowl of *cephalaria tatarica*, a kind of giant scabious, standing in a corner of their sitting-room and being enchanted by the effect of the pale yellow flowers against the mauve wall paper. I recall most vividly of all going to lunch with Arthur and Dorothea Ponsonby at Shulbrede Priory; she was a daughter of Sir Hubert Parry. Arthur Ponsonby was at this date Private Secretary to Campbell-Bannerman a long way then, it seemed, from his leadership of the Labour Opposition in the House of Lords. He had had a tremendous success in the O.U.D.S. production of *The Frogs* of Aristophanes and had wanted to go on the stage, but family influence had prevailed on this former Page of Honour to Queen Victoria to enter diplomacy. I was fascinated by him and by his wife.

Lunch was in the old refectory and there must have been well over a dozen guests. We were all kept waiting for a while because Donald Tovey and Schiller, the pragmatic don of Merton, were expected. At last it was decided not to wait any longer and we all sat down. Round about two Tovey and Schiller came in.

"Oh, what a wonderful room for sound," Tovey exclaimed in that absurd voice of his and, making a trumpet of his hands, he began to tootle at the top of his voice. Little Elizabeth Ponsonby, aged four and a half, eyed Tovey with open-mouthed distaste, and turned to come to her father who was sitting at the head of the far end of the table with his back to the gothic windows; I was next to him. Between Elizabeth and her father was Donald Tovey, and she was not prepared to pass this tootling monster. I see her now in her long Kate Greenaway dress turning to walk with short quick steps all the way round the long table to reach her father without passing Donald Tovey. Pitter-pat. Pitter-pat. At last she reaches him from the other side of the room and I can see her now shaking her head and hear her say, "Elizabeth does not like that man." And I'm bound to say that after what I considered a ridiculous piece of exhibitionism I agreed with Elizabeth.

George Montagu's wedding was on July 20th; the reception was held in a house in Bruton Street which had been rented for the season. The bride looked lovely and George himself was obviously the happiest of men.

"Monty, my dear, I must show you Uncle Hinch's present."

He took me along to the display of wedding presents in the middle of which was an enormous electro-plated tray from the Earl of Sandwich. "It isn't very twee, is it?" George commented. 'Twee' was the jargon of the moment for something or somebody that was small and jolly.

Perhaps the amount of top-hats fired me to seek a contrast and it may have been after the wedding that I went along to Hilhouse with the idea of ordering a black Homberg hat. In those days the shop was presided over by a centenarian called Cantell. Yes, he really was one hundred years old and must have joined that Bond Street shop before the Regency was at an end.

"I want you to make me one of those squash hats, I thought I'd like a black one." Cantell looked at me in cold reproof.

"No, sir. Hilhouse could not build you such a hat. What you require, sir, is a new bowler." Forthwith that active centenarian mounted the ladder to find the pattern of my head for a bowler hat, the brim of which would be in this year's fashion. I at once surrendered.

What Cantell would say if he entered that Bond Street shop to-day! Tempora mutantur, but I am sure that Cantell would not have changed with them. I suppose when bowlers first came in he must have had to habituate himself with difficulty to such novel headgear. Yet, only in May of this year 1963 I was still able to make Mr Harmon, who is Hilhouse of to-day, wince when I asked him for a beret; indeed I believe if I had not been a customer of that famous hat-shop for sixty years he would have reproved me as Cantell once reproved me instead of offering with obvious distaste to obtain a beret for me.

Hilhouse is still in Bond Street, but round the corner Forster and Son have long vanished from Grafton Street. They seemed very expensive tailors once upon a time; a lounge suit with two pairs of trousers cost over eight guineas. Old Mr Forster in white Dundreary whiskers sat at his desk writing out the bills in copperplate and protected against interruption by a glass screen. There was a wooden horse on which a Cornet may have sat to show the cutter that his breeches and tunic fitted perfectly before he went off to the Crimea.

Credit with Forster and Son was gloriously elastic; if one's bill was too much, one paid half and ordered two more suits. I recommended my father to Forster's and as he always paid his bills by return I felt I was entitled to at least two years' credit.

Edouard and Butler in Clifford Street are still there, and I have had my shirts made there for nearly sixty years. Their other shop was in Paris in the Place Vendôme. A. J. Izod was in charge of the London shop until he started his own business in Hanover Square, after which I divided my custom between Edouard and Butler and Izod.

I recall going into Izod's one day in the middle of August and seeing half a dozen made-up bow ties displayed. This was a shock to me; it was also a shock to Izod when I came into the shop and saw them. "We have to keep them for the Americans," he said apologetically. "We seldom see any of our regular clients in August. It was quite a surprise seeing you."

"Do you sell them made-up white ties?" I asked coldly.

"No, no, we don't go as far as that," Izod said quickly.

Yes, those made-up bow ties were a severe shock both to Izod and myself.

My bootmakers in those days were Flack and Smith in Davies Street. There was a fashion at the moment for patent leather boots with light kid uppers for wear with a tail coat. I hear my father's voice from the past asking me what I had paid for a pair of such boots I was wearing at the time.

"Forty-two shillings," I told him.

"Forty-two shillings for a pair of boots?" he exclaimed. "Well, I can't afford to spend forty-two shillings on a pair of boots." I wonder how much a young man of to-day would have to spend on a pair of boots before he was able to shock his father.

The only letter that remains from this summer of 1905 is one from Ethel Dilke written from 7 Chilworth Street, W. on August 7:

I was so pleased to hear from you and I read it all quite easily. You don't say which of Georgina's children was saved. I think you ought to have got 14/-. *Pigs fetched as much as* 16/- *in my day.*

Georgina was a sow of high intelligence whose great ambition was to bring her litter across a small ford of the Windrush to rout about with them in the orchard. This I forbade her to do. 'You have the whole of the field to rout about in with your family, Georgina, and I will not allow you to bring them into the orchard.' One day Ethel Dilke was in the library with me when Georgina arrived with her family, and I shouted to her 'Go back at once, Georgina. You know you're not allowed in the orchard.' To Ethel's delight Georgina turned round, and with loud grunts of protest took herself and her children back across the ford into the field that was her territory. The letter continues:

Send Daphnis and Amaryllis to Vanity Fair. I hear it's a new man who means to work it up. Mind you send a note with it.

But *Vanity Fair* sent back my long pastoral poem with editorial regrets.

I don't believe in Charles learning wisdom. But if he's even so little less of a fool it's to the good. How *bad is Twinkle's neck? You aren't a bit good at details.*

Charles, of course, was the staghound given to me by Philip Lloyd-Graeme. Twinkle had killed a stray Jacobin pigeon and after biting off its head had strained his neck in pushing it behind one of the espalier pears by which he had sat all day, growling if any of the dogs came near him.

And why didn't you come and see us when you came up for Mr Montagu's wedding? We'd have given you eggs for lunch and done any other little thing. Not very friendly of you. Praps you'll come from Grosvenor Road. It's a long way though. You must sleep the night. No charge is ever cheaper than 7/6 a week which I must say sounds quite cheap. Is it with attendance?

I've just looked it up in my wages table. It's £20 a year.

I had not realized until I read this old letter that Christopher and I had decided as early as this on the move to London. I must have found the two rooms at 7 Grosvenor Road when I was in London for George Montagu's wedding. 1 to 7 Grosvenor Road were a terrace of small houses which began at the end of Abingdon Street. At this date most of Westminster was almost a slum. The beginning of Grosvenor Road was not a slum but the houses from 1 to 7 were all lived in by working-class tenants. Mrs Charnock, the gloriously Cockney landlady of Number 7, was a continual delight to me. Mr Charnock was a brick-layer, and every Saturday night without fail he and his wife came to blows when he returned from the pub. The houses were only two storeys high and we rented the rooms on the top floor. I had the front room papered in apple-green with cherry-red (*not* cerise) curtains to the two windows looking out across a small public-garden to the river with a view of old Lambeth Bridge. Our bedroom looked out on a yard and the stables of the Tilling Omnibus Company, a splendid specimen of William and Mary architecture. But more of 7 Grosvenor Road presently. The letter from Ethel Dilke continued:

Sicily sounds good. Don't you love to say 'Syracuse'? It's like that blessed word 'Mesopotamia'. The word before 'luck' is the one I can't read.

She tried to copy my illegible epithet, but I cannot read it myself. The allusion to Sicily was an invitation I had had from Alec Hood to spend December, January and February with him in his castle of Bronte. He had inherited the Nelson dukedom of Bronte and used to have three months' leave every winter from his job as Private Secretary to Queen Alexandra. For reasons which will appear presently I could not pay that visit to Sicily, and I have always regretted the missed opportunity.

We hope to move next week. I mean we mean to. The pianola comes on Monday next. I gave Fisher your message. He sends his respects and says it truly wasn't him. They did before. Who is doing your book? Goodness, how you leave out details. And all with an air of giving so many. Fisher hasn't had the photographs done. He'll send them as soon as we have a minute's time. Will you tell Mr Whitworth Jones he shall have his too.

The Dilkes had taken 53 Sussex Gardens, which for Ethel was always 53 Sussidge. The message I gave to Fisher has long been forgotten. The 'book' is my first attempt to collect my poems which I was intending to send to Elkin Matthews, the former partner of John Lane, in whose Vigo Street offices John Mavrogordato was dabbling with the idea of becoming a publisher himself one day. The letter concludes:

What have you written lately? Long or short? Lyrics? Sonnets? Not a word about them and only mentioned at all in a postscript. I want, please, to hear them rather soon.

Have you read Oscar Wilde's Happy Prince*? It makes me weep tears of sheer joy when the swallow speaks of Egypt.*

Lavender. I forget if you have it in the garden. It just occurred to me that it should be there. Is it?

This letter brings back poignantly from the past how much I owe to Ethel Dilke's early encouragement of my writing.

It was about now that Luxmoore and Gerald Wellesley came down to Burford to see Hutton about a publishing problem. Hutton was to edit a volume of Ainger's *obiter dicta*; on hearing of this Irving had got in touch with Sir Frederick Macmillan and asked that a criticism Ainger had once written of his Hamlet should not be reprinted. I cannot be sure, but I think it included a phrase that his performance was funny without being vulgar. My mother remembered Irving's being much upset at the time by this criticism, and now thirty years later it still rankled. Macmillan had promised Irving that it should be omitted from the forthcoming volume and Luxmoore was trying to persuade Hutton to refuse to omit it. Hutton said he could not compel Macmillans to include the article and in the end it was omitted from the collected papers. On second thoughts I believe it was then that Gerald Wellesley gave me that piece of damson velvet which had once been Rossetti's.[1]

In the middle of August Christopher's sister Faith came with Kate Whitworth Jones to stay in the Other House. She had gone on the stage and had been with Charles Hawtrey at the Avenue Theatre in

[1] After the last night of the Wexford Festival in October '63 a distinguished looking man of about my own age came up to me and said 'I think we last met at Broadway about sixty years ago.' 'No, Duke, it was at Burford,' I told him.

some minute part in *The Message from Mars*, and later on toured in the United States with him in Anstey's farce *The Man from Blankley's*, in which she had played the parlour-maid waiting at a dinner-party. To be on the stage in those days seemed like a great gesture of independence from a girl brought up in a scholastic ambient. Naturally I was not prepared to be impressed by a young woman's going on the stage, and paid little attention either to her or Kate Whitworth Jones as they lolled in hammocks. Then Hugo Rumbold, a younger brother of Sir Horace Rumbold, came down to stay. He was an amusing youth who used to tell stories of how he had gone to parties dressed as a girl without anybody's finding out. He stammered slightly and when held up for a word used to spell it very quickly. I hear Bobbie Whitworth Jones asking him why he had not been at George Montagu's wedding. "I was at g-g-g—I can't say it—I'll spell it. I was at g-g-g—double o—d-d-dee d-double u—d-d-dee," from which we were supposed to understand he had been at Goodwood.

Mrs Williams was giving a garden party at Taynton; not being too fond of garden-parties I had made an excuse not to go; if I had done I should have been angrier than I was when I heard about what I considered completely outrageous behaviour. Faith Stone (she called herself Faith Reynolds on the stage) and Kate Whitworth Jones thought it would be amusing to dress up Hugo Rumbold as a girl, lending him the clothes, and with Bobbie Whitworth Jones they all went to the garden-party. In spite of Hugo Rumbold's claim to put on a perfect feminine performance he was quickly spotted and none of the Williams family was at all amused. I was furious. So too was Christopher when he came back from the Chinnerys and heard what had happened. We sent an ultimatum to Bobbie Whitworth Jones, demanding Hugo Rumbold's departure from Burford. Whitworth Jones told us we were being rather provincial; I retorted that we preferred to be provincial if behaving like a bounder was evidence of metropolitan behaviour.

Presently Robin Buxton came down to play in a cricket-match between Ladies and Gentlemen. I was out almost at once as usual, and found myself sitting next Faith to watch the play. I was surprised to find her much more intelligent than I had supposed; by the time the innings came to an end with some terrific slogging by Christopher I had made up my mind to see more of her when Christopher and I came to London at the end of September and *vie de Bohême* was to begin.

I had made friends earlier in the year with a girl called Daisy, whose rent and household expenses in Great Coram Street were paid by a commercial traveller and who was free when he was away to frequent the Café de l'Europe and the Café de Provence in Leicester Square without having to earn her living professionally. Daisy was the true *fille de joie* whose world was the underworld. She was not a girl in an office who supplemented her salary by gold-digging from business men. She was not a flash tart who frequented the promenades of the Empire or the Alhambra. Thanks to her, my knowledge of London's underworld became as extensive and peculiar as Sam Weller's knowledge of London. That knowledge I should one day put to use for the fourth part of *Sinister Street*, when Michael Fane was searching for Lily. Neither Lily nor Sylvia Scarlett ever existed in reality: they were completely creations of my own imagination. My friendship with Daisy was not a love-affair, but we shared a sense of humour and she was the perfect guide. Her gift as a *raconteuse* would only be surpassed when I met the original Jenny Pearl of *Carnival* five years later.

Poor Christopher suffered from my absorption with the night life of London. His chief complaint was that when I came back at four in the morning I would sit on my bed and chew away at the Ribston pippins from Lady Ham which lived in a basket under my bed.

"For god's sake *must* you eat apples at this hour of the morning?" he would moan from his bed.

Then at seven o'clock we would be woken by the noise of the bells of the omnibuses being tested, and by the steps being tested by loud stamps before one omnibus after another clattered out of the yard for its day's round.

Christopher was working very hard at writing articles for the weeklies, one of which was occasionally accepted and munificently rewarded with a guinea. Once he even got two guineas for an article and we felt that wealth was in our grasp. I wrote a long poem in *terza rima* called *Life and Death on Chelsea Bridge*, which five years later Henry James would consider much the most promising in my volume of poems and which Quiller-Couch would condemn as the only poem he did not like.

One day we went to see Desmond MacCarthy, who was living somewhere in Chelsea with his delightful German mother. Desmond had been at Stone House before he went to Eton and was a great friend of Faith Stone when he was a little boy and she was a little girl. At Cambridge he had been the golden boy of the Apostles, as Hallam had been once upon a time and Rupert Brooke would be presently, what indeed Milton had been more than two centuries before Tennyson joined that galaxy of major poets of which Cambridge could boast—Marlowe, Spenser, Milton, Herrick, Dryden, Gray, Wordsworth, Coleridge, Byron, Tennyson. What could Oxford muster against such a team? Shelley who was sent down, Collins, Matthew Arnold, William Morris, Swinburne. . . . the only sop to Oxford is that no Cambridge poet did as much for his university as Matthew Arnold did for Oxford.

Desmond MacCarthy was now editing a quarterly called the *Independent Review,* which was the first manifestation of Cambridge cum Bloomsbury. He was charming to Christopher and myself but he did not invite either of us to contribute an article to the *Independent Review.* Christopher had only managed to get a Third in Greats and I remember Desmond's saying to him what a pity it was he had broken with the family tradition of King's, Cambridge by going to Christ Church, Oxford.

Faith Stone was now living in digs at 125 St George's Road, Pimlico, and I thought she might be able to play a part in a Grand Guignol one-act play I had written called *Punch and Judy.* The other woman's part was to be played by Dorothy Scott, who had been my Nerissa in *The Merchant of Venice.* I was to play the third part and it was to be given at some charity bazaar. However, this fell through because the woman who was running the bazaar thought it was too horrible and frightening a one-act thriller for a charity audience.

I found Faith's company more and more agreeable and we took to dining together frequently at the Brice in Old Compton Street, where for 2/- one had a five-course dinner, wine and coffee included. To-day the Brice restaurant is Wheeler's famous oyster-bar and restaurant. We used to come back to Grosvenor Road and wish that Christopher would have an engagement to dine out somewhere. I recall one of those dinner engagements of his when with absence of mind he put a towel round his neck instead of his white silk muffler. A memory of those evenings in Soho remains in a poem which Quiller-Couch included in his *Oxford Book of Victorian Verse.*

> *My dear, what dinners we have had,*
> *What cigarettes and wine,*
> *In faded corners of Soho,*
> *Your fingers touching mine.*

We were growing more and more in love and I began to think that it was hardly reasonable behaviour for me to make love to the sister of my best friend. True, she was five years older than I, and after five years on the stage might be considered able to look after herself.

Nevertheless, I was ill at ease with myself. On my way back to Grosvenor Road on that November afternoon, I saw walking along on the other side of Abingdon Street the Colonial Secretary, Alfred Lyttelton. He was smiling to himself as he walked slowly along on his way from the House of Commons; I wondered what had happened to that now decrepit Unionist party to make him smile. If he could smile at the prospect before a Government on its last legs surely I too could smile at my own prospect. When I reached our rooms in Grosvenor Street I found Faith there alone.

"Why shouldn't we get married?" I asked her suddenly.

"As soon as we can," she replied.

"Christopher will be going to Eton for the wall game on November 30th. We'd better try for that date. Of course our marriage will have to be kept a dead secret."

By now the consternation our marriage would cause was beginning to overwhelm me and I felt that I should have to achieve something before it was made public. I went to Doctors' Commons and found out that a special licence was obtainable for two guineas, but that Faith would have to sign it as well as myself. As soon as we knew for certain that Christopher was going to Eton for St Andrew's Day, Faith wrote to the Vicar of St Saviour's, Pimlico, her parish church; I still have the rough copy of her letter in pencil!

Dear Sir,

Would you be kind enough to let me know if it will be convenient for you or one of your clergy to take a marriage by licence to-morrow, Nov. 30 at 1 o'clock? Also could you let me know what is required in the way of witnesses.

Yours truly

Faith Stone

To this the Vicar replied:

St Saviour's Vicarage
46 St George's Square
S.W.

Dear Madam

I can take a marriage by licence to-morrow (Thursday) at 1 o'clock with pleasure. Two witnesses are required, but if the Parties who come to the marriage come without them, both can be provided without any trouble.

Believe me to be

Yours truly

Henry Washington

I said I would go round to Nevern Square in the morning and see if my brother Frank could be one witness, and we'd leave the other to

C.M. at 24 years

Faith in 1905

Mr Washington. On that Thursday morning I arrived at 1 Nevern Square about nine o'clock to find out if Frank, under the strictest vow of secrecy, could come along with me to Grosvenor Road. He was up in his bedroom shaving.

"Are you doing anything at one o'clock, Frank?"

"No. Why?"

"Well, I'm getting married at one o'clock and I want you to be a witness."

Frank stood the shock as a militia subaltern in the 5th Royal Dublin Fusiliers should. Only a faint nick made in his cheek by the razor suggested a moment of surprise. Then we went off to meet Faith at Blackfriars and get the special licence at Doctors' Commons. After that I bought the wedding-ring at some shop in Cheapside. Frank and I parted with Faith at Westminster Bridge and at half-past twelve he and I reached St Saviour's to wait for her arrival. We got the crossing-sweeper outside to come in and oblige as us a second witness; his name was Richard Robert Primmer. Nobody could have been kinder and more sympathetic than Mr Washington the Vicar; the marriage went through like clockwork.

The wedding breakfast, or rather lunch, was held at the Brice, the bill for which was six shillings; I could not run to champagne after the expense of the licence and the wedding-ring, but the owner, on hearing what the occasion was, stood us a bottle.

Christopher did not come back that night, and we decided that Mrs Charnock might think it odd if his sister spent the night at 7 Grosvenor Road; when Big Ben chimed the strokes of midnight I escorted Faith back to St George's Road. She felt that as Frank knew about our marriage it would be only fair to confide as much to Christopher when he came back from Eton. He scoffed at our notion of keeping it secret for a couple of years and said that if I did not announce it he should do so himself. So on December 4th I told my mother. She was her quickly comprehending self and promised to do her best to keep my father from being too much upset, but urged me to write to him at once. What worried her most was the effect the news of my marriage might have on Ruth Daniel.

"I loved Ruth so dearly," she told me. "And have always hoped that you and she would come together again."

"But it was she who broke off the engagement," I said.

"She broke it off because she loved you too much. She thought she was standing between you and your career."

"Not much of a career so far," I said bitterly.

"You *are* only twenty-two."

"*Only* twenty-two! That's pretty old, you know."

I went on to tell her that all this year I had been haunted by the memory of Ruth and that the reason why I had married Faith was to impose on myself responsibility. I could not face the possibility of another love-affair going wrong. Faith was five years older than myself and would be able to share with me the vital necessity of making our marriage a success.

"I shall write to Ruth," my mother said.

"But you'll write to Faith?"

That December 6th was a day of letters. My mother wrote to Faith:

Will you drive down with me to Bethnal Green to-morrow evening? We can then have a quiet talk.

I am rather bewildered about everything at present and really feel perfectly unable to write about it.

My love to you, dear child, and please always think of me as a good friend.

Her father wrote to Faith:

Helensbourne
Abingdon. *Dec. 6.*

Darling Faith,

I can't quite approve and yet I am not furiously angry as I suppose a sensible parent should be. If Mr Mackenzie had been of the same equable temperament as myself (equable is Arthur Benson's word) no doubt he could have been brought over with the same ease. But I can imagine the charm of a romantic marriage with no trousseau or wedding breakfast. There is a spice of romance in this aged heart, and perhaps it has descended to you. As there was more than a spice in your mother it is not unnatural . . . if you are happy I am happy and my only prayer is that the happiness may be lasting. . . . I should strongly advise you not to keep the matter from Mr Mackenzie: the sooner all bombs are hurled the better.

You are to keep a small corner of your heart for
Your loving Daddo

I hoped I should get even a fragment of as charming a letter as that from my own father, to whom I wrote on December 6th from Grosvenor Road:

My dear Father,

I am afraid that the news in this letter will considerably dismay you, as I know what views you hold on youthful marriages. I have been strongly tempted the past week to keep from you the fact that last Thursday I married Miss Faith Stone. My intention was to keep it a secret from everyone until I thought the 'psychological moment' had arrived for the revelation. However, on second and I hope and believe that you will think better thoughts, I decided that it was not fair or honest to continue in receipt of an allowance from you on false pretences. I have always played a straight game with you in the past and I could not bear to keep such a momentous fact from you.

Now I perfectly admit your right to withdraw that £150 a year which you allow me at present. I am perfectly prepared to go on the stage either on tour or in town. I have no doubt you would do your best to get me an engagement.

On the other hand, if you see fit to continue the allowance, there shall be no further call upon you. Of course I should be more than grateful, recognizing to the full your extreme generosity always so conspicuous in the past.

So much for that. Now for my reasons for what to you and indeed to everybody must seem an unaccountable step. I have always had a somewhat fatal attraction to women and my love-affairs already have been numerous. I have made one girl unhappy and myself as unhappy. Since then I have made two other girls rather unhappy.

I have had no other vices—neither inclination to drink or to gamble, but a petticoat has always been able to whirl me off my balance. For the last year I have longed more passionately than I can tell you to be settled. My eternal philandering since my engagement was broken off was injuring both my work and myself. In this affair I was determined to finish for ever with half-measures. You know my headstrong way, and you will understand that if I have made up my mind I will have my own way. As it appears in this case I have been luckier than I deserve. Your daughter-in-law is handsome, charming, clever and moreover the sister of my greatest friend. Of course the news was as much of a shock to Stone as any one.

If you knew how many times I have been tempted to cut myself off from society and marry some barmaid and be done with love-affairs for ever, you would be glad that I have chosen so wisely. You will remember your own youth perhaps and forgive me more readily for this step.

Of course I pledge myself not to have any children until I can support them without assistance from you. I am not a fool, though you may think I am. When you read this letter remember that I have been frank with you and forgive me more readily.

I cannot tell you what it would mean to me if you could possibly bring yourself to see that this marriage may after all be the finest thing that could have happened. Already I feel free from everything save the most earnest desire and determination to justify your confidence. If you will continue to back me up, I swear you shall never regret it. If I am famous (many are convinced I shall be) you will have done a good deal more for me than fathers usually do for men of genius.

Please forgive

Your loving son

Monty

That very long letter was found by me among a tangle of my mother's papers only a short time ago. I was tempted not to put it into print, but honesty prevailed. Although at eighty I am faintly embarrassed by that cocksure opinion of myself, it represents what I was thinking at twenty-two more revealingly than any attempt to evoke those thoughts from the present.

Having brought myself to put that letter into print, I feel I must print my reply to my father's reception of it.

Helensbourne,
Abingdon. *December 21*

My dear Father,

I understand your feeling of being hurt that I did not tell you before. It was less intentional than it seemed, and really it did not strike me that you would be sensitive to what was really not at all a want of confidence but a desire not to worry you before the event.

Personally I am always much less upset when a thing is done.

I feel that perhaps you don't think I quite appreciate the single-heartedness of your life, your steady unselfishness and the sacrifice of your ambition for the sake of your family. Indeed I do. . . .

It is inevitable that anyone who proposes to stake his fame on literature is bound to convey an impression of dawdling at first. These present years are the ones in which every great man has been criticized for what the world chooses to suppose waste of time.

But it is significant that all the great poets were relieved from the harassing effort of earning their daily bread at this very period. A young man is laying up his experience, pruning his extravagances, moulding his ultimate ideas. I should not write like this, were I not firmly convinced that one day I shall rank high among the English poets. Some intuition is given to men born poets which justifies their contempt of popular success and consoles them with the prospect of ultimate glory . . . . The wear and tear of a violent and oppressive imagination are such that he must have some soothing influence to counterbalance this. Some find it in drink, some in drugs, a few in dissipation. But I am now happier in my marriage than I have been for a year. I have lost the restlessness which prevented me from undertaking irksome drudgery. I can sit down to work with pleasure. I can get up in the morning. I can get to rest at night. I am so profoundly changed by this step that I can only regard it as the most fortunate occurrence in the world.

It is a grief to me that it has upset you so much; it will continue to be a grief until I am assured that you not only tolerate it but are glad *that I embarked upon it.*

You ask if determination to have one's own way is the right way to get on. By Heaven it is! and the only way. I have in the past conquered what seemed insuperable bars to progress by this determination and force of character. I impress my personality on all with whom I come in contact. If I were not the most indomitable optimist conceivable I should long ago have become a bank clerk.

Don't think this letter boastful, self-confident and absurd, but consider what I have already done.

(i) *Practically a volume of poetry which in all circles is considered promising of real greatness in the future.*
(ii) *Successfully edited an Oxford paper.*
(iii) *Successfully managed a financially tottering Club.*
(iv) *Written some decent dramatic stuff.*
(v) *Got a Second in Schools.*
(vi) *Paid for my school-education entirely.*
(vii) *Made the friendship of a very large number of admirable people and finally married a perfect wife.*

I have on hand an enormous number of plays, poems, essays and God knows any amount of work. You simply shan't be disappointed. *It is very good of you to agree to the Jan. allowance and I* rely entirely *on your discretion by what I do in the next 3 months what you decide to do next. I know you to be the most fair-minded man of my acquaintance.*

One thing—I am sure you will be the first to admit that throughout your very strenuous life you have found in your own wife the one certain solace for innumerable disappointments, endless anxieties and some sorrows.

And now with a devout hope that you will come to see that what now strikes you as inconsiderate and disappointing was really as valuable a step as to justify my acting entirely on my own initiative.

I am
Your loving son
Monty

At this moment of all-round tension the drains at 7 Grosvenor Road went wrong and Faith's father asked us to go and stay with him at Helensbourne, that charming house in the lee of St Helen's church, Abingdon, with a garden running down to the river.

That letter to his daughter quoted above shows the sweet core of her father's nature. The Reverend Edward Daniel Stone was indeed the dearest old man I have ever known. He had found it impossible even to swallow, let alone digest, the Thirty-nine Articles of the Anglican Church, and so had never taken priest's orders. One of the pleasures of his old age was his belief that Broad Church views were slowly but surely lightening the obscurantism of High Church and Low Church alike. He was an equally passionate Liberal in politics, and though he was inclined to deplore the leadership of the Liberal

Party's having been handed over to Sir Henry Campbell-Bannerman, rather than to his old pupil Lord Rosebery, he awaited with eagerness what he believed would be the ignominious collapse of the Unionist Party at the General Election in January. He was by now very deaf and used to go stumping through room after room toward his beloved billiards-room, slamming every door behind him to the slight distress of his daughter Ruth who kept house for him. Then he would play match after match between spot and plain, in which the unspotted billiards-ball nearly always won because he could not refrain from giving spot difficult cannons or pockets which spot would miss, whereas his favourite plain was always indulged with easy shots. He was glad to find an opponent in me, but I quickly realised I must give spot the same difficult shots he always gave it, for E.D.S. did not like to lose a game of billiards and if he could win one by a series of flukes, each more outrageous than the last, he enjoyed his victory all the more.

He was up every morning by six, when he would write out the elegiacs or hexameters he had composed for the weekly competition in the Saturday *Westminster Gazette*. He would come stumping down to breakfast, humming away to himself, and fling the fair copy he had made in his own beautiful handwriting for me to read before he posted it off. I do not exaggerate when I say that he won the guinea prize five times out of six so long as the Saturday *Westminster* lasted. I should call the failure of the sea-green incorruptible to maintain itself against the vulgarisation of the British Press the major disaster for British journalism in this century.

In days gone by E.D.S., Algernon Swinburne and Pope Leo XIII had been wont to exchange elegiacs. Eheu fugaces! We shall never read again a volume like *Arundines Cami*. The reeds of Cam have withered; the loosestrife of Isis has faded away.

Apart from Faith's father and her elder sister Ruth, the only other person in Helensbourne when we arrived there at the beginning of that December was a little girl of thirteen, pale and solemn with a tuberculous knee. This was Nellie Baker, whom Faith's mother had adopted when she became a Catholic, one of a large impoverished Catholic family. She may have hoped that one of her own five daughters would follow her into the Church. I was astonished to be told that Nellie had been expelled from two convent schools because of the bad example she was setting the other girls, for I could not have fancied so sedate a child was able to set a bad example. I did not have an opportunity of drawing out this pale solemn child for some time because I was seized with an acute attack of jaundice, the result presumably of the mental agitation of lifting the lid from that secret marriage.

I am glad I had that vile jaundice because it taught me what it was to feel that life was not worth living, and I have been able ever since to feel compassion for people whose excess of bile spoils existence for them. I have never since experienced any bilious attack or even the mildest liverishness; with the memory of that jaundice I realize that a well-behaved liver is the secret of happiness. I have never known jealousy and I am convinced that jealousy is the result of misplaced bile. At least two of my most successful and distinguished fellow-authors, with no excuse at all for jealousy, cannot hear of another's success without that tell-tale yellow creeping into their eyes. I am sure that Shakespeare when he called jealousy the green-eyed monster must have noticed that faint discoloration.

I lay in bed with jaundice, wondering if I should ever be able to taste anything again, wondering whether before me stretched a life of eternal drabness, whether I should ever again be stirred by the touch of a woman's lips on mine, whether my tongue would ever cease to feel like mangy fur, whether I should want to talk to or hear anybody talk to me again.

A letter from my mother to Faith dated December 10th suggests a fear of typhoid:

Thank you for letting me know how Monty was and I shall be glad to hear when his temperature goes down. Christopher tells me the landlord is to do the drains at No. 7—so that can be a relief to all our minds. I think it was most kind of your father to have you and Monty to stay with him just now. Monty must repay him I hope in making you very happy.

I am glad to have seemed kind—I want to be but feel curiously incapable of being anything. *My love, dear.*

I knew at the time how much distressed my mother was over Ruth. Indeed, she had not yet been able to bring herself to tell my little sisters, Katie and Fay, who had adored Ruth, about my marriage. Yet it was only just over a month ago that I found in a sealed envelope two letters to my mother from Mrs Daniel and Ruth written in that December nearly sixty years ago. I never knew at the time what a shock my marriage had been to Ruth; if my mother had shown me that letter from her it might have wrecked my marriage with Faith. Instead she thought of a way by which I might justify to my father what he was considering the reckless imprudence of what I had done.

In 1904 he had produced at Paisley a play called *To-Morrow* by an anonymous writer. It had an original idea but the play itself was poorly constructed and poorly written. He took it out of his repertory almost at once, but he was now considering having it rewritten after Addison Bright, who was J. M. Barrie's agent, had told him that the idea was so good that it would be worth his while giving it a London production if it could be pulled together. He had even approached Barrie on the subject. Barrie, however, had too many ideas of his own to be bothered with other people's. The idea was that an English peer, who had been a rip, was on the eve of marriage to a sweet young ingénue and that on the night before his wedding he found himself and his valet back in the eighteenth century.

As soon as I was able to get up from that bed of jaundice I sat down to tackle *To-Morrow*, and somehow I managed to rewrite it in time to give it to my father as a birthday present on January 14th. I certainly got quickly down to work in spite of jaundice. I find a letter to my mother in that December:

I'm up but not able to get into Oxford to take my degree as I intended. Let me have a word to say what you think of the new scene. I think it much improved. Since I have been up I have written 50 *lines of a new poem,* 3 *sonnets, a lyric and also the 'Posy' to let friends know about our marriage. . . . I hope Father will understand my letter. Looking back on it, it seems a little self-confident, but I really do believe in ultimate success and I don't like him to think I am playing with life.*

Just after Christmas Logan Pearsall Smith told me Philip Morrell was looking for somebody to help him with his electoral campaign in South Oxfordshire, and I went to call on him and Lady Ottoline in Bloomsbury.

"What I want," said Philip Morrell, "is somebody to edit and write a four-page journal appearing every day during the campaign. Then you would have to make two or three speeches in different places every day and prepare my speeches for me, and of course be at hand to keep any meeting going until I arrived. If you could fit in a bit of canvassing so much the better. This will be quite a bit of hard work for a fortnight but it will be a useful experience for you."

"Shall I have a motor-car at my disposal?" I asked.

Morrell smiled. "No, I'm afraid I shall be using the only motor-car available. You'll have to manage with a bicycle. But I shall be paying you handsomely."

The sallow face of Lady Ottoline nodded graciously above that floppy form of hers.

"I'm sure you enjoy bicycling," she said. "I think young people always enjoy bicycling." She uttered this great thought in what she evidently supposed was the impressive tone of the Pythian priestess herself; I thought it was merely a very affected way of talking.

The prospect of bicycling all over the Chilterns in the middle of winter did not appeal to me, but I felt it would be wrong at this moment to turn down a handsome fee.

"Yes," Philip Morrell went on. "I am prepared to give you £20 for what will be just a fortnight's work. That surprises you, doesn't it?"

"Yes, it does, Mr Morrell." But I did not add that my surprise was due to the nerve of asking anybody to do what he was wanting me to do for £20.

"Well, when can you come along and discuss the plan of campaign?" Philip Morrell asked with the complacency of somebody who has just made a good bargain.

"I'm afraid I won't be able to accept your offer, Mr Morrell. I could not accept less than fifty guineas for what will be rather an exhausting job."

As I followed the butler out of that earnestly artistic Bloomsbury room I heard Lady Ottoline say: "What a very farouche and conceited young man, Philip."

Faith and I decided that the best way of letting our friends know we were married was to send a card of New Year's greetings:

Montague and Faith
Compton Mackenzie
send
A Posy of Sweet Months
to all their friends
for
MDCCCCVI

7 Grosvenor Road
Westminster
S.W.

Lady Ham
Burford
Oxford

The stripling January comes in cold:
But never let your hearts grow cold or old.

When February pours her silver rain,
May February fill your purse again!

When March blows in the Spring with windy weather,
Let Love blow in your heart light as a feather.

Clouds and lambs! Blue and white is April's token!
May your antique blue china ne'er be broken!

Columbines dance in May with dancing hours:
Dance you with columbines and all sweet flowers.

And now comes June with azure eves and morns,
Go gather roses, heedless of their thorns.

When hot July comes in with flaming lilies
We pray that you may meet your Amaryllis.

Swart August suns and tall wheat turning yellow!
To such a harvest may your wishes mellow!

September with dew-dabbled cobwebs dressed;
May ne'er a gossamer your locks molest!

October with red apples! leaves astir!
We pray your cheeks may be even rosier.

And when November wraps the town in mist,
You shall be bright as a bright amethyst.

So that when Spring's forgot in drear December,
Us twain with kindly thoughts you may remember.

M.C.M.

I give a few extracts out of some of the letters I had from round the world from friends, all but one of whom (Lord Swinton) are now gone:

Mrs Overton wrote from High Cross:

You have certainly succeeded—probably beyond your wildest expectations in startling all your friends. Dear lunatic, what can I do but wish you good luck and give you my blessing! What else could I do, whatever you did! . . . Speak kindly to your Lady for me and mine.

Always your loving
Mum

I look back to that precious year at High Cross when I had rescued myself from school and just begun to search for a path that would wind its way up Parnassus.

Ethel Dilke wrote from 53 Sussex Gardens:

We just never heard of such a thing. How could *you get married without us and to someone we've never seen in spite of her lovely name. . . . I hope she's as charming to honeymoon with as you were. We give you the best of characters from experience. The posy is charming. I couldn't have kept off 'amethyst' myself.*

I look back to that precious friendship with Ethel Dilke and think of those afternoons at 53 Sussidge with her and Viola Taylor who would marry, first my friend Maurice Woods and later Charles Garvin. I look back to the birth of Ethel's eldest son and to her telling me that when Sir Frederick Pollock came to see her after John was born he had asked what he weighed at birth, and when told nine pounds had observed "Ah, that's exactly the weight of a rifle."

Archdeacon Hutton wrote:

What a wonderful man you are! May all things ever go well with you. When shall you return to your country seat? It's bad to begin with influenza and jaundice, but good to get the worst over. . . .

Ever thine

W. H. Hutton

I look back to those wonderful dinners with him in the Great House and much regret that I never visited him when he became Dean of Winchester.

George Montagu wrote from Chalfont Lodge, Chalfont St Peter:

Indeed I congratulate you with all my heart and am so glad that you are happy and at peace. Please tell "Miss Faith" that I think she is a very lucky person, and you are too, you old sinner.

You must both come here in January after this election is over. We should both love to have you. Alberta always speaks of you as "that dear boy".

I look back to that visit at the end of January and I see the present Lord Sandwich being wheeled about in his perambulator just six months old.

Raymond Wavell-Paxton wrote from Windsor, where he was now a subaltern in the Coldstream Guards:

Fortunately I have long since given up being surprised at anything you may do, so was able to bear the shock with fortitude. Accept my blessings and genuinely sincere good wishes for your success. I really am damned glad.

I look back to that first term at Magdalen and to the flowering of a wonderful friendship sixty-two years ago.

Francis Underhill wrote from Oxford:

I have given up being surprised: therefore I accept your marriage with equanimity tempered with hope. . . . I am going down to High Cross for the inside of the week: pupils are not to be back, or I could not have borne it.

I look back to that pink-faced Exeter undergraduate with fair curly hair when I was a pupil at High Cross and to the last time I saw him in that glorious Palace at Wells.

Hugh Francis wrote from Edenbridge, Kent:

I have heard scraps of news about you now and then, the most important of which was that you habitually wore a brown wideawake and a large green tie. Your news is more important.... I have been up to Magdalen twice this autumn. The College is going to the Devil ... we won the Fours and never had a bump supper. Alban Hood went up and took a fond farewell of everybody. It is a grievous pity that he should go and bury himself in Burmah. I do not believe his health will stand it.

I look back and see Hugh Francis in that pink Leander tie refusing to go out and cox the Eight when the *Daily Mail* rag was at its merriest, and I see him later on as the portly Master of a City Company.

Alban Hood wrote from *Camp somewhere on God's earth, Upper Burmah.*

March 7, 1906

I suppose you are the respectable married man now.... I am doing the hermit touch ... if you were here you would write like hell about the place.... I can't make head or tail out of the damned language, which is a nuisance as I have no one to talk English to for two months at a time.... I shall probably get the sack from the firm I am working for as I haven't the heart to curse my men, they're such jolly people.... Think of me judging timber and inspecting elephants and buying buffaloes and enjoy a gentle laugh.

I look back to dear Alban Hood playing so exquisitely on that grand piano of his in Chaplain's Quad. Perhaps the Great War for Civilization was kind when it took him.

Tom Spring Rice wrote from Sloane Street:

It's all very great and wonderful and I've hardly got over my surprise but (if you'll forgive patronizing) I do think it's a splendid plan altogether. I only wish you hadn't got jaundice.... Christopher tells me he has been converting everybody with much success. You are too splendid and romantic getting married without Christopher knowing when he was in the house!

I look back to dear Tom Spring Rice playing as beautifully as Alban Hood on his grand piano in Balliol. He sacrificed music not for teak but for diplomacy.

Philip Lloyd-Graeme wrote from Bridlington:

You are luckier than you have any business to be. If you have not been divorced by the time it arrives accept the Upton Letters as a mark of my esteem.... I hope during this season you will reincarnate in yr person all the desired virtues. The best of luck to you both.

Malcolm Hogg wrote from Bombay:

On this auspicious day, the anniversary of that glorious Jan. 17, when you and I both cried our first tears to an unheeding and unappreciative world, it would be ridiculous not to be able to express myself on paper and send you my very warmest wishes for the best of luck and happiness. . . . If you have time write and tell me of your plans and doings. How is Joan of Arc prospering? Out here I still feel uprooted and do not much care for the life or the people on the whole. I suppose I ought to consider myself lucky from a worldly point of view, but I can't get here any of the things that interest me. . . . I won't tell you in stereotyped fashion that you're a very lucky fellow, because you see, in this case, I think you both very lucky.

I have quoted from enough letters, and as I read through them I am humbly amazed at the warmth of good-will shown to me by my friends, and I realize with an equal warmth of gratitude how much I must have owed to the confidence shown by them in my ultimate ability to make a name for myself.

The exhilaration of that 1906 General Election had the quality of Wordsworth's poem about the French Revolution.

Bliss was it in that dawn to be alive,
But to be young was very heaven.

I cannot help regretting the present method of a simultaneous poll; the excitement was protracted for over a fortnight in those days. I recall the Liberal slogan 'Vote for'—whatever candidate it was—'and swell the flowing tide' and the excellent Tory retort 'Vote for ——and DAM the flowing tide.' How splendid it was to hear that A. E. W. Mason was in for Coventry and Hilaire Belloc for South Salford. At last, at long last we were burying the remains of Victorianism and building a brave new world. I borrowed my mother's brougham and went down to West Ham to convey voters for C. F. G. Masterman to a triumphant poll. Charles Masterman was one of the most brilliant of the young Liberals, married to a daughter of Gen. Sir Neville Lyttelton, and not merely a young Liberal in politics but a pillar of Anglo-Catholicism. Ten years hence he would be one of those whom Asquith would have to sacrifice to that Tory intrigue in 1915, led by Bonar Law, which achieved a coalition and wrecked the Gallipoli Campaign with the help of the Generals in France who had decided that, whatever happened, Winston Churchill and Johnny Hamilton should not have Constantinople. When I reach my fifth Octave, I shall hope to make it clear that the responsibility for prolonging the war for three years of slaughter rests primarily on that disastrous June of 1915.

Two days after Charles Masterman was elected as a member for West Ham I was waiting to hear what my father and Addison Bright thought of my reconstruction and rewriting of *To-Morrow* and entering my twenty-fourth year, hoping that at last I had achieved something worth while and that I should be able to justify that 'amazing marriage'.

TWENTY-THREE YEARS OLD: 1906

ADDISON BRIGHT approved of the changes I had made in *To-Morrow* and was anxious that if my father succeeded in getting a London theatre to produce it Pauline Chase should play the young heroine.

"But," he said, "you will have to get Barrie on your side."

Whenever Bright spoke of Barrie he lowered his voice reverently. To Bright Barrie was a god. J. M. Barrie was not a big man in the physical way; Addison Bright was even smaller but he had a tremendously forceful personality. I went to see *Peter Pan* and was able to tell Bright without too much insincerity that Pauline Chase would be ideal for the part of the heroine. *Peter Pan* as a play I found as intolerable as indeed I imagine anybody else in his early twenties would have found it at this date.

Barrie came to dinner at Nevern Square and perhaps in self-defence against my mother's American notions of hospitality he agreed to find another Peter Pan next year if *To-Morrow* was a success. However, he guarded himself by insisting that all depended on Charles Frohman, with whom Pauline Chase was under contract. I was amused to watch poor Barrie's attempts to avoid being given a second helping of every dish. I recall that he was very sweet to Fay, who was now eleven years old and fourteen years away from being his Mary Rose.

I have not mentioned that Canon H. C. Beeching had taken the house that stood near the gate of the ruined Priory in Burford. Once upon a time it had been lived in by the painter of that popular picture *The Empty Saddle*, which shows the servant of a Cavalier bringing back his master's horse to the Priory at Burford. There was a big print of it hanging in the hall at Avonmore Road. Beeching used to be the Vicar of Yattenden in Berkshire, where he and Robert Bridges had fallen out over a hymn-book they produced. He wrote the best monthly commentary on contemporary topics that Blackwood's ever published in my time; he was now a Canon of Westminster to become a year or two later Dean of Norwich.

I sent the Beechings a copy of my Posy and Mrs Beeching wrote to invite Faith and me to dinner to meet another young poet. This was Walter de la Mare, who hardly said a word either at dinner or after it. I remember being much impressed by his face and I hope it was not my loquaciousness that kept him so silent; it may have been, I reflect apologetically.

Soon after that dinner in the Cloisters of Westminster Abbey, Faith and I went down to Eton to stay with her housemaster brother, Ned Stone. Ned, the very soul of kindness, had always been held up by his younger sister as a bogey because from time to time he had to write her letters of brotherly admonition, usually about some extravagance of hers. He was inevitably shy with me at first; no doubt I was shy with him. The ice was broken at a dinner party he gave to which Ronnie Knox, the Captain of the School, was invited and with whom I immediately formed a friendship that would last until his death. Then in his last term at Eton he seemed a very sprite of humour, an iridescent bubble of wit. Ned was not yet married and I remember his telling me how lucky I was compared with him. This was after Ronnie Knox and I had been making everybody laugh by our complementary sallies.

I was less successful with Ned's eldest nephew, John Carter, whom I met in his perambulator next day. I have never been able to emulate Swinburne's success with babies; to be candid I have never understood their attraction for so many people. My brother Frank was equally unsuccessful until he had a baby of his own. I remember Sidney Crowe's coming to Avonmore Road with Leah, her first daughter, at whom Frank gazed with evident distaste before he told his cousin that her baby was very like a monkey.

To return to John Carter in his perambulator. I decided to try the effect of putting my finger in my cheek and making it pop. It was a disastrous gesture. John Carter yelled loudly in affright and yelled even more loudly when Christopher leant over the perambulator and grinned to reassure him. Christopher's glasses at close quarters on top of that pop from my finger was more than poor John Carter could stand. His father, the Reverend Thomas Carter, was then living in Eton with Margaret, another of Faith's elder sisters.

When Christopher and I apologized to Tom Carter for frightening his son he told us his hope was to have three sons, one for the Army, another for the Navy and a third to carve out for himself a career in the Colonies. I am glad to-day that John Carter decided to find his distinguished career in books rather than barracks.

My father decided to try out the new version of *To-Morrow* in Paisley, where the original version had been produced two years before, and in mid-February I went to Scotland to attend the final rehearsals. The night train was crowded; a hard-headed, soft-faced business man from Glasgow asked me if Faith who had come to see me off at Euston was my sister; many people perceived a likeness between Faith and myself in those days. After this he went on to say he had heard Harry Lauder sing and from that went on to wonder how any girls accustomed to wearing tights could keep straight. I told him I did not think tights any more provocative than nightgowns. He continued to fidget with pruriency; at last I told him I was used to meeting itinerant puritans and that Bunyan would certainly have put me into Vanity Fair and that I would just as certainly have pitched him into the Slough of Despond.

"Ah, the Pilgrim's Progress. There's a great book."

"You think so? I think the Pilgrim's Progress and Foxe's Book of Martyrs have done more harm to British morals than any books ever written." This silenced him.

My sister Viola was now my father's leading lady, dropping the Compton and appearing on the programme as 'Miss Mackenzie'. It was ridiculous of my mother to persuade my father to start her off as Lady Teazle, Lydia Languish, Kate Hardcastle and the rest when she was still eighteen, and particularly ridiculous to give her love scenes with my father in some of the plays like *To-Morrow.*

I remember nothing of the rehearsals in Paisley except that I was infernally tired and was starting an abscess in one of my teeth. Indeed, all that I remember of those days in Paisley was a story told me by Miss Marie Hassall, who had succeeded Elinor Aickin about ten years ago as Mrs Malaprop, Mrs Candour, Mrs Hardcastle etc. and who would be with the Compton Comedy Company for at least another ten years.

In 1880 Marie Hassall had married Charles Boote, who had deserted a puritan home in Nottingham to go on the stage and had then still further disgraced himself by marrying a young Irish Catholic actress. A year later he had been killed by a star-trap when playing Harlequin, leaving Marie Hassall with a little girl of three. She had been out of an engagement for some time and at last in despair of money she decided to take her little girl to Nottingham and ask Charles's brother Jesse to take her into his house. This was refused: he could not be responsible for a Catholic child. Back to London went Marie Hassall and in the train she met a nun who took a great fancy to her little girl Rosie, so much so that when she heard Marie Hassall's story she said she was sure the Mother Superior of her convent would take her in her charge.

Back in London, with all that she could pawn pawned, there

arrived by the same post a day or two afterwards two letters; one was from a manager offering Marie Hassall a part in a touring melodrama with her little daughter; the other letter was from the Mother Superior offering to keep Rosie at school until she was eighteen. She would lose the part if she did not have Rosie with her but Marie Hassall did not hesitate. She took her little daughter to the convent and somehow existed until she got an engagement.

She saved money year after year until she had enough to send Rosie to a finishing-school in Paris, and then at nineteen Miss Rosie Boote was picked out from the chorus at the Gaiety by George Edwardes to sing 'Maisie is a Daisy' in which she had a triumphant success and was proposed to by Lord Alfred Taylour, who presently became Marquess of Headfort. "And I still put something aside every week out of my salary for my second grandson," she told me.

This story fascinated me; twenty years later I should use it as the foundation of my novel *Rogues and Vagabonds*.

I came back from Paisley at the end of the week and when the train stopped in the morning at Willesden for tickets to be collected I threw mine out of the window as if I were going to get out of an omnibus. Fortunately the inspector was a sensible fellow and was content to take my name and address and the date when I bought my return ticket. I was rather prone to fits of absent-mindedness in those days, because I was always being seized with ideas for a new play or a new poem. However, I never managed to equal my father's feat of lighting a cigar, putting the match in his pocket and throwing a gold match-box out of a railway train.

In March we went to Sandown in the Isle of Wight, where Christopher was staying in Shanklin to tutor the second Chinnery boy. This was the first time we met Mrs Chinnery, who was now in her mid-forties and a perfect example of the fashionable type of Edwardian beauty. Wealthy, beautiful and prodigiously generous, she was the centre of life in that Shanklin hotel. Various young women competed jealously with one another to be favourites of Mrs Chinnery, and Alyce Chinnery herself loved to be the object of such competition. I was terribly tired, and the confounded neuritis whose attacks were becoming more frequent must have made me dull company. Faith enjoyed the whirl of intrigue and gossip but I used to protest at coming in to Shanklin for eternal parties. What I did enjoy, however, was making friends with Mrs Chinnery's four-year old daughter Felicity who, outrageously spoilt though she was both by her mother and her nurse, was an enchanting child.

I have a relic of that fortnight of lovely March weather at Sandown, to be paid for by a foul May, in a note to my mother of what a palmist told me:

15 *Guadaloupe Terrace*
Sandown, I.W.
March 9, '06

A queer female I met at one of Mrs Chinnery's parties asked me to let her read my hand. She told all about Addison Bright and this play but said something would happen to prevent its final success and that my success would not come for five years. This was discouraging but I shall have to believe it in order to believe what she said next. I had a mark of genius, a mark which influences a whole nation, the mark of all my ambitions achieved and also a title! Ha-ha!

"*In fact you have the most remarkable hand I have ever seen for absolute success.*" *She said this with such conviction that I began to wonder if she could possibly possess clairvoyance. I cannot believe that the lines made in the palm of a hand by the way it was clenched as a foetus can possibly foretell the future.*

Addison Bright had been up to see *To-Morrow* in Scotland and came back with various suggestions for improvements, and my mother thought I should go up and discuss them with my father. I was getting fed up with *To-Morrow* by now, and had started to write a play of my own. I quote from a letter to my mother:

The Divorce Court play is taking shape. It is to be a sinister Elizabethan tragedy of modern times—Jealousy and Revenge.

Man=A marries girl=B. They are devoted but B foolishly tells him about an affair she had in the past with a married man. A has fearful moods of retrospective jealousy. One is seen in the first act. Suddenly C who has tried to divorce his wife has a counter charge made against him in which B is the co-respondent. C and A meet face to face in the Divorce Court, A holding a brief for C's wife. C in a fit of jealousy gives away B to all the world. Then the rest of the play is A's revenge. C is ultimately murdered in a dancing saloon in Morocco by A and two friends. Last act is the New Life.

It is hardly surprising that my mother wrote to say she thought it would be wiser if I postponed this bloodthirsty drama and joined the Compton Comedy Company in Greenock.

When I did start to work on Addison Bright's suggestions I got interested, and enjoyed myself during the three weeks spent in Scotland. After the Greenock week the Company played three nights in Stirling and Falkirk and a week in Perth. In Stirling I went to the first cinema theatre I ever visited. Indeed, it must have been one of the first cinema theatres that anybody ever visited, certainly in

Scotland. When I was last in Stirling I tried to find out where that old cinema had been; nobody had any notion. I recall only one of the shorts presented to the accompaniment of a tinny piano. This was a farce about a girls' school where the pupils behaved far worse than even the girls of St. Trinian's. The final scene showed one of the mistresses chasing about half a dozen of the girls in their nightgowns all over the school until they reached a window out of which they were leaning to see if they could climb out and escape, when the mistress caught up and shut the window down on them, leaving half a dozen girls in the right position for the spanking she was going to administer. Then just as she began to roll up the first nightgown the film came to an end, and above the tinny piano one heard a disappointed 'oh' from the audience. I must have been a bit disappointed myself, or I should hardly have remembered that ridiculous farce of 57 years ago.

In Perth I recall going to lunch with Archdeacon Aglen, whose wife was a Mackenzie first cousin of my father. I recall too the shops in High Street, nearly every one of which had a fascinating eighteenth-century sign outside it. Alas, the signs of Perth have vanished with the snows of yesteryear. My father was a friend of the Pullar-Phibbses and we had two jolly supper parties with them after the show in their delightful house on Kinnoul Hill looking down on Perth.

One evening I was walking beside the Tay on the North Inch. A full moon was shining and the air was full of Spring. Presently I overtook a charming girl and with some excuse about asking my way I got into conversation with her. At last all too soon we reached the gate of the small low house where she lived, on the outside of which was a placard saying CAMPBELL'S MINERAL WATERS.

"And this is where we part," she said, and quite spontaneously we kissed each other good night. I watched her walk along the garden path to her front door; she turned a moment and waved a farewell before she went in. I hope, if that young Miss Campbell of long ago, who will doubtless be a grandmother today, chances to read this piece of kissing and telling, she will forgive me for recording this long treasured memory of what can have been hardly more then than a quarter of an hour in the Perth moonlight.

I was up in Manchester in the last week of April to do some more tinkering at *To-Morrow*. There must have been another argument with Addison Bright for I find a note I scrawled about this time:

Surely the point of the play is that a young man with the feelings and passions of to-day finds himself transported to a time when he can give vent to them, unhampered by the restraining influence of Eton and Oxford. It is not so much 'ancestral voices prophesying war' that haunt his thoughts, but his 'alter ego' desiring war against the principles of his 'ego'. The point of the play is not hereditary criminal instincts coming down from one's forefathers, but tries to show the result of a strong imagination working on a basis of fact. Laidlaw knew his great-great-grandfather was a blackguard, and long dwelling on the knowledge had half-persuaded him that he was one too. When he found himself in his ancestor's shoes his mistake was proved to him. The play has nothing to do with heredity. I'm getting awfully tired of the way people are blaming everything on heredity to-day. Heredity only exists so far as we think it exists and surrender to it. We expect a penchant for high play, we expect a taste for alcohol. We expect cancer or tuberculosis, and we inherit the sins of the fathers because we expect to.

The temptation to-day is to surrender to the unconscious which psychoanalysis claims to reveal. Calvinism, communism, fascism, freudianism, behaviourism, existentialism, they are all various aspects of the attack upon man's free will.

When I got back at the end of April there was a telegram from Abingdon to say Faith was ill. It was a duodenal ulcer. There were tenants in Lady Ham until the end of May, and she went down to Alton with a nurse.

Then came tragedy, ruthless and sudden. Barrie had discovered that Addison Bright had been sending out a company in Canada in a repertory of Barrie plays without letting the author know and without paying him any of the royalties due to him. It must have been a great shock to Barrie, and perhaps it was asking too much of him to forgive Addison Bright. Nevertheless, he may have wished that he had not immediately dismissed him as his agent, after Addison Bright went out to Switzerland and shot himself. I have two or three letters of Barrie's written to my mother at this time, from which it appears that he and she were trying to decide what to do about Mrs Bright, who had been overcome by the shock. The death of Addison Bright meant that any prospect of producing *To-Morrow* in London was out of the question for this year.

At this moment Bobbie Whitworth Jones's financial affairs got into a tangle and he asked me to take on all responsibility for the Lady Ham property, being unable to pay his half of the insurance premium on Harry Pirie-Gordon's life. I was in no position to do this, and in the end the problem was solved by Christopher taking over Whitworth Jones's share. We had hopes of letting both Lady Ham itself and the Other House for August and September.

Then my mother suggested that in the autumn Faith and I should go and live with Mrs Addison Bright at her house in Russell Square. It would be a kindness to her and it would save us money. Mrs Bright was most anxious to have us and we should not have to pay anything; perhaps I might do a little tutoring of her small son. 7 Grosvenor Road was given up that May; the parting with Mrs Charnock was sad. I have been particularly fortunate all my life in being able to win the affection of those who were looking after me domestically or serving under me. This may be due to my always becoming the other person, so that a position of perfect equality is created. I was much distressed by having to give notice to Mrs Charnock. I owe to her my first impulse to preserve ripe Cockney figures of the past, who even already seem to belong more to the London of Dickens than to the present, and who will soon be quite extinct.

By this time Faith had developed colitis, and when we went to Lady Ham in that June she was put on a diet of poached eggs, asparagus and digestive biscuits. I thought it would be easier for her if I put myself on the same diet, but I substituted bread for the digestive biscuits. Although I must have eaten at least ten poached eggs a day during that June, I still enjoy poached eggs, and asparagus is still, with globe artichokes, my favourite vegetable. I did not like digestive biscuits then and I do not like them any better to-day.

I was at work on two plays and polishing my poems for the volume I was hoping to get published. Christopher was in Oxford staying with a Stone uncle who had a fine library which he would inherit one day. He was working on an anthology of sea-songs for the Clarendon Press.

Logan Pearsall Smith had not approved of my marriage because he thought the desperate need to make some money would divert me from the austere novitiate to literature from which he had such high hopes. He had now taken Iffley Lodge, where he had been joined by his mother who had left Philadelphia. Mrs Pearsall Smith was a formidable matriarch and ruled not only Logan but also Mrs Bernard Berenson and Mrs Bertrand Russell, his two sisters. She was no longer able to walk but propelled herself along in a wheeled-chair in which she indulged in what could almost be called furious driving about the house; I can see her now suddenly shooting into a room at top speed. She had been the friend, indeed she could have been called the protector of Walt Whitman, for whose *Leaves of Grass* I had fallen completely. I recall John Mavrogordato's arguing with me that Walt Whitman was not as good as all that and my reading to him *When lilacs last in the door-yard bloomed* and bringing tears to his eyes and John's retracting all he had said against Whitman. Mrs Bernard Berenson had been Mrs Costello before she married the great B.B.; she had a charming and rather mysterious young daughter called Ray, who would marry a Strachey and write a Bloomsbury novel that would be much admired, but who died young.

There had been a wonderful circle in Florence who published a magazine called *The Golden Urn*, the copies of which given to me by Logan have vanished from my shelves. I recall one in which was preserved all the best poetry of Keats. As I remember, the only line excised from the Ode to a Nightingale as really bad was 'To thy high requiem become a sod'. Then they tackled Milton and I recall being completely knocked over by the glory of 'Busiris and his Memphian chivalry'. Mrs Berenson was the first woman I saw take out a large Havana cigar from her case and light it. One of my pleasures to-day is to see a woman smoke a cigar with genuine enjoyment. It is sad that women did not take to smoking en masse until the pestilent habit of inhaling blended cigarettes, known once upon a time as 'gaspers', had been brought back from the trenches of the First World War. In the eighteenth and early nineteenth centuries the avant-garde of women smoked pipes. I wish they would smoke pipes and cigars to-day, but then they would have to smoke real tobacco and not swallow a mild approximation to it.

Mrs Bertrand Russell, Logan's other sister, remains in my mind as a figure of sweetness and charity. I used to like hearing them all talking to one another in the Quaker second-person singular.

Logan Pearsall Smith had written a comedy which the Stage Society had refused and which I had tried to persuade my father to take, tempting him as I hoped with the bait of Arthur Ponsonby's acting in it. There was a moment when Arthur Ponsonby played with the idea of giving up being Private Secretary to Campbell-Bannerman and returning to his first ambition of going on the stage. However, Logan's play was never produced and Arthur Ponsonby never went on the stage.

I recall walking round that lovely garden of Iffley Lodge with Logan when the Siberian irises were in full bloom beside the river, growing more lavishly than I had ever seen *Iris siberica* grow before or have ever seen since. It was Logan's last effort to persuade me that if I was to be a poet I must not waste my time writing plays, unless I should feel an inspiration to revive poetic drama. He said that the fragments of Joan of Arc I had written showed I had in me the promise of being able to do that.

"Yes, but, Logan, I'm beginning to ask myself if it is too late in the day for the kind of poetry I can write. When this first volume of mine is published we shall see what the critics say, but I have an uncomfortable feeling that the pre-Raphaelite approach to art belongs to a bygone generation. I must find a way to express myself in terms of to-day. I may still find a way of doing that in verse but meanwhile I must earn a living. You have private means; you can afford to perfect your *Trivia.* You don't really understand what it means to be compelled to earn money. You despise the contemporary novel. I think Galsworthy's *Man of Property* is a hell of a good novel; you find it one more example of the second-rate. I think I can do with plays what Galsworthy has done with the novel. You don't think that is worth doing. Maugham has written at least two really good novels; you laugh at them. Somehow I must make money because if I take an allowance from my father and let Faith accept an allowance from her father I must be able to repay them both with evidence that I am not a self-indulgent dilettante. I may be driven to go on the stage, but I am determined to do my utmost to avoid that and the best way to avoid it is to write plays. Writing poetry will not avert such a doom and if I did go on the stage it would be a certain farewell to poetry."

Back at Lady Ham the need for money was becoming ever more pressing. The tenants of the Other House were an intolerable bore after the jolly days of George Montagu and Bobbie Whitworth Jones, but at least they would be there till after Christmas, and Lady Ham was let for August and September at five guineas a week. Faith and I were to go and stay with Philip Lloyd-Graeme at Bridlington at the beginning of August, but Philip's grandmother died and so that was put off. The Kirbys had taken Barrington Park, the Wingfields' house, about three miles from Burford and Claude Kirby asked us to stay there, but I wanted the sea and we went instead to stay with Freddie and Kate Whitworth Jones in Norfolk.

We were at Nevern Square for a bit at the end of July before my father came back from a voyage to South Africa he had taken. One day a carriage and pair arrived at Number One, out of which of all people in the world popped the Reverend Harold Davidson.

"Why on earth are you driving about London in a carriage and pair with a footman on the box?" I asked.

"I'm helping Lady Townsend," he said. "Lord Townsend has just been declared incapable of managing his own affairs, though capable of managing himself, mind you."

"But what have you got to do with Lord Townsend's affairs?"

"A great deal," said Davidson. "I have interested Lady Townsend in the work your mother is doing in Bethnal Green. And I want your mother to meet her."

"Well, my mother's not in."

"I shall write to her. I must be off now. I have a great deal to do for Lady Townsend. I am being given the living of Stiffkey in Norfolk. It will be a change after my curacy in Westminster."

With this the little man went bustling off; I cannot recall a more surprising sight than that minute parson bobbing about in that landau with a marquess's coronet on it.

In July Elkin Matthews had finally turned down my volume of poems, and I must have written reproachfully to John Mavrogordato who had left Elkin Matthews' Vigo Street office. John Mavrogordato's letter to me has survived.

Wallingford
July 19, 1906

Dear Monty,

I enclose a copy of an amazingly mendacious letter from E. M. I found on my return last night.

I need hardly say that his "recollection of handing me your M.S." is without all shadow of truth. . . . and his suggestion that I dissociated myself from Robert Bridges and others is hardly justified by the very last letter I wrote him with my references to your "extraordinary promise and originality". . . . The high opinion of you I expressed was given more force by the fact that I (intentionally) appeared bored at being dragged into the discussion.

You will notice that he gratuitously mentions the good opinion of Pearsall Smith, whose name had not occurred in either your letter or mine.

If it is possible to get down on paper any remarks called forth by E. M.'s letter please let me have them. I suggest that either he suspects a put up job and is lying accordingly or that being separated from his manager and his letter book he is totally incapable of reasonably intelligent action.

Yours ever
John M.

All I can remember of that fuss with what John Mavrogordato used to call the egg-shaped Elkin Matthews was that after accepting my poems for publication he had written to cancel his acceptance by telling me that John Mavrogordato had advised against publication.

My mother, perhaps with the idea of soothing my disappointment suddenly produced an offer from Ben Greet. In my second Octave I told about Ben Greet's giving me that raffle ticket with which I won a revolver. He came to see me in my first term at Magdalen and afterwards sent me a tea-caddy. Here is his letter:

Montague C. Mackenzie must come and look me up when he is able, for I see no reason why he shouldn't be doing something in my way. Only I'm going to Bayreuth and Munich directly I can scramble from here on Thursday. Let him therefore send me a line telling me what he thinks he can do as actor or lecturer or both.

We give our plays in the way Shakespeare wrote them: and the American public—chiefly, I admit, the intellectual small quarter of it—and all the Colleges and Clubs are very eager to hear its claims propounded to them before hand.

I wrote Mrs Daniel at Worcester to know if she could recommend me a young Oxford man who could do this. She mentioned M. C. M. saying at the same time that the engagement to Ruth was off, but she spoke very *nicely of him.*

I had of course met him at Oxford when he was at Magdalen I think (I always forget those colleges) and talked shop etc. Therefore let him send me a line.

I did not at all like the idea of going to America with Ben Greet, but the disappointment over my poems had been sharp, for when Elkin Matthews told me he would take them I had trumpeted the news about. So I agreed to get in touch with Ben Greet when he came back from Germany. Meanwhile, I had just read H. G. Wells' novel *Kipps* and had been seized with the notion of dramatizing it if he would give me permission. I thought I should be able to get it done while we were at Pulham with the Whitworth Joneses.

Freddie Whitworth Jones was completely different from his younger brother both in appearance and character. He had been roaming the world for the last ten years; coming back to find his sister Kate grown up he had persuaded her to live with him and keep house. He had a boisterous manner and a loud voice which used to make his younger brother close his eyes and wince. He had a wealth and variety of information about every place under the sun. For me the bond was his knowledge of butterflies and moths. One little item of information comes back to me from that piping hot August in Norfolk. This was when he told me that the Painted Ladies he found on St Helena were to his surprise not the South African type but the Argentine type. The migratory habits of the Painted Lady are well known but he was baffled to account for migration right across the South Atlantic from South America, instead of what seemed the so much more obvious migration from South Africa.

As soon as we got to Pulham I wrote to H. G. Wells to ask his permission to have a shot at dramatizing *Kipps*; I got a letter back from Spade House, Sandgate, in that small flowing legible handwriting of his to say that three or four people had made the suggestion to him and that Kipps could not be dramatized. At the moment I have been unable to find that correspondence between H. G. Wells and myself and I can only give the substance of it. I fear it has been lost.

I wrote back to ask Wells if I might submit a scenario of the way I proposed to treat his book and he agreed. I got to work at once in that broiling weather and Wells wrote to say that certainly my scenario was much more promising than he had expected. Then I set to work and sent him the finished play in the first week of September. Wells wrote that it was far better than anything he had expected and that now the test was an actor-manager. I felt that the only actor to play Kipps was Weedon Grossmith, and then as ill-luck would have it a play of my uncle R. C. Carton's called *Mr Hopkinson,* was produced, the theme of which was something like the theme of Kipps, in which Weedon Grossmith appeared. I felt that there was little chance of getting Kipps accepted and by now had been caught by the idea of an eighteenth-century play for my father.

That was a fussy and unsatisfactory autumn. Ben Greet would not offer me more than £9 a week for lecturing and acting in his Shakespeare productions. I held out for £12, hoping he would not agree and mercifully he did refuse. Faith and I were at Abingdon until the beginning of November. I had got my scenario and title for the play I was proposing to write for my father; it was to be called *The Gentleman in Grey*, and after being captivated by Faith's playing of Schumann's *Carnaval* I decided to make another effort to 'modernise' my poetry and started what I called in a letter to my mother 'a sort of Wilhelm Meister, an autobiographical, psychological, allegorical fantasy of some 2500 lines; the subjects suggested by Schumann and knit together'. I added, however, that I was finding it hard to go back to poetry again. Evidently I found it too hard, for not a vestige of that magnum opus remains. In the same letter I asked my mother if she had seen my letter in *The Times* on the Book Club war. *I am strongly against* The Times *and am annoying them by only asking for boycotted books*.

I cannot remember now what all the row was about but I recollect that publishers and authors were annoyed at the proposal of the Times Book Club to sell off copies of books prematurely at half-price. We were shocked, too, by what we thought were the American methods of advertizing their Book Club and the Encyclopaedia

Britannica in the hands of an American called Hooper. He was sending abusive cablegrams from New York for the way his attempt to brighten up the book trade had been received in London. Moberly Bell, the Manager of *The Times,* was believed to be responsible for Hooper. C. L. Graves and E. V. Lucas brought out a skit on the whole business which had a tremendous sale.

I sent the *Isis* a parody of Shelley's *Skylark* in that very week in which I wrote I was finding it hard to go back to poetry. Here are a few of the verses:

To Mr Hooper's Lark
(with apologies to the Shelley Memorial)

Hail to thee, blithe Hooper
Man thou never wert—
Swearing like a trooper
In New York apart,
Through verbose cables of Marconigraphic art.

Wire still and wire
To the land thou leavest,
We can never tire,
While the deep thou cleavest,
And heaving still doth wire and wiring ever heavest.

At thy Yankee lightening
Of the sinking one
Graves's face is brightening,
Lucas has his fun
In a new-published joy whose rage has just begun.

What thou art we know not:
What is most like thee?
From watering-cans there flow not
Drops so bright to see
As from thy absence showers a can of calumny.

Like a poet hidden
Neath a nom de plume,
Writing songs unbidden
Until we presume
Colvin or Archer find, and he achieves a boom.

Book Club, Mober-ly Bell,
Advertising cant
Have produced a Bible
Not exorbitant—
A thing for which they feel there is a grievous want.

Better than the measures
Publishers send round,
Better than the treasures
In the Book Club found,
Thy skill to poet were, if thou couldst but be found.

Teach me the statistics
That Hall Caine must know,
Such wild syllogistics
From my pen should flow,
The Times *should publish then what I am writing now!*

Mr Alden who owned the *Isis* used to pay me ten shillings for parodies and skits that I wrote for the paper, and I was so driven to find money for accounts rendered over and over again that I was glad enough to earn even ten shillings.

A week later Faith and I went to live with Mrs Addison Bright in Russell Square; we soon decided that such a ménage was impossible for us. Mrs Bright was extremely kind, but we had to listen endlessly to her complaints of the way Barrie had treated her husband, of the way Louis N. Parker and all the other playwrights he acted for had treated him. We also had to be careful never to suggest that we thought it had been suicide; we had to keep assuring her how obviously it had been an accident. Russell Square in November was very gloomy. There was no piano. Then mercifully Mrs Bright got worried about her little boy's health and felt she ought to take him to a warmer place than Russell Square. So Faith and I went to Nevern Square for a day or two before going down to Abingdon for Christmas. I recall a visit to the Court Theatre to see *John Bull's Other Island*, which I thought then and still think the best of Shaw's plays, though I found Granville Barker's address to the grasshopper almost intolerably affected in its delivery.

A more important visit was one we paid to Beatrice Bland in her studio at the far end of Cheyne Walk. We had met and loved Beatrice Bland at Burford in July, when she was painting there with two gawky pupils. "Why don't you come and live at 127 across the road?" she asked. "There's a nice big room on the second floor with a glorious view over the river, which I haven't got in my flat. And there's a little kitchen and a tiny bedroom. Twelve and six a week unfurnished. You can't call that much. And you won't have a porter to tip like me. I have to tip him all the time because he's so rude."

I was taken by the notion of living where once upon a time had stretched the gardens of Cremorne, and when we looked at the vacant flatlet the view of the glittering Thames upon a halcyon December day seemed as rich a prospect as the world could offer. In the flatlet above was a struggling painter from a page of Murger. Beneath us were a Quaker couple. On the ground floor was the studio of Ethel Walker, who looked at us as we passed her on our way upstairs with a frown, the kind of frown a housewife puts on when she sees something that ought not to be lying about.

"She doesn't approve of me," said Beatrice Bland.

"She doesn't look as if she approved of anybody," I suggested.

"She was George Moore's great love," said Beatrice Bland. "At any rate George Moore says she was, but I often think of what Miss Purser once said about him. 'Some people kiss and tell, but George Moore tells and doesn't kiss.' Still, she is a *very* good painter."

127 Cheyne Walk was furnished with what my mother could spare from Nevern Square, and the only purchase was a bed that could be let down for the night and shut up against the wall during the day. Such beds used to be a feature of slapstick films when the comic hero would get shut up inside the bed. Probably Charlie Chaplin in his early days found himself shut up in one of those beds.

We went down to Abingdon for Christmas. Frank Stone was home for a week before he took a party of Radley boys to Switzerland for winter sports, of which he was one of the pioneers in England. He was a much loved master at Radley, where his nickname was 'Bones'. We used to hear accounts of his popularity and accomplishment as a singer of comic songs in Zermatt and elsewhere, but he would never give us a taste of his quality at Helensbourne. He was also the only parson with a motor-car for miles round and used to drive at a furious pace all over Berkshire, a road-hog indeed of the Berkshire breed in his clerical attire and black cap. Another of his accomplishments was the violoncello, which he played beautifully.

My favourite sister-in-law Lucy was also at Helensbourne that Christmas. She was the second violin in the famous Norah Clench Quartet, the first to popularize Debussy's Quartet, the music of which at this date left me wondering whether it was music at all. May Mukle was the 'cello. Lucy Stone had a Stradivarius and was an exquisite violinist. It was a pity Faith gave up her piano studies to go on the stage, for she could never have been even a good actress and she might have been a pianist of the calibre of Myra Hess or Harriet Cohen. She had been a pupil of Fanny Davies, who herself had been a pupil of Clara Schumann. The trouble with Faith had been impatience and lack of ambition. If she could not read a difficult piece of music at first sight she could not be bothered to work at it. To the end of her days she remained an accompanist of the first order, and in those early years of our married life a marvellous inspiration and sustenance of my writing by playing endlessly the Beethoven sonatas and music of Schumann I so much loved. I think I can date the beginning of my appreciation of chamber music from the Mendelssohn Trio which Faith, Lucy and Frank used to play at Helensbourne that Christmas.

I must have worked with a good deal of concentration on *The Gentleman in Grey*. I find a letter written to my father on January 1st 1907:

I have this evening finished the second act of the Gentleman in Grey and the play is much better than I thought it was going to be, and great fun with plenty of dramatic moments. . . . When I have written the last act which I hope to complete this week I shall return to town and read it to Mother. When I have heard her criticism I shall re-write it. I mean copy it out and cut it and get all allusions etc right. Whether you receive it on your birthday rather depends on Miss Bliss the typist. At any rate you shall receive it at latest by January 22. *This you can count on for certain.*

In a letter to my mother on that first of January I wrote:

I hope father will feel inclined to do this play. You might let me know if you think he'd rather not.

The scene of *The Gentleman in Grey* was set in an imaginary eighteenth-century spa called Curtain Wells and the hero was a kind of Raffles, a gentleman highwayman. I had only just mastered the art of writing Cockney dialogue from my dramatization of *Kipps*, but the writing of eighteenth-century dialogue was second nature. In my childhood I had read every play in the many volumes of Oxberry's Drama at least twice and some of them several times. The novels I had enjoyed best were those of Fielding and Smollett. Indeed, my youthful reading was about identical with that of Charles Dickens, except that I enjoyed an advantage denied to Dickens: I was able to read in childhood the novels of Charles Dickens as well as those of Fielding and Smollett.

Faith fell ill just before we were due to go back on January 8th, and Christopher volunteered to stay with me in Cheyne Walk. I quote from a letter to Faith:

So far we have not been able to discover where the knives are but no doubt they will turn up. Two rather mangy specimens were in the kitchen. During the recent snow the kitchen was flooded and was on evidence more like a pond than a kitchen.

Christopher with considerable folly has given all the correspondents 125 *as the number to write to. As a result he is now setting out to the District Sorting Office.*

On January 9th I wrote to Faith after reading the play to my mother and my Aunt Ellen who was over in England.

The play went off very successfully last night. Aunt Ellen and my mother were delighted with the first two acts and could find no fault with them. But the third, as I already knew, fell off a bit. However, we solved the problem, I think. . . .

One of the ladies of the company has had a miscarriage and the result is that my unfortunate mother has set out to-day for Northampton in order to play second Lady to Viola! it being impossible to get anyone at the short notice. . . .

It's becoming very difficult to store away the books in this room. I do wish you were up here. . . . Alice wears more curlers than ever. Her head looks like a quilted counterpane now. Coal is up to 1/6 *per cwt. which is scandalous.*

My mother came back with the welcome news that my father had decided to produce the play in Scotland next month, provided I could get the third act right; this I managed to do. He had given up the foolish experiment of having his nineteen-year old daughter play ingénue parts in which he had to make love to her; these were now played by Miss Phyllis Relph, an extremely pretty and extremely capable young actress. I think one reason for his agreeing to produce *The Gentleman in Grey* were the love-scenes I had written,

I quote from one last letter to Faith when Christopher was staying at Cheyne Walk:

This place is becoming a pigsty and I shall be heartily glad of an orderly temperament at work again. I have proved what I always suspected that I am in distinction from most men of a profoundly tidy disposition. I can't describe the tangle into which Christopher manages to twist the contents of a room within two or three minutes of coming into it. With a somewhat pathetic economy, I had set aside four new collars to be worn on such grand occasions as demand the frock overcoat, the silk hat, the lavender gloves. Alas, I now find that he wore each of them for one short day of this week, having also worn my collars the week before. I find myself reduced to the frayed and undignified relics of such of our friends as found it convenient to leave their worn out gear at Lady Ham.

The bedroom is a jungle of flannel shirts, clammy as the tentacles of an octopus and as sedulous in their attempt to cramp mental progression. Wherever I turn, whatever I move, whenever I sit down, asleep, in dreams, Christopher's silk hat obtrudes itself. Should I want to put the kettle on, that wretched hat sits before the fire; if I fill the lamps, the hat waits for the clean kerosene, if I want a walnut, a biscuit, a lump of coal, I must always search for them in Christopher's beastly hat. It rivals all that has hitherto been held most fertile on earth in its eternal productivity.

Whenever he goes out he buys three halfpenny papers, so that the room looks as if it were hung with bunting for a royal procession. Need I add that such papers as the Referee, Sunday Times, Academy, which I should really like to have read, vanish instantly?

Perhaps I am becoming faddy since marriage, probably I am, but I must say that the dirty, disordered, unwholesome mode of life pursued by young unmarried men fills me with a strange Pharisaic glow of superiority. I get up, at the moment of writing that, to look for a match. Need I say he has taken all the matches? He also insists upon washing his feet in the sitting-room, night and morning—a 'tip', as he oddly calls it, he swears he obtained from you! This to my protest. Alice works as hard as God almighty to evolve a world out of chaos. For my part I begin to find the pseudo-dirt of bachelor freedom irksome. I prefer your frankly dirty man, one who abandons his soul and body to dirt. Mustard and cress dirt, thick grimy black dirt, which dirt can be ploughed, sown with seed and made profitable, but this half-hearted dirt which is neither profitable for agriculture nor pleasant to play in I disown.

And all this, allowing for exaggeration, merely means that, however conscious I may be of the advantages of matrimony, it's not a bad thing to be reminded of them by an unusually untidy brother-in-law.

I will give you an example—perfectly true—of his methods. He wants to read for five minutes in bed. What to read? I suggest one of Hardy's novels. Good. Shortly afterwards I look round the room. I find Jude the Obscure on the piano, the Mayor of Casterbridge leaning against the fender, A Pair of Blue Eyes gazing wistfully out of a plate, Two on a Tower upon the floor, Tess of the Durbervilles interfering with my correspondence, The Return of the Native under my cushion, and Far From the Madding Crowd in the bed! This is what he calls just fetching a book for five minutes.

Last night we went to the Holborn Empire—a very good show. I lunched with Robbie Ross at the Reform Club. Remind me to tell you a marvellous story he told me about Maurice Hewlett and Owen Seaman, the new editor of Punch, and we are both dining with Hugh Sidgwick at the National Liberal and with Philip Lloyd-Graeme on Thursday. . . . It's most abominably cold today with fog and mist and grey nastiness. I shall be going to Leicester next week to read the play to the company.

Alas, I have forgotten what that story was about Maurice Hewlett and Owen Seaman, but it gives me an excuse to tell another of Robbie Ross's stories, this time about Arnold Bennett.

"Arnold Bennett was anxious to become a member of the Reform and so H. G. Wells and I put him up and in due course he was elected. He was duly pleased and asked if H.G. and I would lunch with him on the first occasion of his going into the Club because he always felt very shy of entering a new club for the first time. So H.G. and I agreed on a date when we would lunch together. Then, on the morning of the day, H.G. let me know that another engagement had turned up which would prevent his being at lunch. It was a busy morning at Carfax and I was a little late getting to Pall Mall.

"When I reached the Reform I asked the head-porter if Mr Arnold Bennett had enquired for me and the head-porter replied in a voice of obvious disapproval, 'There is a Mr Bennett waiting for you in the atrium.' I felt a moment of uneasiness as I hurried through to the atrium. Now, smoking is absolutely forbidden in the atrium. Occasionally a very senior member of the club may walk through it on his way out with a lighted cigar, but whatever his seniority he will hide that cigar under his overcoat on his way to the door. Imagine my feelings when on entering the atrium I saw Arnold Bennett standing with his legs apart and a thumb in each armhole of a red and yellow waistcoat, gazing round at the gathering with a large lighted cigar in his mouth as members went past him with various expressions of horrified disgust. And when I greeted Arnold Bennett I could see upon their faces the reflection 'Ah, a friend of Robert Ross. That explains it.' "

TWENTY-FOUR YEARS OLD: 1907

I FORGOT it was my twenty-fourth birthday until a letter came from my father by the second post wishing me many happy returns. I was tired with the effort of copying out *The Gentleman in Grey*, rewriting some of the scenes and finally revising the three typed copies; when I arrived in Leicester in the middle of the following week I felt completely washed out. My father's lodgings were at 169A London Road. I recall nothing of them except that one reached them along one of those jolly cobbled streets which were a characteristic of Leicester in those days. I like to fancy that in one of those cobbled streets I may have heard the early mewling of the infant Snow.

The Opera House, Leicester, of which my father would presently become part owner with Milton Bode, was one of the finest theatres in the provinces; I read my play to the company gathered at noon in the old green-room that was now the manager's office. Usually when an author reads his play to the company the actors and actresses only pay full attention when he is reading their own parts. On this occasion they listened from start to finish with encouraging attention. When I had finished the low comedian, an admirable old actor with a lifetime's experience, whose name I have forgotten but whose very words I remember said to me: "Sir, it is not for the actor to say what the acting capacity of a play is until that great unknown, the public, has approved, but let me congratulate you upon one of the finest literary efforts I have ever heard." I felt like embracing the old boy.

I had been a little apprehensive of my father's reaction to the opening scene in the maze at Curtain Wells., because it would involve carrying scenery, which my father had a strong objection to doing. To my relief he said he thought Glover at the Lyceum, Edinburgh, would be able to produce such a scene.

"Edinburgh?" I repeated eagerly.

"Yes, we'll produce the play at the Lyceum in the last week of February. You can join us at Sheffield and go north to Aberdeen with the Company to attend a week of rehearsals before we go to Edinburgh. You'll have a critical audience there, the most critical in Great Britain, and if Edinburgh approves you'll have nothing to worry about."

I took a couple of rehearsals in order to get the various parts to start on the right lines, and was disappointed by all the men. Phyllis Relph was charming as the heroine, Phyllida Courteen, but the only performance as good as it was in my own conception of it was that of my sister Viola as Betty, the heroine's maid; she did not say a word wrong. My father was anxious to prolong the love-scenes between Charles Lovely, the amateur highwayman, and Phyllida, and against my own judgment I gave him another four pages of love-making with which he was so pleased that he offered to stump up for Faith to come to Edinburgh for the first night.

What with rehearsing and rewriting the love scenes and writing an article for the *Academy* and trying to get into the heads of some of the company what I wanted, and doing this with an infernal noise under the stage all the time made by the advance party of a popular musical comedy *The New Aladdin* preparing for their effects the next week, I was half-dead when I reached Abingdon on the Saturday after a journey with three changes, with an abscess in a tooth, with the stabbing pains of neuritis and with a foul cold on my chest. I found Faith better but still far from well with colitis, worse than it had been before the poached eggs and asparagus diet last summer.

A fortnight later I went up to Sheffield to join the Company for the journey to Aberdeen on the Sunday night. A letter survives written to Faith on the Monday evening from 104 Crown Street, Aberdeen.

We didn't rehearse to-day but begin to-morrow. I have been marching round Aberdeen with the 'Governor' looking up old friends of whom he has an endless variety here. The jolliest of them is John Hay who runs a restaurant in Union Square called for some reason or other the Athenaeum. He's a quite priceless Roman Catholic who is the chief purveyor of my father's cigars and is the very re-embodiment of Bacchus himself. To-night we go to supper wi' a wee advocate.

I had a pleasant journey to Sheffield. There was only one other man in the compartment and he and I talked all the way up. He was a very brusque, hard-faced, puritanical-looking little man aged 70 *and looking not a day older than* 50. *I was astonished to hear that he was a corset-maker, and as a secondary business made covers for hot-water-bottles. He was on his way to Ireland. He told me that Debenhams, Marshall and Snelgrove and Evans gave the best value of any firms in London. The Evans staff were never sweated and all came from the north of Ireland. I enjoy these peeps behind the scenes of shop-windows. He was very down on the way Whiteley had sweated his staff, and though not prepared to defend taking the law into one's own hands implied that if anybody deserved shooting it was Mr William Whiteley.*

I shared a compartment to Aberdeen with Dennis Cleugh who plays Vernon not quite as I see Vernon. I got about three hours sleep and after much confusion and dashing about we managed to get a breakfast hamper at Edinburgh and reached Aberdeen at a quarter to twelve. I had a marvellous second breakfast with superlative porridge made by one of my father's favourite landladies of twenty years standing; an absolutely grand old girl.

I interrupt this letter to say that this was the last time I enjoyed real Scots porridge. In those days Scots folk sympathized with one for having to leave Scotland and endure English porridge. To-day throughout Scotland English porridge is all one can get wherever the oats are grown; it is a grim and gloomy thought that nobody under eighty in Scotland to-day, except here and there in the Islands, has ever tasted Scots porridge. There was a mill in Skye which made oatmeal in the right way until the early 'twenties and when that closed Scots porridge became extinct. I do not feel I exaggerate by calling it the greatest disaster since Culloden.

The weather is glorious. Aberdeen suggests one's idea of a Greek city—all white granite which glitters in the sun. The new theatre here is splendid. I was rather touched to hear my father was writing to his landlady in Edinburgh to ask if she has a piano and if not to get one in. This is for you to play his accompaniments! I'm sure Aberdeen has made him want to sing his favourite song—'Maid of Athens, e'er we part.'

One of the pleasures of that week in Aberdeen was the realization that my sister Viola, now just twenty, had suddenly grown up and had developed into a young woman of singular sweetness with a complete lack of self-preoccupation. She had fallen in love with Henry Crocker, who had been with my father for the last two or three years playing Sir Peter Teazle, Old Hardcastle, Sir Anthony Absolute and the other old men parts. He was only in his late twenties, but by playing these old men parts he seemed to be an elderly bachelor himself. Indeed, he was very much of a bachelor and not in the least anxious to be caught in the web of matrimony by my sister. He used to share digs with two of the juniors, whose job it was to protect his bachelorhood. However, Viola was dauntless and within a couple of years she had married him and it was as happy a marriage as anybody could wish for, Their eldest son is Nicholas Crocker who is head of outside television in the Western Region of the B.B.C.

It was in Aberdeen that week I bought my first Lovat pipe, and as I write these words a Lovat pipe is in my mouth but with a vulcanite mouthpiece not the white bone of the original Lovat pipe.

The weather remained glorious throughout the week; after

rehearsal I used to sit on the sand gazing out at a sea as blue as the Aegean. It was the middle of February and the Riviera could not have provided better weather at such a time of year.

On the Saturday night after playing to bumper business all the week my father's voice sounded tired; in the train next day on our way down to Edinburgh it became a whisper just as we were going along that part of the old North British line which runs above the sea.

"I'm afraid I shan't be able to appear to-morrow night in *The School for Scandal*. Crocker will have to rehearse the understudies."

I was appalled. Joseph Surface playing Charles Surface, Sir Benjamin Backbite playing Joseph, Careless playing Sir Benjamin Backbite, Trip playing Careless and the baggage-man playing Trip. What would become of *The Gentleman in Grey* due for production on Thursday?

"I'll play Charles Surface for you to-morrow night," I said, thankful indeed that the week was not opening as it so often did with *Davy Garrick*.

"Do you think you can get the lines in time?"

"Of course. I played the picture-scene at school seven or eight years ago. I won't be able to sing *Here's to the Maiden*, but I expect one of the others will be up to it."

So that night my sister Viola sat up with me, both of us sustaining ourselves on almonds and raisins until I sent her off to bed about three, by which time I was sure of all my cues and sat up for another three hours getting the lines perfect. The rehearsal was called for ten o'clock, and we had one run through of the various scenes in which Charles Surface appears. Then I went on with the rehearsal of my own play, whose future was of more importance to me than Sheridan's past.

I was curiously calm when the evening came, which is more than could be said for the Company, who were all in a state of jitters on my account. I do not think it occurred to me that an Edinburgh audience might be annoyed to find that their favourite actor of that date was not appearing in a part he had played about a thousand times and that his son, barely twenty-four, was taking his place. Anyway, I got through without a single prompt, though in their nervousness for me one or two of the cast had to be prompted.

I got back to our lodgings at 40 Lothian Road to find my father still voiceless; so I had to sit up again that night and learn Bob Acres in *The Rivals*. Mrs Gillies, the delightful Highland landlady of those wonderful lodgings, had been much distressed to hear of my subsisting on almonds and raisins the previous night and insisted on serving me with a couple of mutton-chops at two in the morning.

Bob Acres was a trickier part than Charles Surface because it included the duel and that meant a great deal of business to master. The traditional business of the duel-scene, going back to the days of Sheridan himself at Drury Lane, has now been forgotten. I was more nervous than I had been when playing Charles Surface the previous evening, and I did have one prompt. Absorbed by the future of my own play, I had refused more than one run through at rehearsal.

Back at 40 Lothian Road I found my father's voice better but by no means better enough to guarantee his appearance at the Wednesday matinée of *She Stoops to Conquer*. So to be on the safe side I sat up that night again and learned the part of Tony Lumpkin, wishing it was Young Marlowe whose nervousness would have reflected my own state of mind. What was worrying me acutely was the possibility of my having to play the leading part in my own play, because knowing all the parts as I did I should be almost bound to make a mess of my cues. Mercifully my father's voice had returned by Wednesday morning and I could sleep all the afternoon till I went down to meet Faith at Waverley Station.

I can remember absolutely nothing at all about the first night of *The Gentleman in Grey*. I fall back on an extract quoted from *The Era*:

"The audience gave an enthusiastic reception to the work of the young dramatist. An attractive agreeable play, in which much skill is shown alike in dialogue and construction. Many of the lines had an epigrammatic ring and freshness, and there are dainty gems of speech which have an almost Elizabethan flavour. The comedy is full of quite exceptional promise. . . . Mr Edward Compton was seen at his best. There are abundant opportunities for the display of his versatility. . . . The robbing of the stage-coach was carried through with an air of gay bravado. There was force in the scenes with Vernon, pathos in the act in which he is recognized by his uncle, and beauty and tenderness in his acting in the love-passages with Phyllida. Mr Compton made a distinct triumph and was loudly recalled at the end of each act. At the fall of the final curtain there were loud calls for the author and Mr Compton led his son on to the stage. Enthusiastic applause followed, and Mr Compton said 'Was the play a success?' A unanimous shout of 'Yes!' came from all parts of the house."

Yet I myself was disappointed; it was not the play as I had seen it in my own mind. I began to ask myself if I was not too good an actor to be a good playwright. Was I going to write plays in the future of which the only good performance from my point of view would be when I read it to the company? After that, were the actors instead of giving life to my characters going to destroy that life?

We went on to Greenock from Edinburgh and there the same doubt assailed me. The only other bit of a notice that survives is from the *Greenock Herald*:

"The dailogue is intellectual—full of the sort of humour that catches one after the manner of Old English Comedy at its best. . . . The enthusiasm of the audience knew no bounds, the appearance of Mr Compton and his modest young son being demanded by the heartiest plaudits and given an ovation."

George Blake used to recall how as an eleven-year-old boy in the Greenock theatre that night he remembered my appearance—very slim and looking like an embarrassed schoolboy as I thanked the audience for their reception of my first play.

I recall from that week my surprise at seeing rhododendrons already in flower, and crossing over to the isle of Bute to visit Edmund Kean's old house with the wonderful wall paper he had had designed from scenes of Shakespeare, that house set among the vivid green of the Bute landscape on which a soft rain of the west was gently falling.

From Greenock we went on to Glasgow, where the Compton Comedy Company played for the first time at the new King's Theatre. My father had found it difficult to bring himself to desert the old Royalty Theatre; I do not believe he ever brought himself to desert the Lyceum Theatre in Edinburgh for the new King's Theatre which would be opened there this very year. My only memory of that week in Glasgow is of Norah Dunn, as she now was, sitting with her husband and her sister Myra Duncan in a box on the prompt side. It was just a year after the birth of Norah's daughter, Doris Valentine, whose ambition to go on the stage I should be encouraging eighteen years later.

Faith and I spent one more week with the Company, in Dundee. I forget where we stayed but the name of our delightful old landlady was Fortune. Here I spent two nights of more acute pain with neuritis than I had hitherto suffered, after which we went back to Cheyne Walk. From that early Spring in Chelsea I recall eating sometimes at a tiny restaurant close to old Chelsea church which was run by Mrs Osborne, a charming widow; she may have been a grass-widow. A naval Commander was in love with her whom she called the Sailorman, and I imagine there must have been some bar to their getting married. She was always a great encouragement to me and urged me to publish my poems at my own expense rather than send them round to any more publishers. She used to write reviews for one of the weeklies. One evening a striking figure came in with gold earrings in his ears, wearing a dark blue Guernsey and we were introduced to Mr Augustus John. I was captivated by his personality and eagerly accepted an invitation to go and see him, but destiny intervened and I did not get to know him for another thirteen years.

I was much exercised in my mind about the trial of Horace Raynor for shooting William Whiteley, whom he believed to be his father. Correspondents in the columns of the *Daily Mail* were arguing against a reprieve for Raynor, and on March 28th I wrote a letter from 127 Cheyne Walk which was not printed but a copy of it I made at the time survives:

"*Sir,*

Most of your correspondents who have expressed a desire to hang Raynor assume that blackmail was proven. So did twelve men probably honest, possibly uneducated, certainly fat-witted. Where was the evidence? Mr D. H. Lambert writes of an "old and respectable tradesman"; he is a fair type of the average unimaginative man, exuding stupidity gross, open, palpable. The Lamberts of this world cannot understand that the life of a man like Whiteley is not to be judged only from his presidency of that emporium in Westbourne Grove, but equally from his property in a mean side-street of Kilburn. He made his bargains also when the shutters were down. He was helping in his own underlife to pave the streets of this grim underworld of London. Men like him breed their parasites, but when they are devoured by their own brood the Lamberts cry 'Sweets to the sweet, farewell.' Whiteley paid the penalty but he was never punished by Society. Therefore Society has no right to punish a man whose crime was first made possible by its own negligence. If the gods really created man to provide great laughter for Olympus, what a very diverting turn will be served by the Lamberts when they hang out their withered little souls to flap in the winds of eternity."

A letter from me would be shorter and less rhetorical to-day, but I should still express the same sentiments. In the middle of writing this Octave I was compelled to send a brief note to *The Times* after a leader inspired by the Profumo case had produced a sackful of congratulatory correspondence:

I wonder if you realize how turbid in the clear air of France appears the torrent of self-righteousness pouring down your columns.

The letter was not printed. Brief as it was, I was informed by the Editor's secretary that there was no space to spare for it.

In the first week of April I was bargaining with a second-hand bookseller in Red Lion Passage, off Red Lion Square, for a huge collection of playbills and newspaper cuttings about various murder cases. I forget what he asked or what I offered but in the end we agreed on a price betwixt and between. I was driving back to Chelsea on the top of an omnibus when halfway down the King's Road I suddenly felt extremely ill. "Oh, no," I said to myself, "not another attack of this damned influenza." Influenza was still *la grippe* in those days. It seized you instantaneously and although it might follow upon a chill it did not necessarily do so by any means. One either had influenza or not; one never heard of influenza colds as one does to-day.

I got down from the bus at the *World's End* public-house and walked in a daze with wobbly knees along Cremorne Road to Cheyne Walk. I kept sitting down on the stairs up to our room and luckily found Faith at home. "I've got another go of this blasted 'flu'," I told her. She let down the box-bed and I threw myself upon it. Soon my throat seemed to be closing up and after an agonizing night Faith telephoned to Frank Wallace, our much loved doctor in Earls Court, tall, handsome and always wise. By now I was beginning to be delirious and the pain from my throat was all over my body. Wallace immediately diagnosed scarlet fever and telephoned to the Western Fever Hospital in Brompton Road for an ambulance. I was carried downstairs over the shoulders of a stalwart ambulance attendant, accompanied by a nurse, and was put to bed in one of the wards with what turned out to be diphtheria as well as scarlet fever and a temperature of 105°. Agonizing pain all over, with ice-packs changed from time to time; my throat so bad that it could not be swabbed but was sprayed hopefully; above the head of my bed a gas jet burning with a kettle on it in case tracheotomy should be necessary.

What a week that was! For some hours my temperature touched 106° and stuck at 105° for four days. The delirium was not violent and consisted mostly in seeing small heads on legs coming up from the floor on either side of my bed, swelling up to the size of pantomime bigheads, and trotting away along the ward. Another curious delusion was that the signal visible from the ward window, on the Clapham Junction line that ran along between the hospital and Brompton Cemetery, had come into the ward and that the post had turned into spirals and was waving about. This worried me and I kept asking the night-nurse to do something about it because otherwise there would be a railway accident. In one of the beds opposite was a merchant-seaman who spent much of his time climbing imaginary rigging, hoisting himself up into the air hand over hand. This worried me, too, because I was afraid he would try to start climbing up that wavy signal post and I asked the night nurse to warn him it was not as solid as it ought to be.

Meanwhile, Faith had been put into strict quarantine in Cheyne Walk, but Mr and Mrs Unwin, that kind Quaker couple below us, insisted she should spend the days with them, and pooh-poohed the idea of any danger from infection.

Then one morning I woke up with the pain in my throat gone and the fever down; there were still the shooting pains in my joints to which was added the familiar stabbing of peripheral neuritis, but I felt so much better that I asked the night-nurse for a cup of tea.

"Goodness me, it would be as much as my life was worth to give you a cup of tea until Dr Menzies has made his round."

"Now, listen, nurse. I am better, and if you'll give me a cup of tea I shall be better still. Indeed, I shall be quite well, but I must have a cup of tea. Otherwise, I'm sure my temperature will go soaring up again, and it will be all your fault." To her credit she took the risk and gave me that cup of tea. I looked at her gratefully.

"My god, nurse, I never realized what a damned pretty girl you are. You really are lovely."

"Will you stop talking such nonsense."

"I'm afraid I'll have to stop talking for the next few minutes. Put the screens round me. I must go yachting about the bed on that bed-pan of yours. It's ridiculous that nobody has managed to invent a foolproof bedpan yet."

To my chagrin I cannot remember the name of that adorable nurse; even now I can feel the pang of disappointment with which I heard her tell me that she would be going off on her holiday next week. When she came back from that holiday she was on day-duty in one of the typhoid wards. However, when I was out of hospital she dined with me once or twice and confided in me the problem of an affair she was having with a married man. I hope I gave her good advice, for I felt I owed my life to her devoted nursing during that critical week. Apparently, so I was to learn later, it had been touch and go for a while. Why should I be able to remember the names of half a dozen other nurses and forget the name of the one to whom I owed so much?

In the next bed to me was a Caius man called Rae, an Old Cheltonian who had been a rugger Blue and played in the Cambridge three-quarter line. He was now in his last year at St Thomas's Hospital and was to be married in August. I really do not know what I should have done without Rae's company during those weeks in hospital. Except for that seaman and a cleaner from Harrod's on the other side of the ward, the rest of the patients were all slum children, the toughest of them being the Duchess of Marlborough's tiger. Do I have to explain that a 'tiger' was a diminutive groom who in livery with a cockaded top-hat balanced himself at the back of a light vehicle, ready to jump down and hold the horse's head when his master or mistress alighted? This particular tiger bullied all the other kids until Rae was able to give him six of the best, after which he behaved himself. The heads of all these kids were combed every morning for lice, and Rae and I had to have our heads combed. Luckily after we had been in hospital for some time a kid developed chicken pox and so for three weeks we had no fresh cases in our ward, being in quarantine. This meant an eternal racket from the convalescents but the combing for lice came to an end.

Nurse Williams, the charge-nurse, was a plump little Welshwoman from Rhyl. She was a brunette barely five feet tall, but a disciplinarian whose word nobody ventured to question. She had a great sense of humour withal. "I never knew I was so popular with the other nurses until you and Mr Rae arrived," she said. "The variety of excuses they invent to come and consult me nowadays is surprising. I am going to put two placards over your beds. 'Married' yours will say, Mr Mackenzie, and Mr Rae's will say 'Engaged.' "

Nurse Stewart, the probationer, was an Aberdonian, a solemn fair girl with a good profile who always looked a little puzzled when we made jokes. In the mind's eye I see her sitting surrounded by about three-dozen flasks of urine of every shade of yellow, which she is testing for whatever signs of nephritis might be revealed. Nephritis was one of the complications that was easily provoked by scarlet fever in those days of its virulence. Five of the children in the ward had it. One poor kid had been there for five months.

A full three weeks passed before I was allowed up in blankets, and I was so unsteady on my legs that two nurses had to hold me up when I started to walk. When the time came to dress, Nurse Williams suggested Rae and I should be sent old suits which it would not matter baking to disinfect them. We would not want to wear the shapeless blue jackets and trousers provided for convalescents by the hospital. So Rae and I made arrangements accordingly. The cleaner from Harrods and the seaman heard about this and, detecting favouritism as they thought, insisted that they were to have suits sent them. I knew this might mean spoiling perhaps the only spare suit either of them had, and I announced I was not going to spoil one of my suits but should prefer to wear the hospital garb. Rae did the same, and after that our two wardmates were content.

Outside the ward was a triangle of asphalt with a plane-tree in which a thrush used to sit, looking as bored with the sparrows as Rae and I were with the noise of the children. Coughing at night was our worst affliction. A child would start coughing; this would start off another child; in a few minutes there would be about a dozen kids coughing.

Nurse Roy, the night-nurse who succeeded my first night-nurse, used to quieten them successfully but after three weeks she was moved to a typhoid ward; the rather dull nurse who took her place had no notion how to keep the children quiet at night. Nurse Roy was an Edinburgh girl who used to sit talking to me until one night the cleaner from Harrods begged us to let him get a wink of sleep. We felt like two of the children who had been coughing.

When Rae and I got up we used to sit in the bathroom and play cards on the bath rest. Cribbage, casino, piquet—game after game. Rae usually won at cribbage; I was his master at piquet; casino found us equal. Casino was a game much in vogue with French cabaret girls. Grand casino was the nine of diamonds, little casino was the two of spades, and the object was always to get rid of one's cards. I used to play the game in Athens when I was there in 1916 but I have completely forgotten it and cannot find it in the totally inadequate guides to card-games provided by the paperbacks of to-day.

The children in the ward were getting noisier and noisier: I recall two of them being put to bed for two days and another's writing home to ask his mother if she could think of a way for him to escape from hospital. The poor little things were utterly bored. Then I had a bright idea. I got Faith to procure sixty boxes of tin soldiers. The penny boxes of the 'nineties were no longer available; they now cost 4½d for a box of twelve. Then Rae and I picked up for our armies and war was declared by one side of the ward on the other. Marbles provided the artillery and the armies moved forward two feet after every six shots, the winner of the battle being the army which reached the middle of the ward with fewest casualties. The game was a great success for about a week until it was forbidden on account of the number of marbles that were falling down the gratings into the heating arrangements. Luckily the weather got better about then and the children were able to play out of doors on the asphalt, where they taught Rae and me to play hop scotch, tibby cat, and several other games I have forgotten.

The scene I recall most vividly from that asphalt is when the cleaner from Harrods made an appointment for his family to come one Sunday afternoon to Brompton Cemetery and climb up the wall to wave to Pa from the other side of the railway line. There was some difficulty in hoisting up a buxom Ma, who disappeared three times in the middle of blowing kisses to Pa.

Rae and I were given leave in the middle of May to play lawn-tennis on the staff's court. Rae, as a Cambridge blue should have been, was much better than I, though to be sure his blue was for rugger. Once a terrific drive by Rae sent the ball right out of the court. At that moment one of the porters was walking along close to the hospital buildings with what I supposed was a sack of waste paper over his shoulder. 'Thank you!' I called, holding up my hand for the ball to be thrown back to me. The porter stopped and glared at me. 'Can't you see I'm carrying a corpse?' he asked indignantly, and walked on toward the mortuary.

In that May my brother Frank had been gazetted to the Royal Inniskilling Fusiliers who were in Crete, where the Great Powers were engaged as usual in coddling the Turks and denying the Cretans union or enosis with Greece; I had a postcard from Malta where he and another subaltern were waiting for transport to Crete.

Poor old chap, I'm awfully sorry to hear about you—I hope you are better now. Having a ripping time here—guests of the Rifle Brigade—ripping good lot—went to the Opera last night in their box—ripping company—get well soon. Love to Faith.

Claude Kirby sent me a copy of Maurice Baring's poems which had recently been published by Blackwell in Oxford and asked me why I did not get my poems published in the same format. It certainly was an attractive volume with a grey paper back and perfectly printed. I asked Faith to send the complete collection of my poems, which she had copied out in a specially bound quarto notebook in what was still a legible and beautiful Stone handwriting, to Blackwell for an estimate of what it would cost to print 750 copies. Blackwell's estimate was £40. With great difficulty I worked out what 750 copies at 3/6 would bring, decided that I would not have to sell out the edition to make a profit on the deal and that in any case they would make good Christmas presents. So I decided to do a final revision when we went to Lady Ham for a bit after I got out of hospital, and to find out if Blackwell would be able to publish in October. A month ago I saw a mint copy of those poems advertized in a second-hand book catalogue for eight guineas.

I heard in a letter from Faith that Nellie Baker, who must by now have been sixteen, had not been allowed to visit one of her real sisters, and had run away either from school or from Helensbourne. I wrote strongly taking her part and pointing out that what seemed to her an injustice might have a bad effect on her whole future life. Faith agreed with me; she always had great tenderness for that little adopted sister.

My father had decided to take the St James's theatre from the middle of July for three months in order to produce *To-Morrow*. That play was an obsession with him. He had sent it to his brother-in-law Claude Carton, who had encouraged him in his hopes for it and had offered to put in various bits in the present portion and make some suggestions for the eighteenth-century portion. I knew that this meant more tinkering by me and by now I was sick of *To-Morrow*, but I was cheered up by hearing that Eva Moore was going to play the girl Laidlaw loves. Then James Welch brought out a play called *When Knights Were Bold*, in which the chief character found himself back in the middle ages. This was a highly successful farce and I wrote to tell my father I thought he was running a risk in producing *To-Morrow*. However, he was still obsessed with that confounded play.

The process of peeling began and itching was added to what was now the acute boredom of hospital life. At last came the order for release on Saturday, May 25th, when I was to go down to Lady Ham. On the night before I left, the Matron, a Scotswoman of strong personality and tremendous competence, invited me to play bridge with her.

"Well," I hear her say, "I don't believe we ever had a patient in the Western who was spoilt as much as you. And yet, though really you almost disorganized my working-staff, I am bound to say we shall all miss you, and that includes myself."

With my things from the hospital was a note to say that for another week I ought not to wear other children's socks or play with other children's toys, because the process of peeling was not yet complete. Readers to-day will think I have made a great fuss about a minor ailment like scarlet fever; it is always agreeable to congratulate the present on its advantages over the past.

We had managed to let Lady Ham for a term from August onwards and I felt quite sure these weeks of June and July were the last I should spend there. In that June we acquired a cross between a bob-tailed sheep-dog and some other breed. Bob was then a puppy six months old of great intelligence, and would remain a devoted friend and companion both of myself and even more dearly of Faith for the next thirteen years.

I had to set to work as soon as possible on the reconstruction of *To-Morrow* in which R. C. Carton was taking more and more interest. The first disappointment was the news that Eva Moore was ill and would not be able to play the heroine; her place was taken by Grace Lane. Then there was a long argument about the title and finally in spite of my protests it was decided to call the play *The Eighteenth Century*, which I thought an idiotic title. The first night was to be on July 29th. I remember nothing about it except that Henry Ainley's wife, Suzanne Sheldon, gave a splendid performance of Lady Anthony Frayle, one of the figures in the dream, and, as the White Knight said, my own invention.

A letter from Henry James to my mother has survived:

Lamb House,
Rye,
Sussex.
July 28th, 1907

Dear Mrs Compton,

I am full of regret, but as I wired yesterday to the theatre, I can't be in town for tomorrow night. I was *there for 3 days last week, but had to come home to receive relations on a visit—of which the end will not be for two or three days yet: so in short I'm quite nailed here. I wish you, all heartily, an eminent success with your theatre and Play and am your and Compton's faithful old friend*

Henry James.

P.S. I mustn't forget that I've heard some rumours of the play being your Boy's! I send him and it my blessing. I back him heartily and must see the piece a little later.

Meanwhile, I had arranged with Blackwell to publish my poems in October. That preoccupied me much more deeply than the fate of *The Eighteenth Century* with the shaping of which I had merely played the part of a tinker. The play ran until the middle of September, when my father decided to stage a revival of *The School for Scandal*. In this Henry Ainley was to play Joseph Surface, and I was able to persuade him to play Joseph Surface as I thought the part should be played. By now Joseph Surface was always played as the conventional stage villain, whom nobody on or off the stage could mistake for anything else. On the other hand, if the part were played with grace and elegance and if the asides like 'I have put my hand to so many cursed rogueries that I doubt I shall be exposed at last' were delivered light-heartedly instead of with a scowl, his ability to take in Sir Peter Teazle would make Sir Peter seem less of an old duffer and double the dramatic value of the screen scene. Grace Lane was a moderately good Lady Teazle; Ainley was absolutely first-class, the best Joseph Surface I ever saw, thanks partly to my suggestions but much more to the coaching of his wife who was the perfect Lady Sneerwell.

My confounded neuritis was plaguing me again; having by now completely recovered from that mood of passionate atheism which had succeeded the breaking off of my engagement to Ruth Daniel I turned again to the idea of being ordained, which was a severe shock to Faith who with a parson father, a parson brother, a parson brother-in-law, one elder sister in the Wantage sisterhood and another Ruth, utterly absorbed in devout Anglicanism, felt that a parson husband would be too much of a good thing. So I suggested going to live in the Azores for a year to give myself time to make up my mind whether I really had a vocation for the priesthood. We were staying at Helensbourne and I still have a letter from the secretary of the Sociedade Propagadora Punta Delgada in the island of S. Miguel from which a few extracts may be of interest to-day:

I should advise you to come to an hotel at first, and afterwards look for the house as you require. We have some on the neighbourhood of the twon (sic) of different prices according to the sizes and situation from 3 shillings up to five shillings a week.

Servants girls for home work from 14 up to 18 shillings a month. Men nearly the same. We have splendid landscapes here and the island is a great deal appreciated by those who pays us a visit. Regarding your intention (presumably to write a book) *some thing is tried in the same way by this Society but for that the first thing required is the publication of a law by the Portuguese Government, alowing the play in certain places like St Michael's which can be considered as a spot for tourists, specially for the Americans. The other matter which is very important is the matter of hotels for receiving the tourists.*

The town of Punta Delgada is visited yearly by thouthands (sic) of American tourists of the great steamers of the White Star Line in tours to Italy and Egypt. We have had royal visits, scientific missions, and American milionaires (sic).

There are several ways to come to this island. By Lisbon in direct steamer leaving every 5ths of the months. . . . 1st class passage nearly £6. Directly from London by the London, Hamburg and Azores Line—£6. Hoping to see you here.

The name of the President of that Society for Propaganda about

S. Miguel was Alberto de Monaco and he obviously had dreams of making Punta Delgada another Monte Carlo.

My plan to go and live in the Azores for a year was shied at by Faith. In 1913 we should sail past S. Miguel on board the S.S. *Prinzess Irene*, bound from New York to Naples. That green island in the rich blue of a March dusk was almost intolerably lovely after the weary grey of the North Atlantic. I asked Faith if she did not regret our not having gone to live there six years ago.

"I've been quite sea-sick enough," she said.

In that September when the Azores were turned down as a suitable residential project I heard that Sandys Wason had been given a living in Cornwall, and I wrote to ask him if he knew of any cottages in the district at a low rent which we might take. He wrote back to suggest we should come as paying guests to Cury Vicarage; £1 a week each (excluding wine and washing). So that was arranged and on October 1st we went to Cornwall.

The five-mile drive from Helston in a fly, through the deepening twilight past signposts with strange names, was a completely novel experience. I was overcome by a sense of passing out of the present into the pre-Roman past. It was a form of the original panic. I should one day repeat that panic in the island of Herm. It is impossible to convey the sensation in words with any hope of a reader's responding unless he has had the same experience. I think Arthur Machen came nearest to conveying it. Powys tried and failed. Francis Brett Young tried and failed. I have tried and failed.

When we reached the Vicarage, we found nobody there except a bewildered parish-nurse who told us that Mr Wason was away in Truro doing a retreat. "When you meet dear Wason," I told Faith, "you'll realize how completely like him it is to have forgotten all about our arrival." I went out and asked the driver of the fly whether there was a hotel anywhere in reach.

"There's the Poldhu Hotel near where they belong sending these wireless telegrams over to America. They be full in summer time when the visitors from up along are around but you'll get a room easy enough, now October month be come."

So we got back in the fly and drove to Poldhu. It was now pitch dark and the lamps of the vehicle lit up more strange names on signposts—Landewednack, Mullion, Lizard. We found a comfortable room in the hotel, where next morning I woke with a thumping headache. I had had many headaches during the last two or three years but I had never had one that came near this thumper. It lasted for three days and as I lay in bed I felt I was being hit on the head by a hammer every quarter of a minute. Then on the fourth day I woke up with the headache gone and feeling perfectly fit. I have never had even the mildest headache since that first week of October in the year 1907. I am glad that I did have such a headache once because I can still sincerely sympathize with people who tell me they have a thumping headache.

I was out that morning in good time and walked up the towans, the site of popular golf-links, to Cury. Wason was not yet back from Truro but was expected that afternoon. I was captivated by my first sight of *Amaryllis belladonna* in a rosy stream all round the walls of the vicarage, but what thrilled me even more was a large *Benthamia fragifera* as it used to be called, laden with its large strawberries. In that moment I was dedicated to the pride and joy of Cornish gardening.

On my way back to the hotel I wandered about Gunwalloe Cove, fascinated by the little church separated from its tower, which was tucked away into the cliff that protected it from the full savagery of the Atlantic. All was strange; I did not even know the name of the mesembryanthemum that grew over the churchyard, its glossy fleshy foliage washed by high spring tides. Presently I saw coming down from the cliff between the church and the sea a senior to myself who had been with me at St Paul's.

"Good lord, Roche, what are you doing here?" I exclaimed.

"Searching for dollars," he said. "But I'm afraid we've lost the fight. The glass is falling rapidly, and I think we shall have a gale by nightfall. It was the same last year. By the time our pumps were fixed, the equinoctial gales were on us and all our gear was washed away."

I wondered what on earth Roche was talking about and he took me up to the top of the cliff from which one looked down into a very narrow sandy inlet with a cave at the end of it and rocks on either side on which were fixed wire posts from which a pump went down into the sand at the edge of the tide.

"We started pumping yesterday and got a lot out, and we shall be pumping again when the tide ebbs."

I was still bewildered and Roche explained that just over a hundred years ago a transport laden with a million silver Portuguese dollars had been driven into this inlet and broken up by the waves.

"They're all here," Roche said. "A million of them buried in the sand which we have been trying to pump out. Half a dozen of us formed a little syndicate to finance the treasure hunt, but I'm afraid we've lost the fight again. You see, we can't start fixing up our equipment till April and we only have about four hours to work in between the tides. All our equipment was smashed and washed away last October, and it will be the same again this year. So, I'm afraid some other syndicate will get the dollars one day—perhaps."

I do not know if any attempts to salvage those million silver dollars of Portugal have been made since; anyway, the dollars are still there. I used to walk along and look for them sometimes at low tide; a year after this I remember telling a visitor with whom I was walking of my failure to find even one. "Well, I've found one," he said, and bending down he picked up one of those silver dollars.

I do not propose to tell more tales of wrecks in this Octave, nor to introduce the reader to what was that magical west coast of the Meneage. Roche told me more tales of treasure, and that afternoon I wrote this little poem while Faith and I were waiting for Wason to arrive at the Vicarage:

How many ships have you seen, fair maid,
Swing heavily on to the shore?
And how many tall tall crashing masts
Have you heard above the roar?

I saw a ship go down, good sir,
In the wild October gales,
In a rift of the clouds by the grey moonlight
I saw her tattered sails.

I saw the men upon her decks
Like shadows on a wall
That fade away when the lamp is ta'en
And are never seen at all.

And what was in her shaken hold
That made the men despair?
Bags of guineas and bars of gold
For their sweethearts all to share?

Bars of gold there were, good sir,
Fit for a kingdom's crown,
For we saw them in the summertime
Full six blue fathoms down.

And the second ship you saw, fair maid,
Oh say what carried she?
Silver dollars of Portugal
And silks from over the sea?

Silver dollars she may have had,
Though never a one saw we,
But on the yellow sands lay thick
Green apples from Normandy.

And the third ship that you saw go down,
Was ever a fairer seen?
And was she a barque or a gay corvette
Or a delicate brigantine?

And did she strike at dead of night
Or on a winter noon?
And was it from the wreck of her
You took that great doubloon?

Oh, ask me not of the third tall ship,
For she held nigh all my life,
And this I wear around my neck
Was cut with a sailor's knife.

I do not understand, fair maid,
You stole this from the dead?
Oh sir, the sailor lying there
In March I should have wed.

I was rather pleased with this poem and felt that Cornwall might perhaps be going to turn my mind back to poetry. We should soon be getting reviews of that grey volume finely printed on handmade paper, price 3s 6d.

I quote from Faith's volume of autobiography *As Much As I Dare*:

"The house was pleasant, newly painted and papered, and our bedroom comfortably furnished. The Vicar had the smallest room in the house with a hole in the ceiling over his bed. His study was for the moment the only living-room, and here we were sitting when he suddenly appeared after dark, with a spine of mud up his back, because it had begun to rain and his bicycle had no mudguard.

"Hullo, Monty. Bored to death? Do you play bridge?"

"They sat down at once to two-handed bridge. I was glad they did this, for I was as nervous of the Vicar as he was of me. The evening passed very easily for us all.

"If I had had any misgivings about life in a remote country vicarage they soon vanished. It was at once obvious that entertainment would be the principal feature of existence. There was no order in the household except the early Mass which the Vicar of Cury and Gunwalloe said daily. Servants were almost out of the question, and a woman from the village was generally our only help. We had a strange married pair for a time, the Barkers. He was silent but for his peculiarly heavy tread, and she a faded beauty with a fleck of foam at the corner of her mouth from endless talking. But they passed on after two months. This was their limit, for they were doing a leisurely tour of the British Isles free of any expense whatever, and they had a desire to see Wales."

Some of the reviews of the *Poems* were long and enthusiastic; some were short and crushing. I was far away at this time from learning to pay no attention to critics. When the *Daily Chronicle* said, "We really do him little injustice by thus cutting off his sonnet above the knee, for in a style like this it is impossible to express anything whether in fourteen or a thousand lines", I felt the reviewer was merely being offensive; but when *Country Life* said "of real passion or feeling Mr Mackenzie's effusions do not give a single hint. . . . his work is inspired by literature rather than by life," I was shaken. Was this true?

It was no doubt gratifying to be told by various critics that my poems recalled Herrick or Rossetti or Keats or Spenser or William Morris, but I did not want to recall any of them. I wanted to express myself; reading coldly through my poems, I decided that they only expressed my cleverness. My poetry was not really inspired: it was a pastiche. It was on a par with my ability to write good Greek iambics or good Latin prose once upon a time. Many of the reviews had praised my sense of melody and my felicitous use of words and hailed my work as work of high promise for the future. Such praise merely stressed for me the danger of fancying myself inspired by life when I was in fact inspired only by literature. I had supposed that my continually turning away from poetry to write plays had merely been an effort to earn enough money to let me persevere with poetry. But in fact, were not plays the logical way for me to express myself and could I not count with reasonable security on taking my place among the leading playwrights of the twentieth century? But how was one to become a leading playwright if all the parts one wrote could only be *played* by oneself? Should I not have gone on the stage? If I had accepted Arthur Bourchier's offer four years ago I should now be getting £20 a week in a West End theatre. But I should be so bored. It would be all so much too easy. Or should I have taken the law seriously? No, I could not have brought myself to defend a man whom I believed to be guilty and I never could have prosecuted anybody; I should always have felt sorry for the poor devil. Why was I continuing to eat odd dinners at the Temple which should have been eaten long since? I sat down and wrote to resign from my student membership of the Inner Temple.

I had told my mother that I was again considering the notion of being ordained. She of course was delighted. My complete withdrawal from religion after the breaking off of my engagement had been a sharp grief to her, and the recovery of my faith as sharp a joy. However, although the possibility of being ordained was still working in my mind I was sensible enough to keep it as merely a possibility for at least another year, and decided to become a lay-reader in the diocese of Truro in the new year. That would be a test. I was well aware my present humour might prove to be no more than a temporary reaction against the uncertainty I was feeling about my fitness to be either a poet or a playwright. I was not prepared to be one more literary amateur. If I were to go on waiting, I must feel completely confident of my ability to become a recognized figure of literature. I knew that if I had surrendered to the stage I should probably be on the way to success by now, but I did not want stage success. It was lucky for me that at this date films were still in their infancy. I cannot feel so sure that I should have had the strength of mind to resist them. The films would have been a new form of dramatic expression to conquer.

Faith was wonderful while I was in this mood of tangled uncertainty. Without letting me know what she was doing she had asked her father to advance her £500 from the £3000 she would inherit one day and beloved old E.D.S. had immediately agreed. That £500 had cleared all debts and we were now in a comparatively easy financial situation with my £150 a year from my father and the £50 a year from hers, and of course my mother giving presents from time to time. £2 a week for the pair of us to be paying guests of dear Wason could not be considered extravagant living. The two houses, Lady Ham and the Other House, were let for at least a year, and Christopher was becoming almost permanently attached to the Chinnery household.

It must have been about the middle of October that Bob, our sheepdog, arrived from Lady Ham. Faith described his arrival in *As Much As I Dare* when she went to meet him in Helston:

"The platform was empty except for an old lady seated on the ground with Bob's chain wound round her waist and Bob sitting beside her, smiling apologetically. Somehow he had swept her off the bench to which the porter had tied him, and there they were linked together. This was the least tactful episode in the whole long life of a perfect dog whose manners and benevolence were only matched by his humour and devotion."

On the evening of that day I went for a walk by myself down across the towans to Gunwalloe Cove, deeply preoccupied about my future.

I had by now made up my mind that my future in literature did not lie in poetry and I was still feeling doubtful about my future as a playwright unless I was prepared to be an actor as well. I was not ready to commit myself yet to taking Holy Orders.

It was a calm clouded evening without moon or stars; the only light visible was away on the western horizon where the Wolf light twinkled its warning to mariners outward or homeward bound. The tide was high and I sat on a sandy tussock of grass close to the water's edge. Suddenly a glow-worm, not an arm's length away, challenged the darkness with its tiny lamp. I was awed by the contrast between this minute creature and the huge night above it and about it. I suddenly felt ashamed of my own doubts and hesitations. I suddenly realized where my path in literature lay.

On the following evening when tea was over and Wason was setting up the dummies for two-handed bridge I asked him whether he'd mind if we did not play our rubber till after dinner as I wanted to write something.

"Another poem in your head?"

"No," I told him. "I think I'm going to start a novel."

How I supposed I should be able to sit down and write a novel without previous meditation on the task I do not know. I had written only one short story in my life, and that was in Charnay when I was seventeen. Yet I felt completely confident and I remain puzzled by such confidence.

I lit two candle swith red shades on either side of a sheet of foolscap and with one of Hardmuth's copying-ink pencils I wrote the first page of what in my fancy was to be the ideal performance of *The Gentleman in Grey*. This novelization of my play should be called *Curtain Wells*. I remember the sense of freedom at escaping from the thrall of narrative verse into narrative prose, and the elation of writing dialogue that no actor would have to speak and in speaking destroy that dialogue as I heard it being spoken in my head.

On that October evening in 1907 I wrote the first two pages of the novel that would one day be called *The Passionate Elopement* and would still be in print fifty-six years later.